The Accidental SysAdmin Handbook

A Primer for Entry Level IT Professionals

Second Edition

■ ■ ■

Eric Kralicek

Apress®

The Accidental SysAdmin Handbook, Second Edition: A Primer for Entry Level IT Professionals

ISBN-13 (pbk): 978-1-4842-1816-7

ISBN-13 (electronic): 978-1-4842-1817-4

Managing Director: Welmoed Spahr
Lead Editor: Steve Anglin
Editorial Board: Steve Anglin, Pramila Balan, Louise Corrigan, Jonathan Gennick, Robert Hutchinson, Celestin Suresh John, Michelle Lowman, James Markham, Susan McDermott, Matthew Moodie, Jeffrey Pepper, Douglas Pundick, Ben Renow-Clarke, Gwenan Spearing
Coordinating Editor: Mark Powers
Copy Editor: Kezia Endsley
Compositor: SPi Global
Indexer: SPi Global
Artist: SPi Global

Distributed to the book trade worldwide by Springer Science+Business Media New York, 233 Spring Street, 6th Floor, New York, NY 10013. Phone 1-800-SPRINGER, fax (201) 348-4505, e-mail orders-ny@springer-sbm.com, or visit www.springeronline.com. Apress Media, LLC is a California LLC and the sole member (owner) is Springer Science + Business Media Finance Inc (SSBM Finance Inc). SSBM Finance Inc is a Delaware corporation.

For information on translations, please e-mail rights@apress.com, or visit www.apress.com.

Apress and friends of ED books may be purchased in bulk for academic, corporate, or promotional use. eBook versions and licenses are also available for most titles. For more information, reference our Special Bulk Sales–eBook Licensing web page at www.apress.com/bulk-sales.

Any source code or other supplementary material referenced by the author in this text is available to readers at www.apress.com/9781484218167. For additional information about how to locate and download your book's source code, go to www.apress.com/source-code/. Readers can also access source code at **SpringerLink** in the Supplementary Material section for each chapter.

Contents at a Glance

Contents

About the Author

Eric A. Kralicek has worked in the field of computer technology for over two decades, specifically with computer networking since 1984. He has been employed in companies large and small, public and private, using a variety of network operating systems in mixed environments. As a networking professional he has written numerous internal documents that have guided other professionals in their use of technical applications both on and off networked systems. Eric has been employed by Digital Computer Corporation as a Senior Information Management Specialist, Compaq Computer Corporation as a Senior System Software Engineer, dot com companies as an Information Technology Manager, and educational institutions providing network management and system integration. In every instance he has provided both technical skills and training documentation. Eric has a Bachelor's of Science degree in Computer Networking from Regis University, Denver, CO. He is Microsoft, ITIL and PRINCE II certified. Eric worked for the California State University system as a Network Analyst supporting administrative computer operations in a mixed network environment prior to working for NATO as an IT Engineer.

About the Technical Reviewer

Mark Beckner is a technical consultant specializing in business development and enterprise application integration. He runs his own consulting firm, Inotek Consulting Group, LLC, delivering innovative solutions to large corporations and small businesses. His projects have included engagements with numerous clients throughout the U.S., and range in nature from mobile application development to extensive backend integration solutions. He is the author of The Coder's Path to Wealth and Independence and a number of technical books on BizTalk and Dynamics CRM. Beckner, his wife Sara, and his boys Ciro and Iyer Blue live on a farm in a high desert town in Colorado. His website is http://www.inotekgroup.com and he can be contacted directly at mbeckner@inotekgroup.com.

CHAPTER 1

■ ■ ■

Introduction

The *Accidental SysAdmin Handbook* is designed to give new system administrators an understanding of concepts, processes, and technologies that will aid in their professional development. It is assumed that you have little to no experience in a professional information technology environment. While every information technology culture is specific to its parent organization, there are commonalities that apply to all organizations. This book looks at those commonalities and provides a general introduction to critical aspects associated with system administration. It further acts to provide definitions for common computer terms and acronyms.

System Administrator Duties

Each organization has uniquely defined system administrator roles and responsibilities. The scope of those duties can change from organization to organization and often change as an organization matures. But there are some basic tasks that all system administrators share.

Task List

- Installation of servers and clients
- Application installation and maintenance
- Creation of user accounts and security groups
- User support
- Shared drive mapping
- Backups and disaster recovery
- Security
- Housekeeping
- Automating tasks
- Printer installation and queue management
- Network operation support/management
- Change management

This list can contract or expand depending on the size of the information technology support team. However, someone will end up responsible for most if not all of these tasks. Many organizations add the role of technology mentor to the list. A growing use of the ITIL v3[1] framework has helped to standardize information system roles and responsibilities as well as processes.

Many information technology support teams divide tasks into roles. This allows each role to build a deep knowledgebase for processing tasks and resolving issues. There should be a deliberate effort by management to balance the workload so that all tasks can be completed effectively without overloading team members.

Task Management Roles (Example)

User Services

- User support (level two support)
- Printer installation and queue management
- Application installation and maintenance
- Installation of workstations or clients

Server Administration

- Installation of servers
- Creation of user accounts and security groups
- Shared drive mapping
- Backups and disaster recovery
- Housekeeping
- Automating tasks

Information Assurance

- Network operation support/management
- Security
- Change management

In this example, roles are separated into three sections (user services, server administration, and information assurance). These sections provide a separation of responsibilities to better facilitate operations and troubleshoot. This allows better management of skillsets and technical training programs so that each role is properly managed. Members of each section are better able to manage their responsibilities and respond to changes in the organization as technologies evolve.

Smaller organizations may merge many of these roles. The balance is found in the number of servers and services as well as the size and complexity of network operations. In this case, many of the tasks that system administrators must perform are automated and generic (meaning that canned scripts downloaded from vendor web sites do most of the common task required to maintain system services). This usually requires the understanding that issues may arise when generic scripts cause unforeseen damage. Further, standardization in creating servers and clients is imperative. The more each server and client looks and feels

---

[1]ITIL v3 home web site: http://www.itil-officialsite.com/home/home.asp

the same, the easier it is to resolve problems that can crop up from daily use. This also requires longer hours for a smaller number of staff. The possibility for employee turnover is greater and the quality of support is less than that of a more complete IT department.

Larger IT departments can provide greater scrutiny for testing and approving scripts, service packs, and hot fixes. They can deploy updates through a process of downloading, testing, and pushing updates with less risk. Services are managed by sections trained to support role-based tasks. This results in a more cohesive deliberate formal process that benefits the end users and operations. Security can be monitored more consistently and issue resolution can be methodically processed. The larger the team, the more focused each team member can be.

Operational Awareness

Whether the IT department is large or small, creating daily/weekly/monthly checklists to ensure that services and tasks are completed and managed methodically will benefit operational awareness.

In larger, more mature IT departments there are well established procedures and mechanisms in place. These processes are integrated in service support applications (such as BMC's Remedy) and integrate both operational aspects of service delivery and document key service management processes (such as change management, configuration management, asset management, service catalogue management, service level management, incident management, and feed a service knowledge management system). Solutions such as Remedy are expensive and require advanced understanding of business process management and technical integration. Because the service support application is interactive and part of business as usual, IT personnel feed the data as part of their daily activities.

In small or new IT departments, the maturity level for documenting processes and recording service knowledge management can be ad hoc with no standardization in place. Appendix A provides sample templates for daily/weekly/monthly checklists.

The Monday checklist found in Appendix A is meant to be simple one page list that would be performed at the beginning of each day by a selected system administrator, who would coordinate with other system administrators to ensure that all listed services were operational.

The weekly checklist is done during the weekly maintenance cycle.

The monthly checklist is compiled over the month and acts to produce a series of reports to ensure that management has an audit trail of changes, issues, and usage of all services and assets. The monthly report is used to evaluate the current operation performance of services rendered so that remediation can take place when discrepancies are noted.

Monthly reports are tied to the internal trouble ticket system, SOPs[2] in place to perform each of the checklist items, and internal report templates.

Communication

All too often people forget that communication is a two-way street. Many IT departments absorb information, act on that information, record their actions, and then move on to the next issue. The user community is left outside the process. Keeping the person who first notified the system administrator of the progress of each ticket (including a follow up after the ticket is finally resolved) benefits the initiator and the team resolving the issue.

---

[2]SOP – Standard Operational Procedures: *"A Standard Operating Procedure is a document which describes the regularly recurring operations relevant to the quality of the investigation. The purpose of a SOP is to carry out the operations correctly and always in the same manner. A SOP should be available at the place where the work is done"*. FAO Corporate Document Repository, "2 Standard Operational Procedures"; 1998, Natural Resource Management and Environment Department. http://www.fao.org/docrep/W7295E/w7295e04.htm

Internal communication is also extremely important. Many IT departments fail to share information internally, even though much of what they are doing crosses over between projects or solutions to issues for the customers. Keeping everyone informed about what's going on can prevent multiple system administrators from stepping over each other in working issues or projects.

As IT professionals depend on e-mail, phones, remote video sessions, and portals for communicating, the value of face-to-face collaboration can be lost. The need to have frequent and well planned meetings with team members is critical to maintaining momentum.

E-mail and video conference sessions tend to limit discussion and cooperation. E-mails are either too short or too long. E-mail content can be misinterpreted. Video conferencing is often time-limited and focused, not allowing detailed conversations to evolve.

A good IT department tends to have weekly meetings to coordinate activities, share information, understand what each teammate is working on, and assist as needed when another team member needs help. They document meeting minutes, keep their internal portal up to date, and coordinate all change management activities transparently. When applicable, they include stakeholders from outside the IT department to fine-tune service delivery and propose improvements.

Providing user education is almost as important as keeping users in the loop regarding issues. A well trained user group makes the job of system administrators easier and helps facilitate the troubleshooting process. It also helps by making everyone aware of housekeeping and preventative maintenance. There is a goal in IT to have a 90-8-2 policy[3] in effect. If users can resolve 90 percent of their problems, and the service desk can solve 8 percent of the more difficult problems, then the system administrators can focus on the most complex 2 percent of the issues. This leaves much of their time allocated to maintaining servers, services, and network security and operations.

Research

Keeping in tune with what's current in IT helps make you proactive with potential external issues. There are lots of free technical magazines (i.e., *TechNet*,[4] *Information Week*,[5] *Redmond Magazine*,[6] *Information Security Magazine*,[7] *The Journal*,[8] etc.). Additionally, you can find excellent research sites on the web (i.e., Whatis. com,[9] a service by Tech Target, EventID.net[10] and Tech Republic,[11] etc.). Expanding your pool of research materials will greatly add to your understanding of how to manage your network, servers, and users base. Along with all of the free research resources out there are paid vendor services (such as Microsoft's MSDN and TechNet subscriptions, which give you test software and in-depth technical support). Each vendor provides added technical services and can be a great advantage in keeping the IT environment up to date and secure.

---

[3]This is the 90/8/2 rule, that is 90 percent will be self-directed, 8 percent will be provided by a "generalist resource," and 2 percent will be provided by a "specialist resource," "Computer Technology Planning," paragraph 5.12; Langa College, December 6, 2005; http://www.langara.bc.ca/about-langara/policies/media/pdfs/B1004.pdf
[4]http://technet.microsoft.com/en-us/magazine/default.aspx
[5]http://www.informationweek.com/
[6]https://subscribe.1105pubs.com/sub/MI?WP=NEWFREE&TC=1
[7]http://searchsecurity.techtarget.com/
[8]http://thejournal.com/articles/2000/09/01/sun-microcomputer-systems.aspx
[9]http://whatis.techtarget.com/
[10]http://eventid.net/
[11]http://techrepublic.com.com/

Training

Attending vendor-specific courses for certification not only helps your professional development but also benefits the organization by increasing your depth of knowledge in handling IT issues. In fact, certification makes you and your IT operation more respectable to your customers and user base. It provides in-house expertise that is recognized by the IT industry and assures those who use your services that you conform to IT standards. It also allows those who attend courses to network with other IT professionals and build relationships that would be hard to build otherwise.

Maintaining certification[12] ensures your organization that its IT department is prepared for the present and the future. Having in-house experts (developed through certification coursework) also provides a wealth of knowledge that can be shared in the IT organization community and its user base. This knowledge can also help build operational policies and directives that further improve performance and reduce the amount of personnel needed to maintain services. It also reduces the dependency on outside experts to support major projects.

Leadership

System administrators provide the organization with a stable information platform in which to conduct business. System administration provides a technical layer in which the user base can conduct daily operations without the need to understand information architecture, infrastructure, or administration. Guidelines set by the IT community help the user base to use complex communication resources without having in-depth knowledge about what goes on behind the scenes.

Developing simple-to-understand processes and IT policies that simplify daily routines for the user base acts as both a standardization mechanism and organizational cultural foundation where everyone knows what is expected from IT and from the user base. This in turn promotes trust and cooperation between IT and the rest of the organization.

When they combine training, research, and communication with simple-to-follow rules, system administrators have a professional presence in the organization. Establishing daily routines to ensure service availability enforces this perception of professionalism. Acting quickly and completely to resolve user issues builds respect and cooperation between the IT community and its user base. Knowing that no one knows everything and being willing to let users know when you don't have the answer but will take the time to learn builds a sound IT/user relationship.

History in Brief
General

History is cyclic. This holds true for information technology and system administration. Policies, processes, and technology cycle between centralized and distributed management. Early on in the development of automated information processing, everything was centralized and system administration was performed in a bubble. As networks evolved, distributed information systems broke the bubble and complicated system administration and security.

---

[12]Example certifications: Microsoft MTA, MCSA, MCSE, MCSD. Cisco CCENT, CCDA, CCNA, CCT, CCNP. VMware Certified Associate, Professional, Implementation Expert, and Design Expert. SANS Institute GICSP, GIAC, GCCC. ITIL Foundation, Service Operations, Service Transition, and Service Design.

As networks matured, an appreciation for centralized management reemerged. This recreated a centralized environment that reined in the less controllable distributed management technologies and grew a host of system administration tools that have defined today's IT world. Understanding how this cycle affects the modern IT organization builds appreciation for all of the thought that has gone into the industry.

IT Timeline

- 1947 – The first electronic computing system was the ENIAC[13].

- 1951 – UNIVAC[14] computer became the first commercial computing system

- 1953 – IBM 701 EDPM[15] led to the FORTRAN programming language

- 1960 – The IBM 7090 was the first electronic computer to use transistors

- 1963 – Douglas Engelbart[16] invents the mouse

- 1969 – Arpanet was born,[17] which was the early Internet, and UNIX[18] was developed

- 1971 – Intel 4004, the first microprocessor,[19] and e-mail[20] was invented

- 1973 – Ethernet computer networking, TCP/IP[21]

- 1975 – Microsoft[22] was founded

- 1976 – Apple I[23] II and TRS-80

- 1978 – VisiCalc spreadsheet

- 1979 – WordStar word processing

- 1981 – IBM PC, MS DOS

- 1982 – Sun Microsystems[24] was incorporated

---

[13]"The ENIAC Story", Martin H Weik, 1961, Ordinance Ballistic Research Laboratories, Aberdeen Proving Ground, MD. http://ftp.arl.army.mil/~mike/comphist/eniac-story.html
[14]"The History of the UNIVAC - J Presper Eckert and John Mauchly", Mary Bellis, 1997, http://inventors.about.com/library/weekly/aa062398.htm
[15]"The History of International Business Machines and IBM Computers", Mary Bellis, 1997, http://inventors.about.com/od/computersandinternet/a/IBM701.htm
[16]1963: "Douglas Engelbart invents the Mouse", Berkley Engineering, 2007, http://www.coe.berkeley.edu/about/history-and-traditions/1963-douglas-engelbart.html
[17]"History of the Internet", Hilary Poole, Tami Schuyler, Theresa M. Senft, Christos J.P. Moschovitis, May, 1999, http://www.historyoftheinternet.com/chap2.html
[18]"UNIX, LINUX ,and variant history", Computer Hope, 1998-2009, http://www.computerhope.com/history/unix.htm
[19]"Intel's First Microprocessor – the Intel® 4004" , Intel Corporation, 2009, http://www.intel.com/museum/archives/4004.htm
[20]"The History of E-Mail & Ray Tomlinson", Mary Bellis, About.com, 2009, http://inventors.about.com/od/estartinventions/a/email.htm
[21]TCP/IP History; http://www.tcpipguide.com/free/t_TCPIPOverviewandHistory.htm
[22]"Microsoft Corporation", International Directory of Company Histories, Vol.63. St. James Press, 2004; http://www.fundinguniverse.com/company-histories/Microsoft-Corporation-Company-History.html
[23]"The Beginning", The Apple Museum, 2009, http://www.theapplemuseum.com/index.php?id=55
[24]"Company Profile", Sun Microsystems, 2009. http://www.sun.com/aboutsun/company/history.jsp#1982

- 1983 – Apple Lisa, Novell[25] Networking
- 1984 – Apple Macintosh
- 1985 – Microsoft Windows
- 1989 – HTTP[26] was created to share files
- 1991 – Linux[27] was introduced
- 1992 – DEC introduces the Alpha[28] 64 bit processor
- 1993 – Microsoft Windows NT[29]
- 1995 – OpenBSD and Windows 95 released
- 1996 – Microsoft Windows NT 4.0
- 1998 – Microsoft Windows 98, and Solaris 7, and VMware Inc. founded
- 1999 – Apple OS X (Darwin) was released
- 2000 – Microsoft Windows 2000 and Active Directory, Red Hat Linux 6.2
- 2001 – Microsoft Windows XP
- 2003 – Microsoft Windows 2003, Red Hat Enterprise Linux 3, ESX Server 2.0 released
- 2004 – Microsoft Windows XP Sp2
- 2006 – Microsoft Windows Vista, VMware infrastructure 3 released
- 2008 – Microsoft Windows Server 2008, Vista SP1
- 2009 – Microsoft Windows 7, VMware Vsphere released
- 2011 – Microsoft Windows 8
- 2015 – Microsoft Windows 10

Personal Computing and Networking

Many people tend to look at the IBM PC as the beginning of personal computers and networking, but in 1973, Xerox introduced not only the concept of personal computers but also networking. Xerox created a computer that introduced Ethernet, mice, and an icon-based graphic user interface. While the concept was expensive and power hungry, it was to be the base for all modern business computers. But, not until the Apple Lisa did the concept of a point-and-click desktop really take off.

---

[25]Novell, Inc. History of the Company, http://www.fundinguniverse.com/company-histories/Novell-Inc-Company-History.html

[26]"Hypertext and CERN", Tim Berners-Lee, CERN, March 1989, May 1990, http://www.w3.org/Administration/HTandCERN.txt

[27]"UNIX, LINUX ,and variant history", Computer Hope, 1998-2009, http://www.computerhope.com/history/unix.htm

[28]http://www.cpu-collection.de/?lo=co&l1=DEC&l2=Alpha%20AXP

[29]"Windows History", Microsoft Incorporated, 2009, http://www.microsoft.com/windows/WinHistoryDesktop.mspx

IBM looked at the personal computer in a very different way—text based and individual (not networked). IBM also put a heavy price on its interpretation of what business needed. IBM executives did not take the concept of home computers seriously until IBM clones flooded the market. IBM used public available technology to engineer most of its product (a mistake that would cost them dearly). Further, they contracted with a little known company (Microsoft) to manufacture their operating system. Both of these choices are now realized to be dramatic failures in forecasting the market.

The birth of the IBM PC clone started the personal computer boom and the public's interest. This interest grew exponentially. For a while there was the family computer store that made cheap IBM clones and flooded the market. From these came more elaborate "national" brands (such as Compaq and Wise) with newer technologies that included portable computers. Companies like the Sinclair and HeathKit promoted cheaper reliable systems that introduced the concept of non-technical people building their own systems from scratch.

Apple, with founders Steve Jobs and Steve Wozniak created educational systems such as the Apple II series, which led to the Macintosh. Apple tried to corner the market on graphic-based operating systems (GUI[30]), suing Microsoft when they manufactured the first versions of Windows. Apple lost the suit given that they themselves had copied Xerox in order to create their popular GUI. The failed suit opened the door for Microsoft to battle head on with Apple for that market share.

Novell Inc. (to be referred from this point on as Novell) and Sun Microsystems (to be referred from this point on as Sun) built a strong market for network operating systems (aka NOS[31]). For many years it seemed that no one could compete with Novell for PC networking systems. There were specialized networking systems such as PICK and LANTastic, but these did not compete on the same level as Novell. UNIX, ULTRIX, and VMS were expensive to own and manage. They required specialized knowledge that was not common to the layperson. Microsoft challenged all of these with its release of Windows for Workgroups, which made peer-to-peer[32]networking possible at a fraction of the cost.

Novell, in an attempt to corner the market on personal computer software (to accent its networking strategy), started buying up companies such as WordPerfect to build an office suite. This strategy over-tasked Novell and took its eye away from its core business (networking). At the same time, Microsoft enlisted the aid of a software engineer from the company that made VMS[33] and incorporated its technology into its Windows GUI, creating what is now known as NT technology. Since VMS was a mature operating system used for large-scale networking operations, the marriage of technologies became the downfall of Novell as the leader in the networking marketplace.

Novell tried to regain ownership of the networking marketplace by creating an innovative directory concept, NDS.[34] Novell had touched on an area of networking management that would set the level of administration for many years to come. Unfortunately for Novell, Microsoft quickly engineered its own

---

[30]GUI stands for graphical user interface.

[31]NOS is a computer operating system that is designed primarily to support workstations, personal computers, and, in some instances, older terminals that are connected on a local area network (LAN). Artisoft's LANtastic, Banyan VINES, Novell's NetWare, and Microsoft's LAN Manager are examples of network operating systems. In addition, some multi-purpose operating systems, such as Windows NT and Digital's OpenVMS, come with capabilities that enable them to be described as a network operating system.

[32]Peer-to-peer is a communications model in which each party has the same capabilities and either party can initiate a communication session. Other models with which it might be compared include the client/server model and the master/slave model. In some cases, peer-to-peer communications are implemented by giving each communication node server and client capabilities. In recent usage, peer-to-peer has come to describe applications in which users can use the Internet to exchange files with each other directly or through a mediating server.

[33]VMS (Virtual Memory System) is an operating system from Digital Equipment Corporation (DEC) that runs in its older mid-range computers. VMS originated in 1979 as a new operating system for DEC's new VAX computer, the successor to DEC's PDP-11. VMS is a 32-bit system that exploits the concept of virtual memory.

[34]NDS (Novell Directory Services) is a popular software product for managing access to computer resources and keeping track of the users of a network, such as a company's intranet, from a single point of administration. Using NDS, a network administrator can set up and control a database of users and manage it using a directory with an easy-to-use graphical user interface (GUI).

version of directory services (Active Directory) and packaged it with their common server package Windows 2000. While Active Directory was a less mature technology than NDS, it was cheaper and backed by a company on the rise in the market place. It can be said that NDS was a better directory service but Microsoft turned out to be a more viable company. Today Microsoft commands a 75 percent market share on all software sold throughout the world. If you were to bet your company's IT budget on any one company, it would be very difficult to choose someone other than Microsoft at this point.

Apple has built a significant place in the market. Apple has a strong user base that will not give up on the company and a growing multimedia market. They have re-tooled their operating system to incorporate UNIX and have made a strong showing by doing so. They have also deversified creating the iPad, iPhone, and a host of other well received products.

Summary

The timeline presented depicts sample milestones that have led to current modern system administration. Footnotes are added to help the reader go more in-depth on select topics. While this list is in no way complete, it is intended to act as a beginning to understand what has transpired over the years.

Much of what is taken as "best practices" is the result of trial and error with great economical cost. As time goes on and technology moves forward, more errors will take place and money will be spent.

It is true that people who do not learn from history are destined to repeat it. Taking time to explore the development of technology, including who designed it and why, helps in understanding procedures and processes that have developed over time.

It often seems that policies and procedures are over complicated, tedious, and time consuming. Experience tells us that this is necessary. Trial and error fine tunes each process to the point that anyone can follow. What is required from the system administrator is the ability to work with issues caused when the procedures fail to give the expected results.

Here is a short list of some books that may prove helpful:

- *PowerShell in Depth: An Administrator's Guide,* by Don Jones, Richard Siddaway, and Jeffrey Hicks

- *Microsoft Windows Networking Essentials,* by Darril Gibson

- *Windows Server 2008 Inside Out,* by William Stanek

- *VMware Horizon Suite: Building End User Experience,* by Paul O'Doherty and Stephane Asselin

- *Essential Virtual SAN (VSAN): Administrator's Guide to VMware Virtual SAN,* by Cormac Hogan

- *Cybersecurity for Dummies*

- *Cyber Security Essentials 1st Edition,* by James Graham (Editor), Ryan Olson (Editor)

CHAPTER 2

■ ■ ■

Home Networking

Like it or not, the majority of users often compare performance of an organization's network to the network in their home. Knowing how to explain the fundamental difference between the two benefits users and system administrators. Being able to present the many layers of administration overhead may lead home users to adapt some of the practices that organizations use to protect and maintain their IT investment. This chapter covers the fundamentals of the home network and builds the foundation for understanding an organization's network.

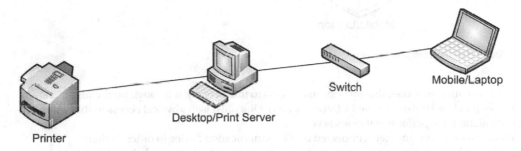

Figure 2-1. *Basic home network*

In Figure 2-1, there are four primary devices:

- Printer
- Desktop computer
- Networking switch
- Laptop computer

Each device presents a type of physical asset. The printer can include a scanner, fax, and more. The desktop provides access to the printer device and may also act as central storage for the laptop. The networking switch can connect desktops, laptops, and even printers if they are networkable and share the same communication interface. The laptop acts as a mobile office device to either work outside the home or transport data. The network connection can be wired or wireless.

Computers purchased for the home are consumer products, preconfigured and simplified for the mass market. They are quickly configured and brought online with little technical expertise. Consumer computer products differ from commercial computer products purchased for office use. They are essentially *turn key* products that have a shorter life span and come with a lot of sample software that eats up disk space and advertises vendor preferences.

Wired Networking

The four basic network home devices can be configured several ways. The various options have their pros and cons. In Figure 2-2, the desktop acts as print server and is connected to the printer via a USB cable. The desktop and laptop computers are connected by Ethernet cables via a networking switch.

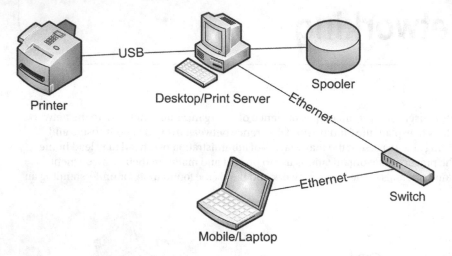

Figure 2-2. *Wired network with print server*

Since there is no Internet access, the only external access to this network is through physically connected devices (such as USB devices and CD/DVD disks). One must gain physical access to this network or provide physical media to perform malicious acts.

A network is *two or more* computers connected by a communication device in order to share information and peripherals (printers, modems, etc.). Even in the most basic network there is the foundation for all networks:

- Network interface (the technology that connects computers)
- Protocols (the way in which computers understand each other)
- Shared devices (printers, modems, hard drives, etc.)

These three things (network interface, protocols, and shared devices) work together to form an alliance of resources that combine their software and hardware to extend the capabilities beyond that of a single computer. Instead of a single desktop anchored to one physical location, the combination of laptop and desktop expand resources to include both a home office and mobile office extension.

In Figure 2-2, there is a shared disk drive on the desktop labeled "spooler". For the desktop to share the printer, it must also share a common folder for print jobs to be staged so that the printer can process them. The print server (desktop) must allow the laptop to process print jobs through this shared folder. In order for that to take place, the laptop must have permission granted by the desktop.

Permission is granted through shared user accounts. The desktop must allow select laptop user accounts to place print jobs into its spooler folder (see Figure 2-3).

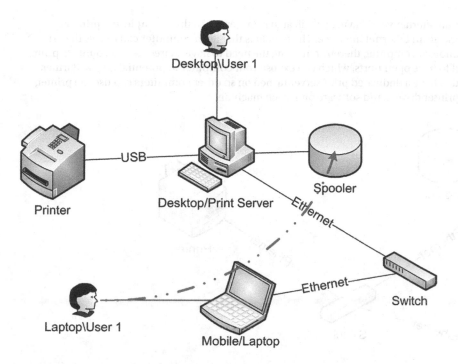

Figure 2-3. *Shared user accounts*

The shared user accounts only provide part of the solution. The desktop and laptop must also share a common print driver that can communicate with the printer in order to process the final print job. The complication arises from the fact that the system administrator must maintain common user accounts on both computers as well as print drivers and any special software that operates any secondary functions the printer provides (such as a scanner or fax).

There must also be an open port[1] granted by the desktop computer so that the print application can communicate between the desktop and laptop. Ports are numbered and have standards by which system administrators can evaluate their purpose. Port 35 is used for "any private print server".[2] All external communication goes through ports, and every open port is a potential security threat. Knowing the basic port numbers and their associated application helps you better understand the threat level associated with the number of open ports on a desktop or laptop.

The de facto protocol for modern networks is TCP/IP.[3] A product of the U.S. DOD in 1973, it is both *the* Internet protocol and the default protocol for all modern networking systems, personal computers, and servers sold today. All consumer computers auto-configure TCP/IP to connect to any visible workstation and/or network device, whether the device is wired or wireless.

---

[1]"In programming, a port (noun) is a "logical connection place" and specifically, using the Internet's protocol, TCP/IP, the way a client program specifies a particular server program on a computer in a network." See http://searchnetworking .techtarget.com/sDefinition/0,,sid7_gci212807,00.html.

[2]IANA Port Assignments, 1998-2009 Network Sorcery, Inc. See http://www.networksorcery.com/enp/protocol/ ip/ports00000.htm.

[3]Introduction to TCP/IP; H. Gilbert, Yale University, 1995. See http://www.yale.edu/pclt/COMM/TCPIP.HTM.

Figure 2-4 provides an alternative to having a dedicated print server. In this example, the printer is connected to the network via an Ethernet interface. The benefit is that each computer can access the printer without going through another computer, thereby removing the need to have shared user accounts to print. It also removes the need to have open ports, which can expose your computer to potential attack. Further, it also removes the need to have a dedicated print server turned on so other computers can use the printer. You still have to install printer drivers and software onto each machine.

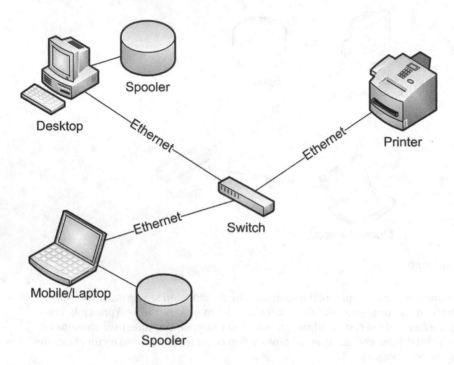

Figure 2-4. *Network-enabled printer*

There are some multifunction printers that won't allow computers to remotely use their extended functions (scanners, faxes, etc.). By setting up network TCP/IP printers, every computer is considered to be directly connected. This eliminates that limitation.

Since each computer has its own spooler, there is no single point of failure other than the printer device itself. The drawback is that whoever prints first, prints first. With a print server you can queue print jobs, set priorities, and override priorities. In Figure 2-4, each spooler ignores the other.

Wired Network Pros

1. Physical security

2. Reliable bandwidth

3. Easy to troubleshoot

Wired Network Cons

1. Cables restrict mobility
2. Clutter
3. Not easily scalable

Wireless Networking

Wireless networks (Figure 2-5) have become very popular for home use. They provide mobility and ease of use, and get rid of all those cables that clutter up the house.

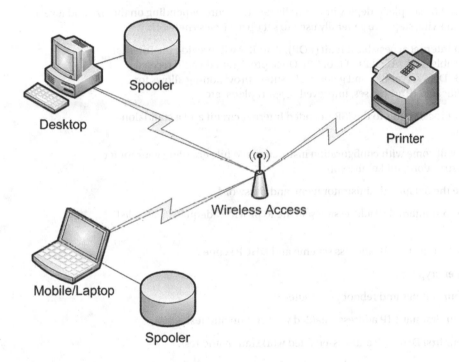

Figure 2-5. *Wireless home network*

In Figure 2-5, the Ethernet switch has been replaced with a wireless access point. Instead of wires, radio waves act to transmit data. There are currently six technology standards in place to support wireless networks (see Table 2-1).

Table 2-1. *Wireless Technology Standards*

Technology	Coding	Modulation Type	Speed
802.11b	11 bits (Barker sequence)	PSK	1Mbps
802.11b	11 bits (Barker sequence)	QPSK	2Mbps
802.11b	CCK (4 bits)	QPSK	5.5Mbps
802.11b	CCK (8 bits)	QPSK	11Mbps
802.11a	CCK (8 bits)	OFDM	54Mbps
802.11g	CCK (8 bits)	OFDM	54Mbps

Wireless networks can be simple to deploy but complicated to secure depending on the size and level of security required. The following steps are generally used to set up a wireless network.

1. Establish an Internet accessible circuit (POP). Your ISP will provide the Internet POP (fiber, cable, DSL, ADSL2+, T1, or T3). Once provisioned you'll receive a dedicated IP, DNS server list, and gateway. Business provisioning allows for multiple dedicated IP addresses, improved support plans, etc.

2. Connect your local router to the ISP-provided Internet circuit and a standalone workstation.

3. Your router will come with configuration instructions. While enabling your router using the instructions, make sure you:

    a. Change the default administrator name and password.

    b. Define your internal IP addressing scheme to provide adequate available IP addresses.

    c. Establish your static IP address scheme and DHCP scope.

    d. Enable encryption.

    e. Save your settings and reboot your router.

    f. Add your first static IP address-enabled workstation and test.

    g. Add your first DHCP IP address-enabled workstation and test.

4. Add other workstations as needed.

5. Back up your router configuration as needed.

Wireless networks provide lower bandwidth than wired networks (Ethernet networks start at 10Mbps and can support up to 1Gbps of bandwidth), which results in lower data transfer speeds. But for the home office, 54Mbps is usually acceptable. The distance between wireless access point and computer (or networked device) has a direct effect on how fast data can be transmitted. Generally speaking, the farther the distance, the longer it will take to download the same data package using the same hardware.

Distance can be defined using four categories (see Figure 2-6)[4]:

1. Short range is about 12 feet

2. Medium range is about 40 feet

3. Long range is about 50 feet

4. Very long range is about 100 feet

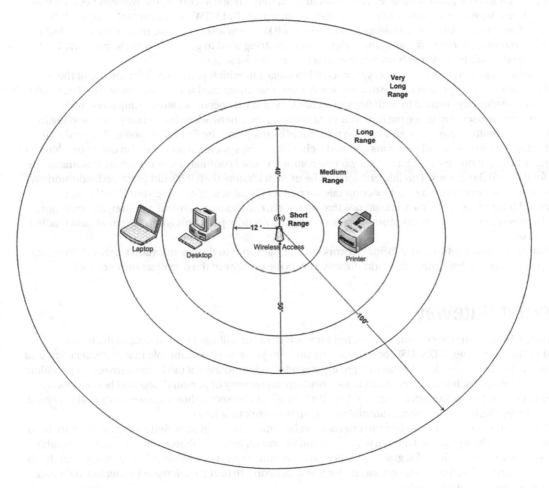

Figure 2-6. *Wireless access range categories*

The quality of equipment is also important. While technology standards apply to all vendors producing wireless components, reliability issues arise from poor manufacturing.

---

[4]Joe and Jack's comments on various commercial 802.11 (a, b, and g); January, 2004. See http://gpsinformation.net/articles/80211ap.htm.

Wireless Security

Wired networks require physical access to the network. Wireless networks require that you be in a close proximity to the wireless access point in order to connect to that network. Wireless networks require additional security measures in order to keep unwanted guests from accessing the network and/or devices on the network.

By encrypting the access point using WPA[5] or WEP,[6] access to the wireless network can be made more secure. WPA and WEP provide sufficient initial security, in that anyone accessing the wireless network will be challenged to provide an access key to establish a connection. But WPA[7] is more secure than WEP. If someone has the time and the knowledge to hack the WEP key, over a short period of time they can deduce the key by monitoring network traffic and isolating the key string used to gain access to the network. WPA is much more difficult to hack and is usually the preferred choice for security.

In either case, wireless access encryption is only a means by which you can restrict the use of the network and not a complete security solution. Every computer connected to the wireless or wired networks should be individually secured by both firewall technology and user accounts with strong passwords.

Many home users fail to see the importance of securing their network or home computers and log in using a local administrator's account with no passwords enabled and the firewall disabled. This makes it easy for the user to download programs and make changes to the system ad hoc, but also opens the door for anyone wanting to do mischief. Since many home computers hold confidential information, this practice is both foolish and dangerous. This information can be used in identity theft if it's not protected. Additionally, open wireless networks can be used by criminals to conduct illegal activities using your IP address, or they could have access to home workstations that do not have sufficient password and firewall protection. Luckily, most consumer products prompt users to establish security protocols when they are being readied for first use.

For the system administrator, home networks pose a backdoor to the organization's network. Working to help users secure their home networks directly affects the security of the organization's network.

Internet Gateway

Everyone who has a home computer either has Internet access or will have it sometime in the future. Whether through cable, ISDN, DSL, or modem, the Internet plays an important role in the use, security, and operation of home networks. The Internet greatly extends the boundaries of the home network by providing a wealth of resources, but it also poses a greater threat to the security of personal data and home network security. Ensuring security is clearly impossible. Promoting a more secure home network is a goal everyone (including the organization's system administrator) should work to achieve.

When you open your network to the Internet you become part of a greater network. Your network is no longer protected by a physical boundary. Your computers are no longer isolated from strangers being able to access your personal files. You gain the ability to communicate with others outside your home, but that is a two-way street. It becomes more important for home networks to build a defensive barrier between your computers and the outside world.

---

[5]WPA stands for WiFi Protected Access
[6]WEP stands for Wired Equivalent Privacy
[7]"The Difference between WEP and WPA", IT.Toolbox.com, B. Wilds, 2007. See http://it.toolbox.com/blogs/unwired/the-difference-between-wep-and-wpa-20092.

In Figure 2-7, there are three basic layers of security:

1. Local Workstation Protection Layer
2. Boundary Protection Layer
3. Unsecured Layer

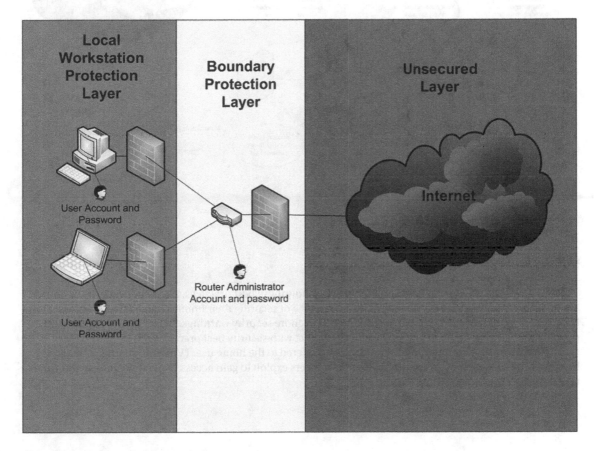

Local Workstation Protection Layer

User Account and Password

User Account and Password

Boundary Protection Layer

Router Administrator Account and password

Unsecured Layer

Internet

Figure 2-7. *Internet access security layers*

In a perfect world the home network would have at least two firewalls (local workstation and boundary); user accounts with strong passwords; a masked Internet gateway address with WPA encryption for wireless access; and encrypted disk drives. With all of that in place, the home network is only reasonably secure. It protects you from average crackers. This is much like placing several locks on the front door to your house—it keeps out those who are stopped by a locked door.

The perfect world would include up-to-date operating system patches, hot fixes, and service packs. It would include a well maintained antivirus/antispyware solution. There would be weekly scheduled deep scans for malicious code and restricted use of Internet browser activity. Users would log on to their home computers with limited user accounts and only use *root* or *administrative* accounts for maintenance or upgrades. These actions protect you from the more aggressive crackers—they keep out those who are stopped by home alarm systems, locked doors, and a home owner with a gun (see Figure 2-8).

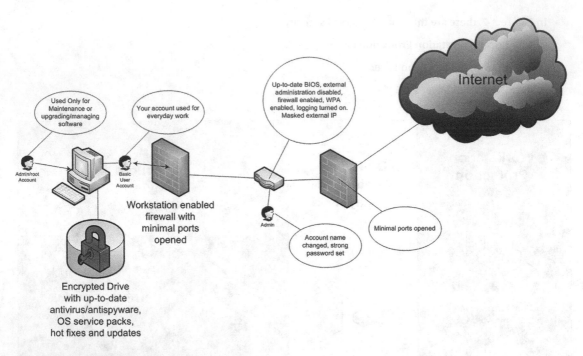

Figure 2-8. *Home security best practices*

But in reality, very few (if any) home networks follow these best practices. Home networks by definition are unsecure. People generally don't see the importance of securing their home against outside access. Most home users find security to be an inconvenience and ignore security warnings. In fact the very goals most people have for their home networks constantly conflict with security best practices.

The vast array of communication technologies offered to the home user (VoIP, file sharing, e-mail, Internet browsing, etc.) open security holes that crackers exploit to gain access to personal information and take control of system resources (Figure 2-9).

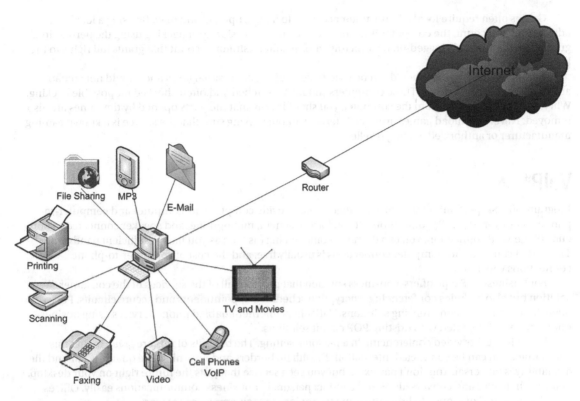

Figure 2-9. Multifunction home computer services

There is a constant struggle between keeping things patched and thwarting the next malicious attack. But the average home users don't see the danger; they feel the frustration when a program on their computer keeps questioning them when they choose to do something that might be dangerous, such as installing uTorrent.[8] If their credit card company was as lax about protecting the same data as what they keep on their home computers, those users would be outraged and speechless.

The versatility of home networks drive users to believe that they should have the same technologies in their office as they have at home. They should have the same ease of use in the office as they have at home. But this versatility and ease of use comes at a price. It opens holes in home security. It compounds the cost of operations. For the home network, the cost is absorbed over time. The growing cost is not managed. The growing lack of security is ignored and forgotten. The threat to security from the outside world through the Internet gateway is someone else's problem.

Gaming

If you have children on your home network, you likely have online gaming taking place. Online gaming is one of the greatest security threats that home networks currently face. Many of the games played on a computer use online gaming or online validation when a game is played. Ports are opened and holes in security are created. Many games offer add-ins that open even more ports. Players often communicate with each other online, which further exposes the system to more security holes.

---

[8]uTorrent, Bit Torrent, Inc. 2009. See http://www.utorrent.com/.

Games often require local administrator accounts to install, update, and play. By using a local administrator account, the computer is further exposed to the possibility of hacking using the permissions granted by the currently logged-on user (in this case, an administrator account that grants full rights to the local system).

Computers with games should not be used to do banking or personal taxes and should not contain any confidential information. These computers should be watched and often checked for possible hacking. When a game is removed from the computer, you should verify that the ports opened by the games are also removed. Never download games from the Internet without making sure that the source is a known gaming manufacturer or authorized gaming reseller.

VoIP[9]

Programs like Skype,[10] Yahoo Instant Messenger,[11] etc. provide computer-to-computer and computer-to-phone voice over IP (VoIP) connections. If you have a camera, microphone, and speaker connected to both ends of the VoIP connection, you can do video conferencing (as long as you have a sufficient bandwidth). The cost of computer-to-computer connections is usually free, and the cost of computer-to-phone connections very low.

For businesses, Skype offers a business solution that provides all of the services of the consumer Skype solution but also includes conferencing, encryption scheduled appointments and secure circuits. Polycom offers high-end video conferencing solutions. VoIP offers Internet-enabled phone services using business phone systems integrated with existing POP circuit solutions.

VoIP gives users video conferencing in a personal setting. The benefits of this are great, in that this communication can be conducted internationally with no borders and no limits. The quality is fair and the availability is universal. You don't pay extra, but you get a service that puts the future right on your desktop. You can share files and conversations and conduct personal or business communications easily. Offices spend a great deal of money to bring the same technology to their employees at work.

---

[9]"VoIP (voice over IP) is an IP telephony term for a set of facilities used to manage the delivery of voice information over the Internet. VoIP involves sending voice information in digital form in discrete packets rather than by using the traditional circuit-committed protocols of the public switched telephone network (PSTN). A major advantage of VoIP and Internet telephony is that it avoids the tolls charged by ordinary telephone service." TechTarget, 2009. http://searchunifiedcommunications.techtarget.com/sDefinition/0,,sid186_gci214148,00.html
[10]http://www.skype.com/intl/en-gb/welcomeback/
[11]http://messenger.yahoo.com/

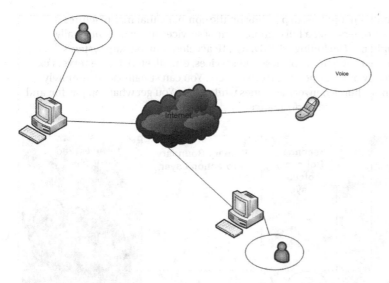

Figure 2-10. *VoIP*

Home Servers

Home servers provide backup solutions, centralized storage, and centralized multimedia management. They can also provide personal web pages available to the Internet. They can act as proxy servers[12] to further protect the local area network from external intrusions.

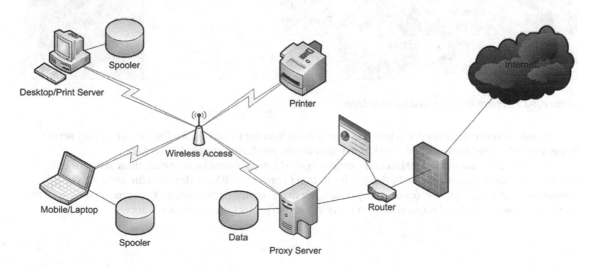

Figure 2-11. *Proxy server and home page*

---

[12]"A proxy server receives a request for an Internet service (such as a web page request) from a user. If it passes filtering requirements, the proxy server, assuming it is also a cache server , looks in its local cache of previously downloaded web pages. If it finds the page, it returns it to the user without needing to forward the request to the Internet." *Tech Target,* 2009. See http://whatis.techtarget.com/definition/0,,sid9_gci212840,00.html.

Home servers come with many different options, depending on the company that manufactures it. Some are glorified NAS[13] systems, while others offer a full complement of services that would normally be provided in a centralized office appliance (including DNS, DHCP, IP acceleration, backup systems, synchronized user data storage, advanced encryption, print server services, e-mail, etc.). Home servers can also give you access to your data remotely or act as personal web servers. You can stream video, remotely back up data while roaming, and monitor home network activities while away. You get what you pay for, and saving money usually means less functionality and performance.

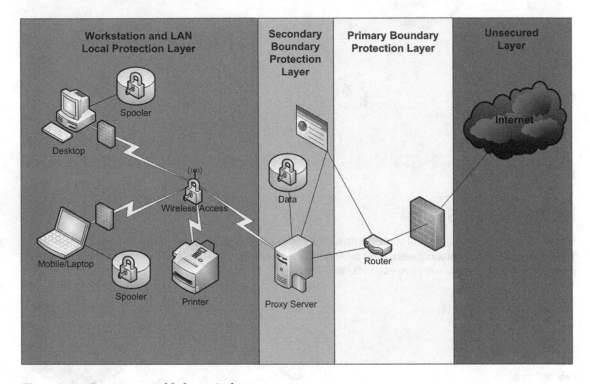

Figure 2-12. *Proxy server added security layer*

Home servers can be used as a further security layer in order to add a third firewall. The proxy server helps shield internal network addresses from external Internet-based attacks by crackers.

In Figure 2-12, there are four layers of security against Internet attacks. However, there remains only one layer against wireless attacks. In this it is important to provide WPA, workstation firewalls, strong passwords, antivirus software, up-to-date patches, hot fixes, service packs, and disk encryption to ensure the workstation and LAN local protection layer provide suitable protection against local access.

---

[13]"Network-attached storage consists of hard disk storage, including multi-disk RAID systems, and software for configuring and mapping file locations to the network-attached device." *Tech Target*, 2009. See http://searchstorage .techtarget.com/sDefinition/0,,sid5_gci214410,00.html.

Backups vs. Archives

Backing up data is a process of duplicating data with compression as a snapshot for future retrieval. Backup data is not accessed in day-to-day work, but used in case data becomes corrupt or is accidentally deleted. Backup data is not modified in normal work activity. It is only modified when a new backup is made using the existing backup file as the target destination.

An archive of data is the extension of the backup process where the data backed up is located in an offline storage facility and usually offsite. The purpose of an archive is to have backups of your data is a safe place in case an environmental disaster destroys your work/home environment. Being offline, archives are generally safe from day-to-day operations and can be retrieved when necessary. They should be deleted only when archival data space runs out or the value of the data stored is no longer relevant.

Few home networks successfully archive data. But when they do, it is done either through removable storage (thumb drives, external disk drives, DVDs, or tape) or using web based storage (such as Microsoft's Azure applications and online storage). Backups stored on home servers are not archives.

In any case, RAID arrays are neither backups nor archives. RAID[14] is used to provide failover for hard disks so that when a disk fails, data is protected. Corruption or accidental data deletions are not protected using RAID since every change made is actively updated by the RAID set. Anyone who thinks that RAID is a type of backup technology will find out quickly they are mistaken.

Cloud Computing

Cloud computing is an idea that has been in the works for some time. The basic concept is that an online technology vendor provides application and data storage online (such as Microsoft's Azure product) so that data and applications you use are always available no matter where you are and what computer you use. Cloud computing offers backup technologies, archival processes, and automatic application updates as a single package to customers. Using secure Internet connections, cloud computing offers security in a corporate environment.

The benefits of cloud computing are impressive. The drawbacks are that customers do not own but use the software and data space. Many home users do not trust corporations with their most personal data. They find the possibility of losing access to their personal data and applications because of billing errors or bad network connections a deal-breaker. Many people will find cloud computing a frightening concept.

---

[14]"What is RAID?", *Tech Target*, 2009. See http://searchstorage.techtarget.com/sDefinition/0,sid5_gci214332,00.html#.

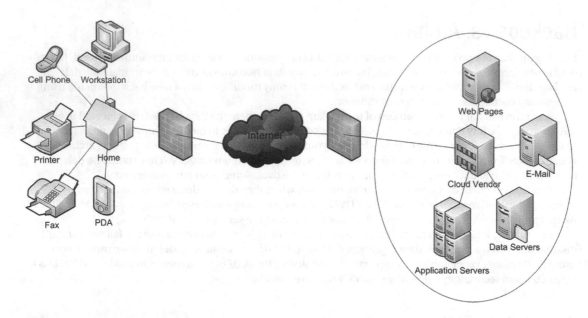

Figure 2-13. *Cloud computing*

Figure 2-13 shows a simplified depiction of a cloud computing relationship (i.e., Amazon Web Services, Azure, and Apple iCloud) where all of the front end computing components are part of the home while all of the applications and data services are remotely located through the cloud vendor's corporate site. An encrypted connection between both sites provides security.

Summary

With all that technology for the home, employees expect even more in the workplace. But there is more at home than in the office because home networks don't apply the same safeguards as organization do. The "perfect" home network is just a dream for most people. While they add more and more technology to their network, very few people apply the security as described in this chapter. Most people ignore the potential dangers. Most people don't bother to make or archive their backups, or even care about how or where their data is stored. They don't secure access to their hard drives via encrypted drives and they don't even set strong passwords (most try to avoid passwords altogether). They don't set wireless access encryption (via WPA or WEP) and they don't enable firewalls. They don't download patches for their operating systems and they often fail to keep their antivirus software up to date (if they even have antivirus software).

Simply said, home networks are usually open territory for hackers and crackers, with data available for anyone with an interest. So when the same users expect the same ease of use and variety of technologies in their offices, they don't take into account the overhead that security places on their workstations, servers, and network. Education is the best method for helping users understand the difference. Maybe through education, users will try to build more secure networks at home. And having more secured networks at home will make the workplace network more secure. Helping home users build "network healthy" habits will lead to better employees in the workplace. Securing all networks will greatly reduce the effect viruses and Trojans have on all systems.

CHAPTER 3

■ ■ ■

Planning a Networking Environment

Many new organizations fail to plan for their network environment. Many simply rent space and plug in a network, never building an environmental analysis for power consumption, circuit failover, temperature control, or security. They don't envision a naming convention designed to simplify troubleshooting. This chapter looks at all of this and more. The goal is to build a strong environmental plan that defines a baseline for equipment to be managed as well as growth potential.

Pre-Site Inspection

Before any network is put in place, there needs to be an inspection of the potential facilities supported by existing floor plans, power distribution diagrams, and predefined modifiable space, unmovable barriers, and restrictions.[1] The IT staff and operations, along with other stakeholders, should complete a walkthrough so that a plan for network deployment can be developed in agreement. A basic network environment floor plan should be designed from the result of this inspection. Detailed plans can follow when the network environment plan is formally adopted.

Support documents should be combined in an environmental operations folder along with all generated documents that will be used to develop a network deployment model. Secure any potential agreements to modify the building in writing prior to contracting any cabling work.

Many times the owner of the building has a cabling vendor who knows the building and may do the work at a discount. Many new buildings are pre-designed to support network equipment.

An alternative to building your own network infrastructure is contracting infrastructure architecture to companies like Rackspace. Everything (servers, routing services, security, web hosting, etc.) can be managed through a contract that simplifies site planning and may help lower the overall cost of hardware.

---

[1]See Appendix B, "Network Environment Inspection Templates"

27

General Environment Considerations

- *Floor space* (entrance, exit, electrical outlets, open space, air flow, etc.)

- *Power distribution* (amps, voltage, circuit distribution, and labeling scheme)

- Available *conduits* and *cable trays* (leftover networking products from previous tenants)

- *Phone access ports* (existing, cable type, etc.)

- *Air conditioning* (current load, potential load, and maximum load)

- *Fire equipment* (fire exits, fire extinguishers, etc.)

- *Water access points* (bathrooms, kitchens, water fountains, etc.).

- *Facades* (false walls, floors, ceilings, etc.)

- *Neighbors* (other businesses that are adjacent to your new office space)

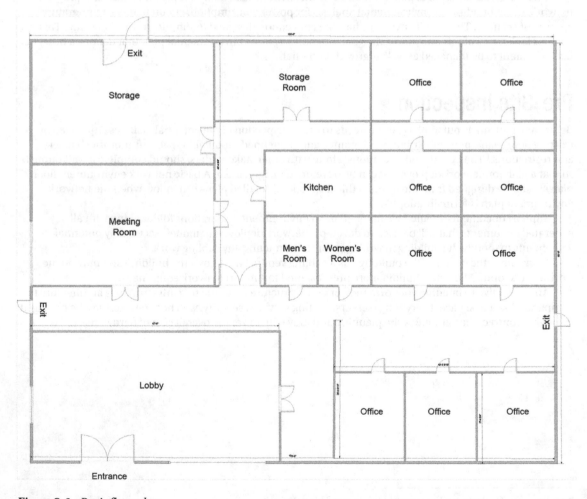

Figure 3-1. *Basic floor plan*

Figure 3-1 diagrams the workspace that will become a networked office space. It is important to get the basics right before you select any space for equipment. Power and air conditioning should be the first consideration. For a server room, the more electrical circuits available the better. Secondly, there needs to be excellent ventilation and air conditioning. Third, there should be a security barrier between customer space and operations. If possible, changes to existing power and air conditioning should be put in place prior to any server equipment.

Take inventory of the office space, including:

- Room numbers

- Electrical outlets in each room

- Circuits distribution (and amps per circuit) for electrical outlets

- Check grounding for each of the outlets and note any issues

- Ventilation associated with each room

- Lighting for each room (check to see if the built-in lights are on separate circuits from the outlets)

- Locate air conditioning and check circuits for the air conditioning to ensure that they are separate from the outlets and lights; find out what the BTU[2] rating is for any air conditioning unit

- Look for any signs of water damage; note any issues and verify that all issues are resolved quickly, before moving in

Make several copies of the floor plans so that you can use them to map out all of the environmental elements that have may affect the deployment of equipment. In the end, you will need to build electronic documentation of your maps but for the mean time, hand-written maps should do the trick.

---

[2]BTU calculator. See http://hearth.com/calc/btucalc.html.

Power Distribution

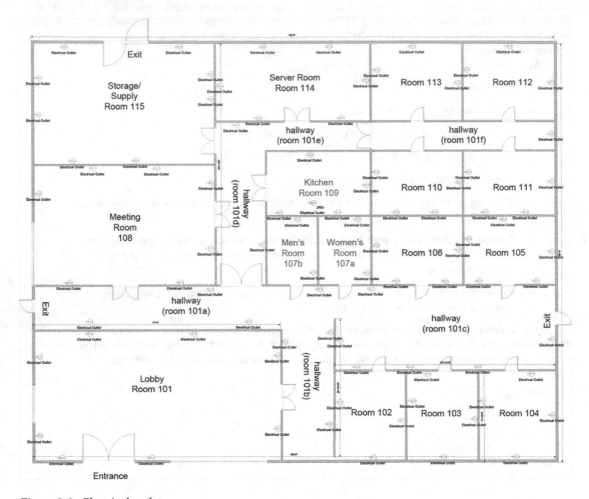

Figure 3-2. *Electrical outlets*

Figure 3-2 represents a first round walkthrough with room numbers and location of electrical outlets in each room. The number of electrical drops (six sets of two outlets) in room 114 provides well-spaced access and an ability to modify circuit layout to enable two or more circuits in support server equipment in the room. Each outlet should be labeled to annotate location and circuit/fuse association (i.e., 114-3-a-data-1A-20, 114-3-b-data-1A-20 for the first part of data outlets). One labeling scheme (the one presented here) labels each circuit by room number, then clockwise ascending number, first or second outlet per pair, type of electrical device, fuse number, and circuit ampere.

- Room number = 114

- First port = 1

- Port (a/b)

- Type = Data / Common

- Fuse #

- Available Amps

Much of the electrical information gathered in the initial facilities inspection should go into three separate documents (the DRP,[3] Facilities/Operational Maintenance Plan, and Network Architecture Development Plan). Appendix C provides an electric circuit form to help you document electrical outlets.

If at all possible, separate all other office equipment from the network equipment (workstations, servers, switches, etc.). This will help you better manage the load and circuit diagram. Users tend to bring in personal stuff (like coffee makers, personal heaters, etc.), which can overload circuits and cause fuses to blow. Keeping those personal devices off the network power distribution will help maintain power continuity and promote a more stable network power distribution environment.

Uninterrupted Power Supply (UPS)

Plan to put uninterrupted power supplies (UPSs) between the network equipment (servers, switches, and routers) and the power outlets. If at all possible, put personal UPSs between the workstations, printers, faxes, and the power outlets. You will need to keep a record[4] of when to replace the UPS batteries so that they are ready when you need them. UPSs also provide surge suppression and power filtering to further the life of the networked equipment. All of this is important in maintaining a stable environment.

Return on Investment

Spending time and money to make sure power is properly distributed, clean, and protected from surges, brownouts, and blackouts helps protect data and productivity. Brownouts and surges damage equipment and can result in loss of data. Blackouts can also damage equipment and result in data loss. Both cost time and money to resolve. Building a strong power resolution plan, providing an effective maintenance procedure, and setting predefined limitations to populating networking equipment based on power distribution helps reduce overall cost in loss of equipment, time, and energy. Time used to rebuild network services when power failures occur take away from daily maintenance and revenue generation.

Having a clear and easily understood description of power distribution and limitations to growth will ensure that surprises don't catch you off guard when you're updating equipment or recovering from power issues. Keeping power distribution documentation up to date will help you to keep system distribution issues under control. Using power distribution documentation to help dictate what can be added or updated on the network will make the decision making process more real.

Air Conditioning

You cannot depend on existing air conditioning to support a server room's potential hardware. Office air conditioning is meant to support workstations, printers, and other standard office equipment, not servers, routers, or other heat-producing systems. It is important to contact an HVAC specialist to have them evaluate additional air conditioning services that will be needed to support your core equipment.

---

[3]DRP stands for Disaster Recovery Plan
[4]See Appendix D, "Uninterrupted Power Supply Maintenance"

There are two paths your organization can take in equipping the server room with proper air conditioning:

1. Install independent air conditioners to supply the server room.

2. Purchase air/power conditioned server racks.

In either event, you will have to get permission to modify the building to support the new equipment. Option number 1 is a semi-permanent solution while option 2 is mobile and can be easily moved if the time comes to relocate.

Option number 2 will be covered first.

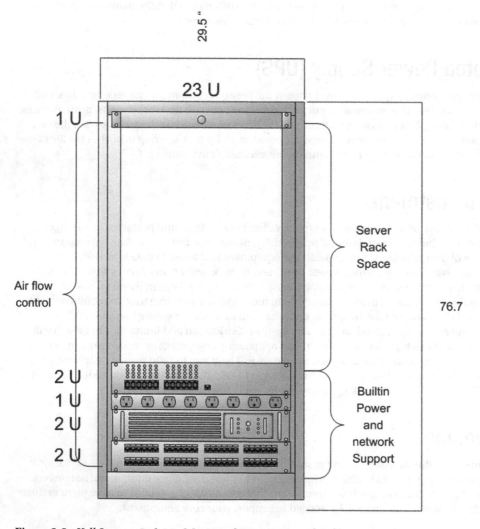

Figure 3-3. *Kell Systems Ltd. Model PSEi37[5] Environmental Cabinet*

---

[5]See http://www.kellsystems.co.uk/37u_rm_server_cabinet.asp.

Racks such as the Kelly Systems Model PSEi37® provide more than simply air conditioning. They provide noise reduction, dust filtering, uninterrupted clean power, surge suppression, cable management, and security. They are relatively expensive but easily reusable. They provide an environmental monitoring system that helps manage systems and automate graceful system shutdowns during natural disasters or unscheduled power outages. And they come in four sizes. They can look like office cabinets or high-tech storage devices. They are perfectly tuned to support core networking hardware that fits inside the box, making them simple to plan and implement.

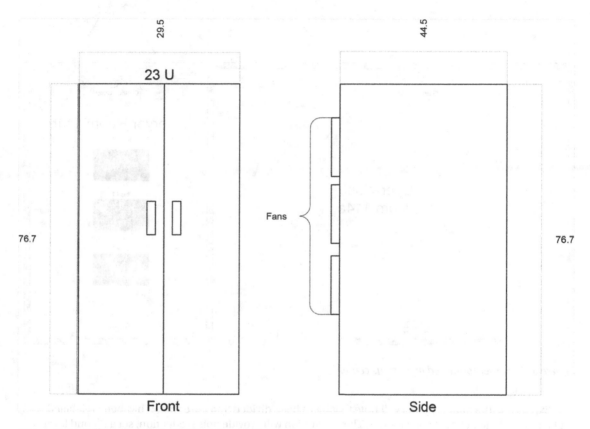

Figure 3-4. *Kell Systems Ltd. PSEi37 external dimensions*

There are many environment-managed rack systems out there and they vary in price. They also vary in options. If you take the time to evaluate all the options on the market and compare them to standard rack mount server rooms where air conditioning, noise reduction, dust management, and power distribution are installed independently, you may find the cost to be relatively equal.

Option number 1 requires more time to implement. You have to contract an HVAC specialist to engineer a solution based not only on the equipment you will need on day one, but also the potential equipment you will grow to need. Many organizations install failover systems that provide twice the equipment than what is required to properly cool their systems. This ensures that when a failure occurs, the secondary air conditioning system will be able to handle the load.

You will need to ensure that the air conditioning systems are on separate power circuits, removed from the power supplying the network servers, routers, and switches. You will also need to provide some sort of noise reduction system (usually a false wall partitioning) between the server racks and the system administrator's operating room. You need to evaluate the dust management and uninterrupted power in case of a power outage. You also need to put in place some sort of software that provides a graceful system shutdown when the power is interrupted.

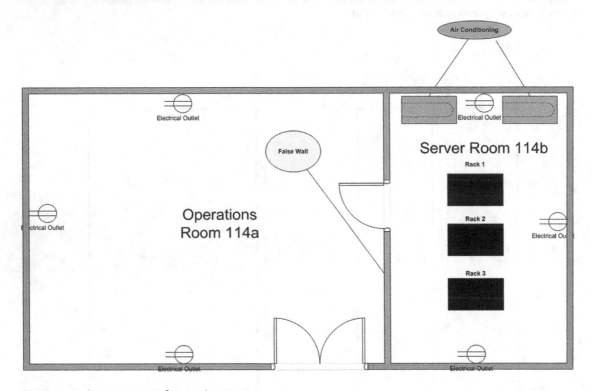

Figure 3-5. *Server room and operations center*

Expanding the room 114, you will note that it has been divided by a false wall. It has been relabeled (114a and 114b) to define the separation. This separation will provide noise reduction, set a second level of security, and minimize the area that will require enhanced air conditioning. The server racks have been placed in the middle of the room to increase air flow and maximize access to the front and back of each rack.

Rack Placement and Power Distribution

If at all possible, there should be at least three feet between a rack and the wall (five feet in the front of the rack to allow for loading and unloading of racked devices). This provides room to access the front and back. The more room the better. Between racks, there should be at least one foot. Many organizations bind racks together for stability and to save room. By having space between each rack, you allow yourself space to open the sides of each rack which may come in handy when power distribution strips are vertically placed on the inside center of the side of the rack. This also makes it easier to add and remove rack mounts for new equipment.

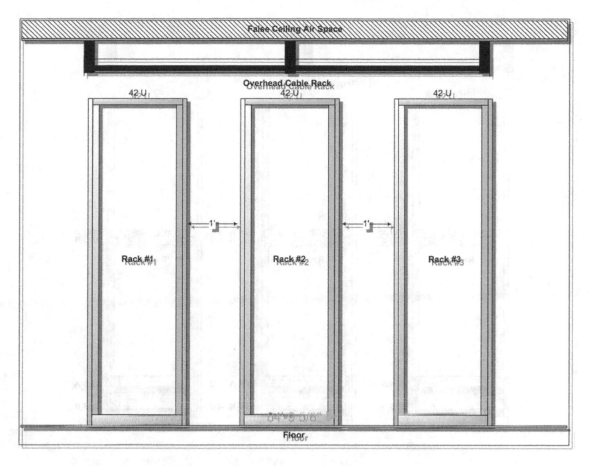

Figure 3-6. *Front view of server racks*

Placing the cable tray above the racks helps keep the cables off the ground, where someone could trip over them and disconnect something.

Power should be distributed per each rack, as shown in Figure 3-7.

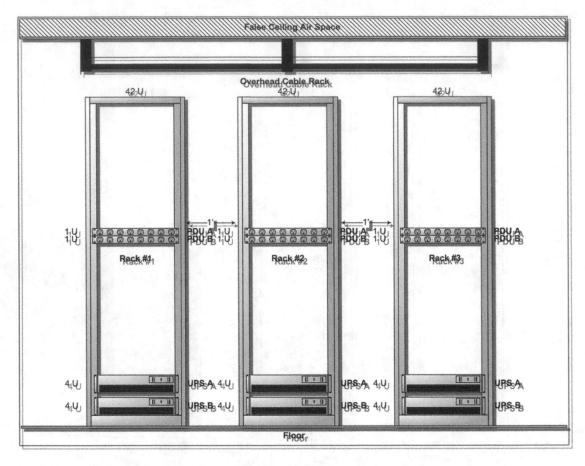

Figure 3-7. *UPS and PDU mounting positions*

Rack mounted UPS systems are heavy. Placing them at the bottom of the rack helps keep each rack from becoming top heavy. There should be two UPS systems per rack for redundancy. There should be two PDU strips (power distribution units or rack mounted power strips) per rack—one for each of the UPS systems mounted in each rack. Each UPS "A" system (as shown in Figure 3-7) is connected to PDU "A" and should be on one power circuit. Each UPS "B" system (as shown in Figure 3-7) is connected to PDU "B" and should be on another power circuit.

Each rack mounted device will have two power supplies. Each device will have one power cable going to PDU "A" of the rack and the other power cable going to PDU "B". This ensures that no one circuit can take out any one device. The PDUs are placed at the center of the rack so that cabling can be evenly distributed top and bottom. Some PDUs are horizontal and others are vertical. Horizontal PDUs offer easy access to power ports without removing the sides of the racks, while vertical PDUs help hide unsightly cables.

An alternative to rack mounted UPSs, central UPS systems are more costly and more difficult to install, but they can free up rack space that could be used for additional networking devices. For simplicity, rack-mounted UPSs will be used in this book's examples.

In large-scale network operating centers there are backup generators that are powered up when the power grid becomes unavailable.

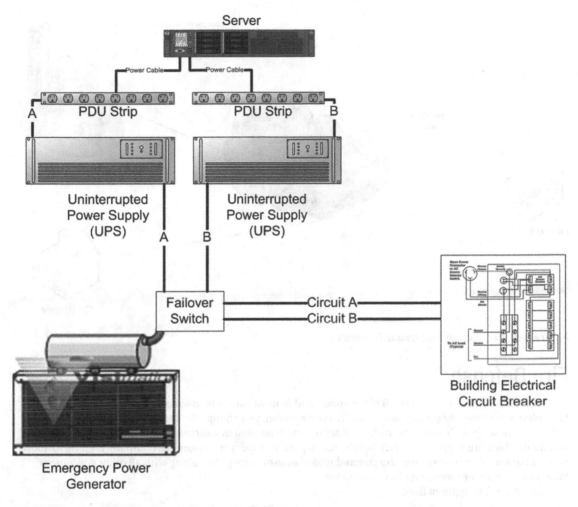

Figure 3-8. Power distribution with generator failover

Some large-scale network operations provide two or more emergency power generators to provide additional redundancy. The generator(s) must provide enough electricity to support all networking equipment connected to the circuits. These failover systems need to be tested annually to ensure they are working properly. A certified electrician is required to build and test this solution.

This solution is for business-critical equipment and usually does not support all office equipment. However, some facilities (such as the military) provide full service.

Another alternative/extension to building an interoffice server room is to rent rack space in a colocation.[6] Your ISP or specialized telecommunication provider can offer high-end server environments with all the power, bandwidth, and IT support your organization can consume. The security is usually excellent and the operational readiness of the facilities and staff is 24x7. This is a costly solution and can have some drawbacks (i.e., accessibility). Business models that put a high price on uptime and customer access (i.e., online services or retail) find colocations a must-have. Some organizations use colocations as a failover site to their internal IT solution, duplicating essential data resources in case of major disasters to their primary site.

---

[6]Colocations: http://searchsoa.techtarget.com/sDefinition/0,,sid26_gci211815,00.html

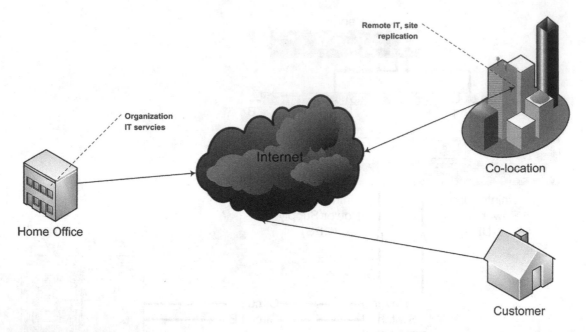

Figure 3-9. *Colocations and remote IT services*

Fire Defense

Fire safety codes set standards for all office space, and in most cases office space comes complete with all fire defense systems. However, when you add a server room, you change the requirements of that room. Standard fire suppression water sprinkler systems cannot be used in a server room. Disabling the sprinkler system disables fire suppression. Neither the fire department nor your insurance company is going to allow that. Make sure that your systems are covered under an insurance policy along with all other equipment located in the server room at replacement value.

There are four types of fires:

1. Type A – Materials such as wood, cloth, paper, and plastics as the fuel source

2. Type B – Flammable liquids, oils, greases, tar, and flammable gases

3. Type C – Electrical fires

4. Type D – Ignitable metals

To have a fire you need three components—oxygen, fuel (as seen in the four types), and heat. You cannot immediately remove the fuel or heat, but you can remove the oxygen. There are several approaches to this but one of the best methods is to use Inergen®. Inergen is safe for humans, equipment, and the environment. It works by displacing oxygen so that the fire has nothing to it keep going. It is perfect for type C fires. You should keep in mind that anything that displaced oxygen will ultimately affect your ability to breathe. All employees should exit the server room quickly. It takes about one minute for Inergen to completely evacuate a room's oxygen.

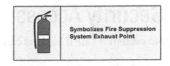

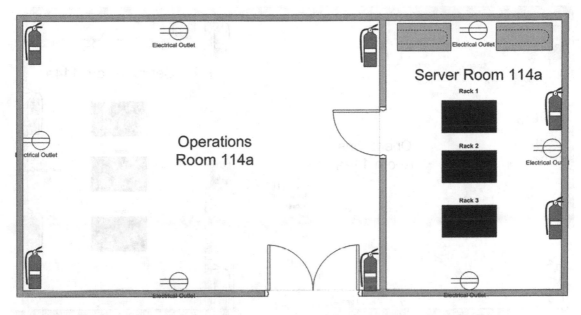

Figure 3-10. *Inergen exhaust points*

There are other fire suppressing systems formerly used in server rooms (such as halon, which was banned in 1995, and CO_2). Many organizations that have installed halon systems prior to 1995 still have them in place. If you are building a new server room you will not have the halon option. If you have a CO_2 system in place (or are thinking of putting one in place) remember that you must completely vacate the server room prior to discharging it. If you fail to get everyone out, you may be extinguishing more than just a fire.

Security Access

No system is safe if hackers can get physical access to it.

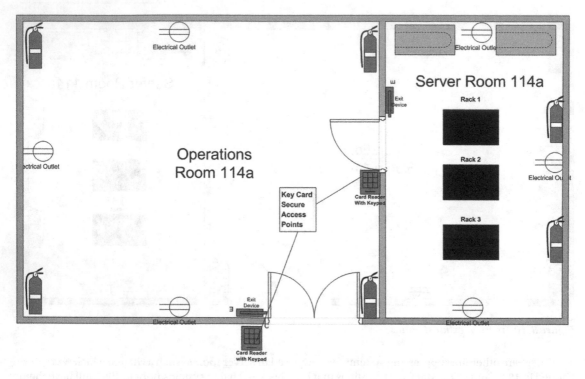

Figure 3-11. *Keycard reader placement*

Access into the operations room must be limited to only those who work for your organization. Access into the server room should be limited to those who work in your organization's IT department. Access should be controlled via access cards and key codes, recorded in a database for review when issues occur. While the operations room may not have direct access to server hardware it will most likely have workstations with open remote access to those servers. This should be managed so visitors do not have direct access to keyboards while remote sessions are open. If someone were to gain access to the server room, anything can happen. Servers are especially susceptible to tampering when physically accessible. Key codes should be changed regularly and key cards replaced annually to ensure security is up to date.

Summary

Whether you are in an organization that has an existing server room environment or you are building one from the ground up, everything covered in this chapter is important in order to keep the network operational. You need to keep everything up to date and well maintained. Keeping logs of fire suppression assets, UPS battery status, air filtration maintenance schedules, and air conditioning equipment is vital to the performance and readiness of your network. Ensuring that all of your network electrical circuits are separated from common office electrical circuits will prove valuable in assessing growth potential and uptime readiness. This is all part of the due diligence that system administration requires.

Having a sound security policy in place to ensures limited access to core networking equipment and will greatly enhance your network's operability and promote user trust in your IT staff. Limiting user access to the operations center were equipment is readied for use and serviced when inoperable will promote quicker response time in servicing your users' IT needs. Having guests in the operations room delays resolution to issues and can cause friction between the IT department and other departments in your organization. Keeping people out of the server room is a must, for security and so that issues don't arise from mishaps or accidents.

All electrical equipment must be redundant. Each network asset needs to be fed by two separate electrical circuits to ensure that no one circuit can bring down any network service. Never run power cables across the floor in the server room. Keep all equipment spaced for easy access and optimized for air flow.

CHAPTER 4

■ ■ ■

Network Layer Architecture

Using industry standards and knowing how and where protocols are applied is essential to understanding your network. This chapter presents the basic standards and protocols used in computer networks and provides diagrams to support their use.

The OSI Model[1]

The OSI model is important for anyone managing networks. It is used to guide the logical and physical structure of network architecture. Knowing what layer is affected by the equipment and software you put in your network helps minimize confusion and simplifies the troubleshooting process. The OSI model is divided into seven specific layers, as shown in Figure 4-1.

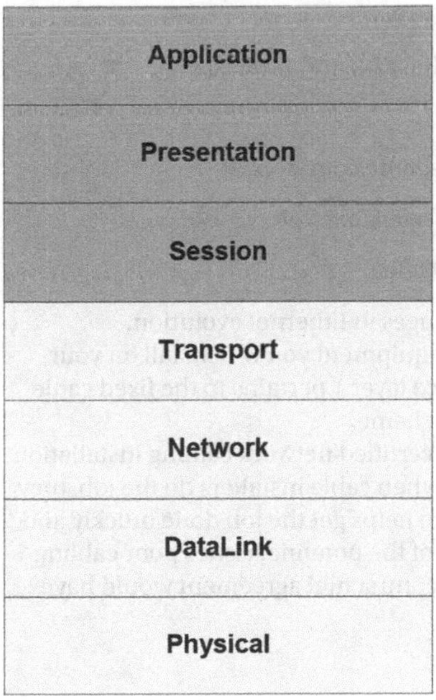

| Application |
| Presentation |
| Session |
| Transport |
| Network |
| DataLink |
| Physical |

Figure 4-1. *OSI model layers*

---

[1]Open Systems Interconnect: http://compnetworking.about.com/cs/designosimodel/a/osimodel.htm; http://www.iso.org/iso/iso_catalogue/catalogue_tc/catalogue_detail.htm?csnumber=18824

Physical Layer

The physical layer (also referred to as layer 1 of the OSI model) pertains to the media that data travels on. Often layer 1 diagrams have layer2 1 and 2 objects mixed; however, there is good reason to keep those assets separate. *Layer 1* objects include:

- Ethernet[2]
- Token ring
- Hubs
- Repeaters
- SAN solution

You can think of "layer 1" as the road that data travels on, but not the highways or freeways. For all intents and purposes, you only need to focus on Ethernet, since there are very few hubs, repeaters, and token ring networks currently being used in IT. Originally designed in 1972 by Xerox, Ethernet has grown into different standards (shown in chronological order):

- 1972 — Ethernet used at Xerox PARC
- 1985 — IEEE 802.3
- 1989 — ISO 802.3a Ethernet for thin coaxial cable (10Base2)
- 1990 — IEEE 802.3i Ethernet over CAT 5 Unshielded Twisted Pair (10BaseT)
- 1993 — IEEE 802.3j defines Ethernet over Fiber (10BaseF)
- 1993 — IEEE 802.1D MAC Layer Bridges (ISO 10038)
- 1995 — IEEE 802.3u defines Fast Ethernet (100BaseTX, 100BaseT4, and 100BaseFX)
- 1998 — IEEE 802.3z defines Gigabit Ethernet over Fiber
- 2001 — IEEE 802.11 (wireless) and Gigabit Ethernet have become common
- 2006 — 10Gbps Ethernet over Category-6 (10000BT) UTP is available
- 2009 — 40Gbps Ethernet (extendable to 100Gbps) IEEE P802.3ba

This list is not complete, but includes all of the most important changes in Ethernet evolution. Ensuring that all cabling conforms to both the latest standards and the equipment you will install on your network is essential to ensuring best performance on your network. Since layer 1 pertains to the fixed cable infrastructure, it would be a costly mistake to install the wrong cabling scheme.

Layer 1 cable, patch panels, and wall ports should be installed by a certified network cabling installation provider. This is not only for technical reasons but for legal protection. When cable installers do the job, they must certify that all cable ends are correct and working. Their experience helps get the job done quickly and reduces the chance of poor cable runs. Doing the job yourself places all of the potential issues poor cabling can produce on your shoulders and removes the legal protection that a contractual agreement would have provided.

---

[2]http://searchnetworking.techtarget.com/sDefinition/0,,sid7_gci212080,00.html

Before you install any network cabling, have a plan for labeling cable ends. What you can't see can make your life miserable. All patch panel ports should have the same label as the wall port they are to be connected to. The label should reflect the location of the wall port and the exact port. There should be at least two ports per person, per office. Common areas should have enough ports to support maximum staffing. There should be two ports per printer (for growth and ready workaround).

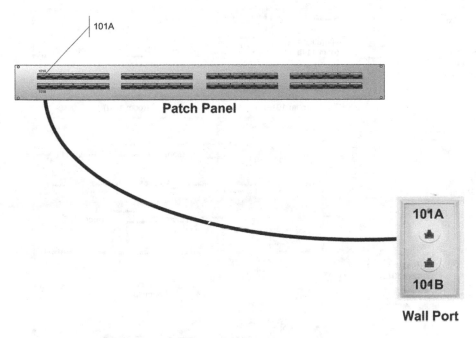

Patch Panel

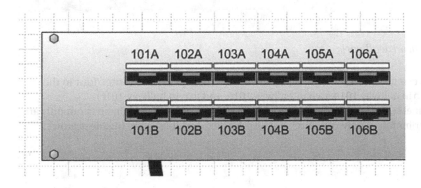

Wall Port

Figure 4-2. *Patch panel to wall port connection*

Keeping port labels as much the same (patch panel/wall port) as physically possible will help make troubleshooting easier and keep things less cluttered.

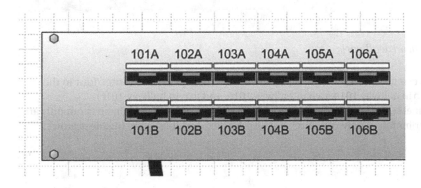

Figure 4-3. *Patch panel sequential labeling*

Your cable installation provider should be able to give you a table for all of the cable drops as well as a map showing the cable distribution.

Whether you install cabling yourself or have a certified cabling installation company do it for you, you will need an appropriate cable kit to test and repair cables when the time comes. Make sure you get the right kit for your installation.

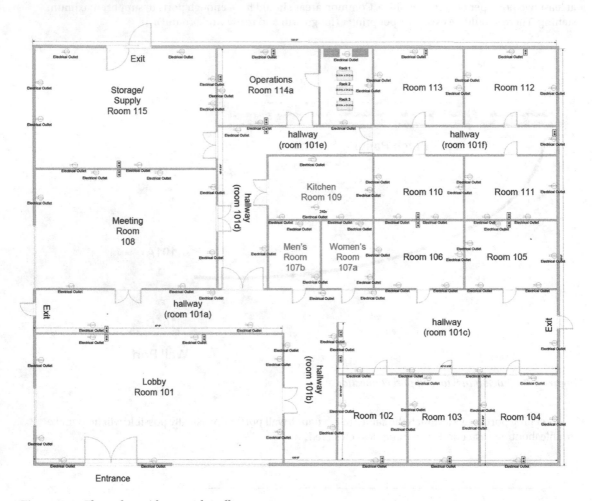

Figure 4-4. *Floor plan with network wall ports*

In Figure 4-4, there are 42 essential wall ports (two per office, six in the operations center, four in the lobby, four in hallway 101c, two in hallway 101a, two in hallway 101e, and two in hallway 101f).

If you look at the patch panel sequential cabling scheme in Figure 4-5, you will find that it is not only an excellent inventory for the distribution of network ports, but also very expandable as the business grows.

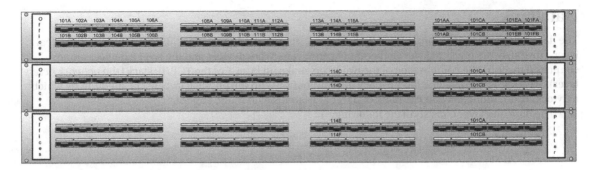

Figure 4-5. *Patch panel sequential labeling scheme*

Patch panels are inexpensive and having more than you think you need is a good policy. There is the capacity for having up to six network drops per room and a total of 18 networked printers total. The first three columns are dedicated to office ports while the last column is dedicated to printers. Splitting up printers from office ports makes it simpler to locate shared resources from independent workstations. At first this looks like a lot of unused ports, but as time progresses, these ports will be used.

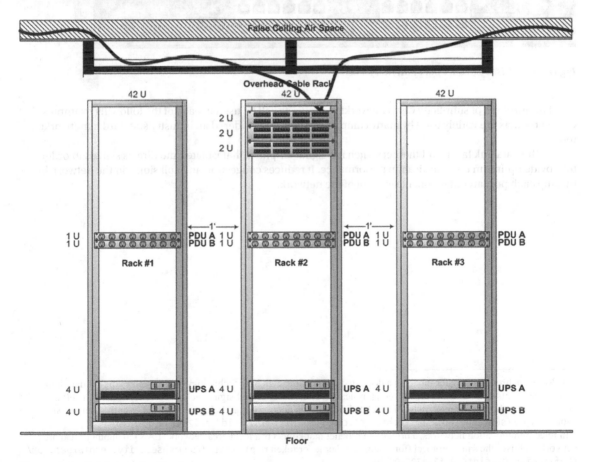

Figure 4-6. *Patch panel cable run*

Data Link

The data link layer (also known as layer 2) incorporates intelligent media in combination with the physical layer. Obviously the physical layer alone cannot connect network devices and the layer 2 devices alone alone cannot do the job. The combination of the two layers make up layer 1 of the TCP/IP stack (the *network access layer*). We look at the data link layer usually in combination with the physical layer as the medium by which networking is conducted. You can think of "layer 2" as roads with traffic control.

The data link layer consists of the following:

- Ethernet
- ATM[3]
- Switch
- Bridge[4]

While all of these layer 2 devices may be used by your organization, this chapter will deal exclusively with Ethernet and switch technologies. Later chapters cover ATM and bridge technologies.

Figure 4-7. *Cisco 2970 24 port Ethernet switch*

For purposes of simplicity Cisco networking products will be used in each of the following examples. Cisco products are widely used by many companies and are considered an industry standard in networking today.

In the data link layer, an Ethernet switch is a signal amplifier that isolates and directs signals in order to provide optimum communication performance. It reduces congestion and collisions on the network by making each port an independent segment of the network.

---

[3]"ATM (asynchronous transfer mode) is a dedicated-connection switching technology that organizes digital data into 53-byte cell units and transmits them over a physical medium using digital signal technology. Individually, a cell is processed asynchronously relative to other related cells and is queued before being multiplexed over the transmission path." http://searchnetworking.techtarget.com/sDefinition/0,,sid7_gci213790,00.html
[4]"In telecommunication networks, a bridge is a product that connects a local area network (LAN) to another local area network that uses the same protocol (for example, Ethernet or token ring)." http://searchsecurity.techtarget.com/sDefinition/0,,sid14_gci211705,00.html

There are five switches found in Figure 4-8—three for the existing office ports and expansion as required, and two for core systems and printers. They provide redundancy in network connections and printer expansion. The core switches are placed at the bottom of the rack to separate core switches from common switches and allow for further common switch expansion as needed.

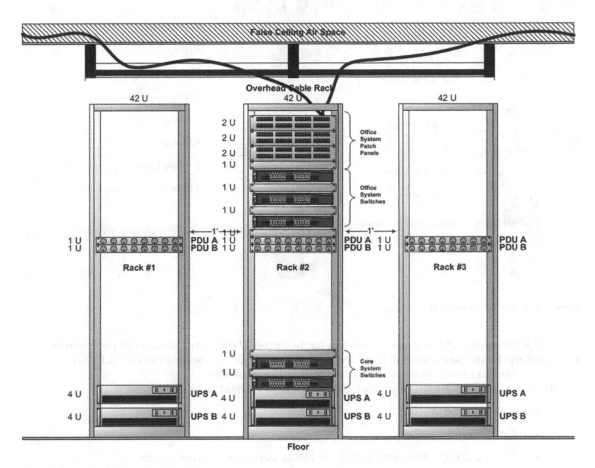

Figure 4-8. *Ethernet switch deployment*

Core equipment in this environment does not need patch panels due to their close proximity. A detailed cable run for core equipment will be examined later in this chapter.

In hub based and bus topology networks, groups of computers shared segments that resulted in higher rates of data collisions. Ethernet incorporated CSMA/CD[5] protocol to manage these collisions.

CAT 5 (100BaseT) cabling is the most common cable type used in networks today.

---

[5]Carrier Sense Multiple Access with Collision Detection (CSMA/CD); *Gorry Fairhurst, 1/14/2004 EG3567*
http://www.erg.abdn.ac.uk/users/gorry/course/lan-pages/csma-cd.html

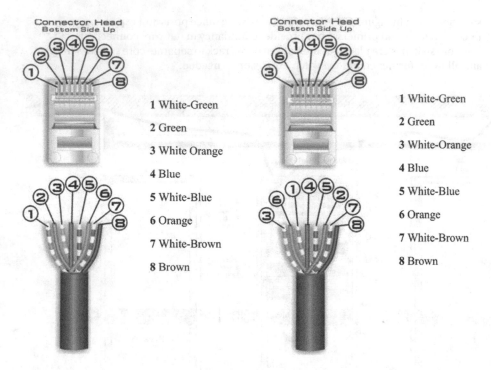

Figure 4-9. *CAT 5 cable ends*

CAT 5 cables (aka CAT 5 A) are used not only for the inter-wall cable runs (from patch panel to wall ports) but also for the patch cables that connect the patch panel ports to the Ethernet switch. CAT 5 crossover cables (aka CAT 5 B) are used to connect one switch to another.

There are limitations to the distance of cable runs and you should be aware of those:

- CAT 5 is rated to 100M

- CAT 5e is rated to 350M

- CAT 6 and CAT 6e are rated to 550M or 1000M, depending on your source

- CAT 7 is supposedly rated to 700M or presumably 1000M

It is strongly suggested that if you are building a new office network, you should look at CAT 5e or above when installing cables. Over planning your network's potential is ultimately investing in its future. There is nothing more disrupting than expanding the network infrastructure while employees are trying to conduct business.

Logical distribution of OSI layer 1 and 2 (layer 1 of the TCP/IP model) is shown in Figure 4-10.

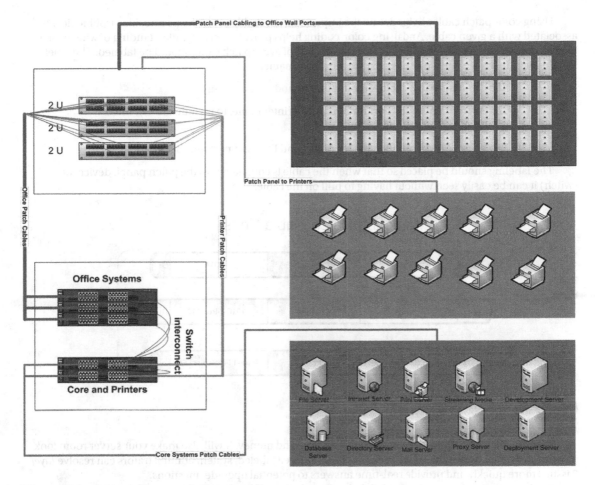

Figure 4-10. *Concept diagram of network cabling*

Figure 4-10 provides a conceptual diagram of general cable runs between all internal networking infrastructures. A presumption of server types is added in the lower-right box. Color-coded cables (red for core systems, green for printers, and blue for office wall ports) are used to categorize network resources. The following color scheme is used:

- Red – Critical systems (shared by all)
- Green – Shared systems (shared by many)
- Blue – Not shared (individual workstations)

Using color patch cables helps define the importance of a cable run. It helps prioritize trouble tickets associated with a given cable. And using color-coding helps provide a visual understanding of what cables may be connected to, quickly and efficiently. Both ends of every patch cable should be labeled. The label should include the wall port it connects to or the device name:

- Office systems patch cables (room number and port number)

- Printers (room number, port number, and printer name, to include the last three digits of the printer IP address)

- Core systems (rack number, device name, and Ethernet port number)

The labeling should be placed so that when the cable is connected (to the patch panel, device, or switch) it can be easily seen without having to pull on the cable.

Labeling Patch Cable Ends

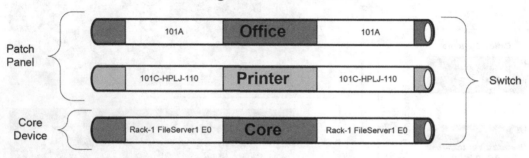

Figure 4-11. *Patch cable labels*

Investing in a good label system will save you time and money. It will also make your server room look more professional. When the server racks are neat and well labeled, system administrators can resolve *layer 2* issues more quickly and provide real-time answers to potential upgrade questions.

It is important to keep up the cable labels when changes occur. Labels that are poorly maintained can cause just as much confusion (sometimes more) than unlabeled cable ends. There needs to be a disciplined process applied to any cable changes made (both upgrades and maintenance). No cable should be added without proper labeling. No cable should be moved without making the proper label changes.

■ **Note** Labeling each and every cable is critical. Failure to label cables will result in time consuming tracing of error points and greatly impact the overall performance of the IT support team in minimizing downtime. It will also affect user satisfaction and may impede business performance.

Figure 4-12 displays the bus/star topology used in the network architectural examples of this chapter. Core switches actually mirror each other when connecting servers (two connections per server—one to each switch for failover and load balancing). Printers are evenly distributed to both switches to reduce the potential for a single point of failure. Since each port of every switch is an independent segment on the network, each node (computer, printer, server, etc.) performs at optimum speed with a minimum of potential data collisions.

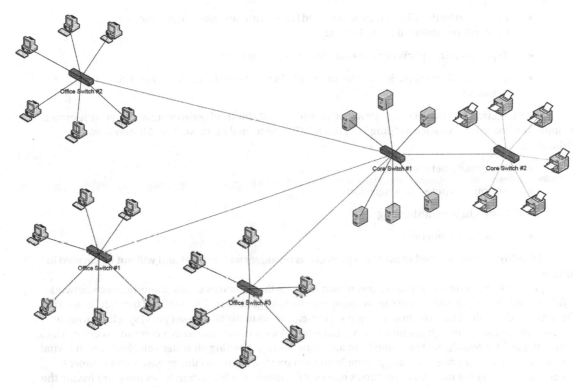

Figure 4-12. *Bus/star topology*

Network

The network layer (layer 3 in the OSI model and layer 2 in the TCP/IP stack) provides extended intelligence and scope to the network media. The following list presents protocols and technology found in the network layer:

- IP
- ICMP
- IPX
- Router

IP (Internet Protocol[6]) establishes a communication standard that will be recognized and understood by all computers on the LAN as well as any connected through the Internet. IP provides the following services:

- 32-bit IP addressing (to identify sending and receiving hosts)

- Fragmentation (this allows packets to be broken down into smaller packets to travel across the Internet and be reassembled on either end)

- Packet timeouts (TTL or time to live field) that terminate lost transmissions and establish the ability to resend quickly

- Type of service (packets can be labeled with abstract services)

- Options (allow the packet sender to set requirements on the path it takes through the network)

ICMP (Internet Control Message Protocol[7]) is used mostly for troubleshooting and reporting errors. Command-line resources such as "ping" require ICMP to be turned on to work. ICMP provides the following:

- Announces network errors

- Announces network congestion

- Assists in troubleshooting

- Announces timeouts

IPX, a Novel Incorporated networking protocol, is no longer widely used and will not be covered in this book.

A *router* is the combination of hardware and software that manages connections between networks. Widely used on the Internet, there can be many routers in larger internal networks. They can be used as firewalls and are often referred to as gateways. They can act as network timekeepers (synching with an online atomic clock through the Internet) so that internal servers can maintain a common accurate clock. Workstations, by default, get their time from an internal server. Keeping all system clocks in synch is vital to a stable network service and having a single point to synch with makes things easier and simpler to maintain. Limiting the number of protocols entering the network is important to security and having the router maintain the time synch with an external device means that other systems don't have to look outside the network for the correct time. Your router (Figure 4-13) can also be referred to as the gatekeeper of your network.

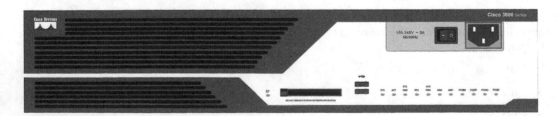

Figure 4-13. *Cisco 3800 series router*

---

[6]Internet Protocol, RFC: 791. See http://www.rfc-editor.org/rfc/rfc791.txt.
[7]Internet Control Message Protocol (ICMP), RFC 792. See http://www.lincoln.edu/math/rmyrick/ComputerNetworks/InetReference/81.htm.

Routers are expensive and redundancy is important. If your organization can afford redundancy, incorporate it. If not, establish a contract that can provide quick repair time. For this example, we will use a single Cisco 3800 series router to keep things simple.

While the patch cables are displayed on the outside of the racks in Figure 4-14, the actual cable runs would be inside the rack using cable trays to manage them.

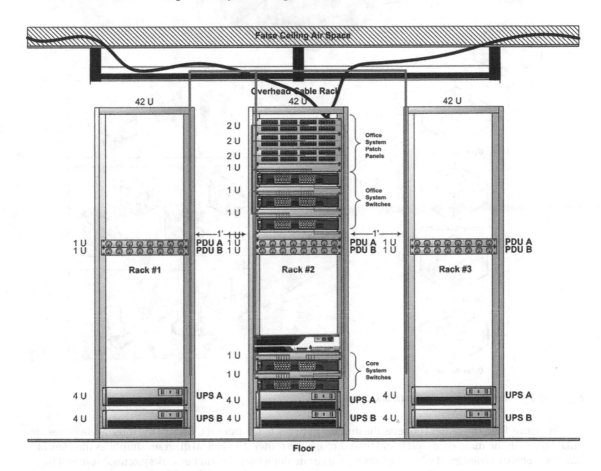

Figure 4-14. Router and cabling diagram

Figure 4-15 looks at the switch<->router<->Internet connection.

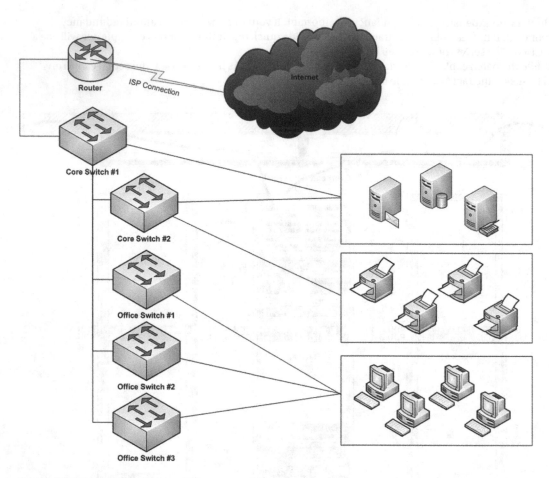

Figure 4-15. *Logical diagram of network connections*

In Figure 4-15, the router connects the internal network to the Internet. Each of the internal switches are linked through the main core switch and then through the router. The logical diagram simplifies the view of how the network is designed while providing an accurate depiction of main network systems. More will be discussed on routers later in this book.

Transport

The transport layer (layer 4 of the OSI model and layer 3 of the TCP/IP stack) is more conceptual than physical (as are layers 1, 2, and 3 of the OSI model). While layer 4 is commonly grouped with the lower layers of the OSI model, it has a lot in common with the upper layers. The transport layer is sometimes referred to as the "end-to-end" or "host-to-host transport". (In fact, the equivalent layer in the TCP/IP model is called the "host-to-host transport layer".)[8]

---

[8]The TCP/IP Guide ver. 3.0, September 20, 2005, Charles M. Kozierok. See http://www.tcpipguide.com/free/ t_TransportLayerLayer4.htm

The following list presents protocols and technology found in the transport layer:

- TCP

- UDP

- SPX

TCP (Transmission Control Protocol—RFC 793[9]) is used by applications that require a guaranteed delivery. It handles both timeouts and retransmissions. It establishes a full duplex connection between network nodes and works with IP addresses to ensure circuit end points.

UDP (User Datagram Protocol[10]), introduced in 1980, is a client/server-based protocol. It is used for video conferencing applications and any other network application that allows individual packets to be dropped without causing substantial communication failure. The UDP checksum protects message data from tampering; however, unlike TCP, UDP checksum is optional. This allows for more versatility in managing datagram transmissions.

SPX (Sequential Packet Exchange[11]) was the transport layer that the Novell protocol used in combination with IPX.

Session

The session layer (layer 5 of the OSI model and the beginning of layer 4 of the TCP/IP model) starts and ends sessions across the network. It allows applications to share information. It ensures that information gets to the right place. It communicates with the presentation and transport layer and can have multiple sessions on any given network. While there are many session layer protocols in existence, only a few are covered in this book.

The following partial list of protocols is found in the session layer:

- AppleTalk Data Stream Protocol (ADSP)

- AppleTalk Session Protocol (ASP)

- Call Control Protocol for Multimedia Communication

- Internet Storage Name Service

- Network Basic Input Output (NetBIOS)

- Password Authentication Protocol (PAP)

- Point-to-Point Tunneling Protocol (PPTP)

- Remote Procedure Call Protocol (RPC)

- Short Message Peer-to-Peer (SMPP)

- Secure Shell (SSH)

---

[9]RFC 793—Transmission Control Protocol. See http://www.faqs.org/rfcs/rfc793.html
[10]See http://compnetworking.about.com/od/networkprotocolsip/g/udp-user-datagram-protocol.htm
[11]See http://www.comptechdoc.org/independent/networking/protocol/protipxspx.html

From this partial list, the following will be examined in this book due to their relevance to modern networking:

- NetBIOS

- PPTP

- RPC

- SSH

NetBIOS (RFC1001) is the protocol standard for a NetBIOS service on a TCP/UDP.[12] NetBIOS is a Microsoft Corporation protocol used for name resolution. A product of the Windows 95 era, it has continued on as a support for older operating systems in a TCP/IP environment.

PPTP (Point-to-Point Tunneling Protocol) was developed by Microsoft Corporation in support of VPNs (Virtual Private Networks). PPTP is used to establish a secure link between two or more nodes on a network communicating over the Internet.

RPC (Remote Procedure Call) is a protocol that applications can use to request a service from a remote computer without having to know the network's details. RPC works on a server/client relationship and is often found as a common part of networking activities. RPC is a synchronous protocol that requires the target computer to complete its request before continuing with other processes.

SSH (Secure Shell or Secure Socket Shell) is a UNIX-based command that allows users to remotely connect to another computer using a digital certificate to authenticate the connection. The connection uses an encrypted algorithm (Blowfish, DES, or IDEA) to provide a secure data path.

Presentation

The presentation layer (layer 6 of the OSI model), sometimes referred to as the syntax layer, is generally used to address and resolve data communication along the seven layers There are several data conversion and compression standards found in the presentation layer:

- JPEG

- GIF

- MPEG

JPEG and GIF are graphic compression standards found in the presentation layer. MPEG is an audio-video standard for streaming media. The presentation layer is also responsible for converting data formats such as PostScript, ASCII, and EBCDIC. There are some encryption methods that utilize the presentation layer scrambling plain text transmission data into encrypted data streams.

Application

The application layer (or seventh layer of the OSI model) supplies network services to user applications (such as HTTP, FTP, or SMTP). These are protocols commonly known to anyone who uses a computer, both on and off the Internet. They support the most widely used resources in IT and often provide basic information processing resources use globally. You can think of the application layer as the "user-friendly" layer.

---

[12]See http://www.faqs.org/rfcs/rfc1001.html.

We will touch briefly on the following selected application layer protocols:

- HTTP
- FTP
- SMTP
- Telnet
- SNMP

HTTP (Hypertext Transfer Protocol—RFC 2616[13]) is the most commonly used Internet protocol for building shared Internet content on web servers. It uses port 80 to communicate between computers over the Internet. Using an Internet browser (such as Microsoft's Internet Explorer©, Mozilla Firefox©, or Google's Chrome©), HTTP is the default protocol to access web content. It was designed by Tim Berners-Lee when working at CERN[14] to share data between colleagues in 1981-1991 along with the development of URLs.[15]

FTP (File Transfer Protocol—RFC 959[16]) provides a basic file transfer protocol between two or more computers over the network. It has been updated by a secure FTP protocol[17] (RFC 2228) in which an encrypted data path is established before files are transferred. The default ports for FTP are port 21 (opening the connections) and port 20 (data sending port). Data sent via FTP is plain text. Data sent via Secure FTP is encrypted. You can use FTP as a command in the CLI[18] or web browser.

SMTP (Simple Mail Transfer Protocol RFC 821[19]) was designed in 1982 and has become the standard by which mail can be transmitted reliably and effectively, both in local networks and across the Internet. The default port used by SMTP is port 25.

Telnet (Telnet Protocol RFC 854[20]) is commonly used to test connectivity between two computers. It is used to verify connections for FTP, SMTP, and other application layer protocols. Telnet is used to test port connections but the default telnet listening port is port 23. Telnet is also widely used to access network devices such as switches and routers remotely.

SNMP (Simple Network Management Protocol RFC 1157[21]) created in 1988 to help manage networking devices in an ever-growing technology industry, SNMP has been embraced industry wide. SNMP uses five simple messages to communicate:

1. GET
2. GET-NEXT
3. GET-RESPONSE
4. SET
5. TRAP

This simple messaging command set is manipulated by the SNMP Manager to monitor devices across the network. Having a well-managed SNMP environment can support a host of network appliances and operations support applications. Before you deploy SNMP, you should have a firm understanding of the pros and cons of the technology.

---

[13]HTTP protocol: `http://www.faqs.org/rfcs/rfc2616.html`
[14]CERN: `http://public.web.cern.ch/public/`
[15]Universal Resource Locators: `http://www.ietf.org/rfc/rfc1738.txt`
[16]FTP: `http://www.faqs.org/rfcs/rfc959.html`
[17]Secure FTP: `http://www.faqs.org/rfcs/rfc2228.html`
[18]CLI stands for Command Line Interface
[19]SMTP: `http://james.apache.org/server/rfclist/smtp/rfc0821.txt`
[20]Telnet: `http://www.faqs.org/rfcs/rfc854.html`
[21]SNMP: `http://www.faqs.org/rfcs/rfc1157.html`

Summary

This chapter presented the installation and infrastructure for network access. It also presented the foundation for building Internet access. It also covered the basic protocols used in the host-to-host and application layers of the TCP/IP model. Figure 4-16 shows a translation model between the OSI and TCP/IP models.

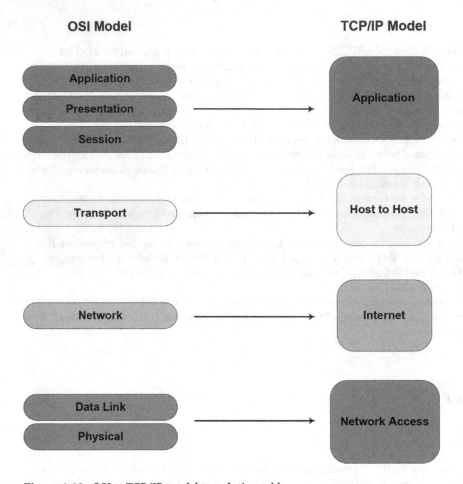

OSI Model

TCP/IP Model

Figure 4-16. *OSI to TCP/IP model translation table*

By applying industry standards, documenting installation processes, and color-coding and labeling network connections/connectors, you build an environment that can more easily be managed and administered. The complexity of networking environments in business can become overwhelming and unsustainable if there isn't a methodical and easy-to-follow plan for installation and growth. This chapter not only presented the installation process but also defined a coding process that simplified tracing network connectors.

While it is one thing to design an installation plan, it is as important to develop a maintenance plan that ensures the installation plan is not forgotten and the coding process is maintained. The need for a change management (CM) process starts with the completion of the initial installation process and continues until the network no longer exists.

CHAPTER 5

■■■

Network Services Architecture

Core network services are found in the upper layers of the OSI model and layers 3 and 4 of the TCP/IP model. They are the basis for common communications used by everyone on the LAN, as shown in Figure 5-1.

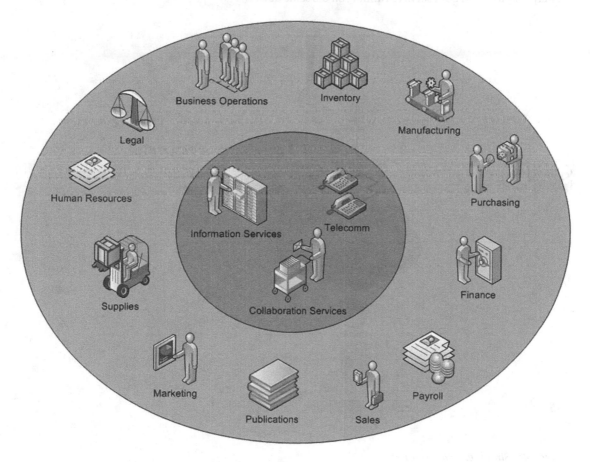

Figure 5-1. *Business information services relationship*

Core network services affect all other services in every organization. When designing those core network services, you should envision how those services are to be incorporated into the overall network services package. The goal for every system administrator is to make network services seamless and transparent to the users. Figure 5-1 represents the core services (in blue in the center) and many of the business services (in green in the outer ring) that directly depend on the reliability of those services.

Routing

The *router* is the digital doorway between the organization's internal LAN and the world. Unlike the physical doorway, the router is on 24 hours a day, seven days a week. And that door remains open long after the last employee leaves for the evening. The routers job is to ensure access (both ways) and provide unsupervised protection from external attacks.

While the firewall may be separate from the router (sometimes not), the router is required to provide basic protective measures to ensure its reliability. We will look at the router separately from the firewall, but you may very well find both services running on the same device.

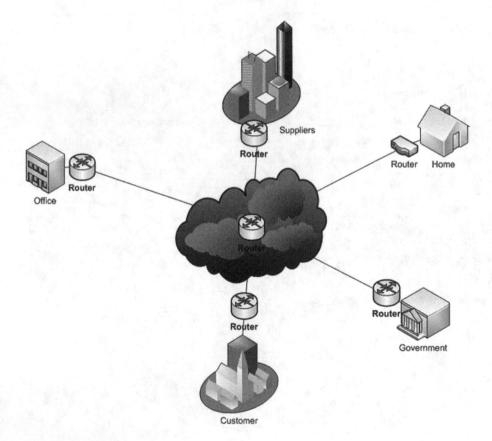

Figure 5-2. *Simple external routing*

Routers manage digital traffic to and from your organization. They provide a public IP address that can be accessed by other routers and in turn by other networks and computers.

A router is basically a computer with two network interfaces connecting two separate networks together. Routers operate as intermediate systems on the OSI network layer.

In Figure 5-3 the Cisco 3800 series router is displayed with two connections (one connecting the internal network and the other connected to an ISP T1 circuit). The Cisco router must be configured with a T1/E1 network module as part of the 3800 series router and must add an adapter card to the default router package.

Router Connections

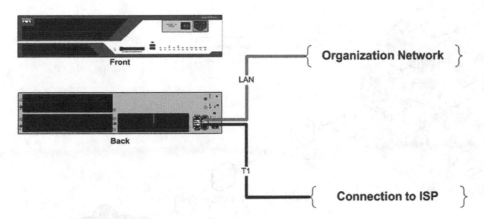

Figure 5-3. Router connections

A T1 circuit is a dedicated 1.534Mbps data circuit. It is important to note that DS0 and T1 may be used synonymously, but they are two distinctly different things:

- DS0 is the contract between you and the carrier and defines the service and cost.

- T1 is a DS0 signal that is sent over terrestrial lines.

A T1 can provide up to 1.534Mbps in digital bandwidth, which can be channelized or non-channelized depending on the circuit provisioning and business requirements. The circuit between the customer and the provider is presented in Figure 5-4.

Basic T1 Circuit Diagram

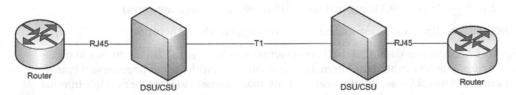

Figure 5-4. Basic T1 networking circuit

The router has a minimum of two IP addresses:

- Public address that interfaces with the DSU/CSU on the T1 link

- Internal IP address (usually a non-public address) that interfaces with the internal LAN

Public addresses can be seen and accessed across public networks (such as the Internet). Non-public (aka *private* or CIDR[1]) addresses are limited to an internal LAN or WAN.

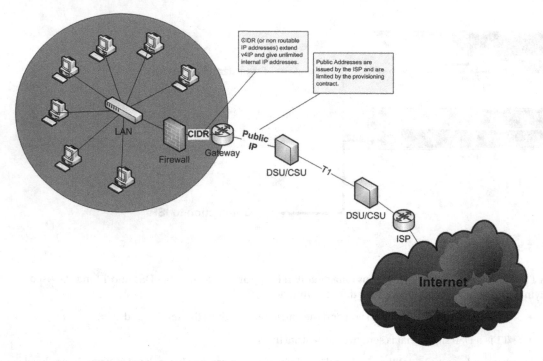

Figure 5-5. *CIDR/public IP addresses*

There are three CIDR IP address schemes:

- 10.0.0.0—Up to 16,777,216 internal nodes (single class A network)

- 172.16.0.0—Up to 1,048,544 internal nodes (16 contiguous class B networks)

- 192.168.0.0—Up to 65,534 internal nodes (256 contiguous class C networks)

NAT (Network Address Translation[2]) is used to convert pubic addresses to CIDR addresses and vice versa. Routers incorporate NAT to bind the internal network addresses with the public addresses issued by the ISP for Internet data exchange. Routers also mask internal addresses to allow for multiple internal addresses to bind with a limited number of public addresses so that the size of your internal network is invisible to the outside world.

---

[1]Classless Inter-Domain Routing (CIDR) Conversion Table: http://kb.wisc.edu/ns/page.php?id=3493
[2]Network Address Translation: http://www.howstuffworks.com/nat.htm

Determining the CIDR IP address scheme that's best for your organization is an important decision and should be planned carefully. For the network examined in this book, we use the 192.168.0.0 IP addressing scheme. This choice allows for an extensive number of node addresses and. in combination with supernetting,[3] we can tailor our network to provide the ability to link current resources with a high performance network mask and expand the network to allow for additional sites to bind with our IP address scheme.

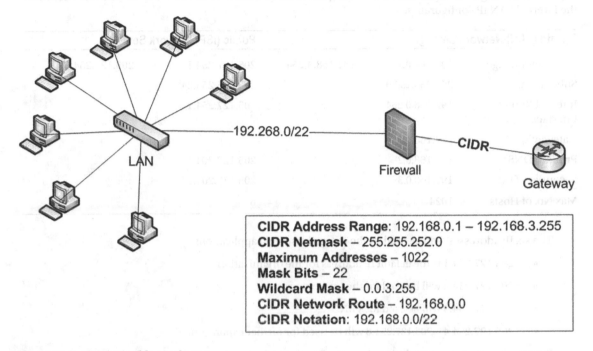

Figure 5-6. *CIDR IP address scheme*

In this scheme, the LAN gateway address would be 192.168.0.1 (firewall). The subnet mask would be 255.255.252.0. There are enough addresses for up to 1,022 network nodes and up to three class C address ranges (from 192.168.0.0 through 192.168.3.255). There is a netmask calculator that can be used to calculate subnets and supernetting:

- http://www.subnet-calculator.com/

Gauging your network size (both current and future) will help you fine-tune the IP address scheme, the response time, and the security of your LAN. Documenting your LAN IP address scheme before building your network will help you envision how your LAN will grow with time.

The ISP gives the public address scheme to the organization. The ISP DS0 package (for the T1 circuit) selected for the example network in this book is fictitious and does not represent any particular IP scheme currently in use. The following IP address scheme will support six public IP addresses to be used by this fictitious organization:

- Host address range: 205.127.254.1 – 205.127.254.6

- Subnet mask: 255.255.255.248

- Subnet ID: 205.127.254.0

---

[3]Supernetting: http://searchnetworking.techtarget.com/sDefinition/0,,sid7_gci854054,00.html

- Mask bits: 29
- Wildcard mask: 0.0.0.7
- Subnet bits: 5

The following table represents basic routing information gathered from both the ISP and that chosen for the internal LAN IP configuration:

Private (LAN) Network Settings			Public (ISP) Network Settings	
IP Address Range	192.168.0.1	192.168.3.254	205.127.254.1	205.127.254.6
Subnet Mask	255.255.252.0		255.255.255.248	
Internal Router Interface	192.168.0.254		205.127.254.1	
Gateway[4]	192.168.0.1			
Primary DNS[5]	192.168.0.2		205.127.204.1	
Secondary DNS	192.168.0.3		205.137.204.1	
Max No. of Hosts	1024		6	

The six IP addresses[6] will be used by the router for several applications:

- 205.127.254.1 is the default IP address for the organization.
- 205.127.254.2 will be used for the Internet proxy.
- 205.127.254.3 will be used for VPN.
- 205.127.254.4 – 205.127.254.6 will be used for further expansion.

Before any servers are actually installed, an IP table can be put together for specific devices that will have direct routes between internal IP addresses and external IP addresses:

Description	Private IP Address	Public IP Address
Default router ports	192.168.0.254	205.127.254.1
Proxy server/antispam	192.168.0.252	205.127.254.2
IP tunneling (VPN)	192.168.0.253	205.127.254.3

---

[4]The internal gateway for the purposes of this book will be the firewall. In this case, it would be a separate computer from the router.

[5]Note: The internal DNS IP addresses were chosen based on which servers would be added first to the internal network. They may change as the LAN matures.

[6]Public IP addresses are routable, meaning that they are visible to the Internet and managed by your ISP. Private IP addresses are not visible to the Internet and therefore managed by the IT department. Static IP addresses are assigned to devices accessed by others (e.g., servers, routers, etc.) while dynamic IP addresses are generally applied to workstations and other end user devices and managed through a DHCP server.

This book's example LAN will use the selected IP address scheme as follows:

- 192.168.0.1 – 192.168.0.254 – Core network devices

- 192.168.1.1 – 192.168.1.254 – Wired network workstations and printers

- 192.168.2.1 – 192.168.2.254 – Wireless network laptops

- 192.168.3.1 – 192.168.3.254 – Expansion (to be used later)

Figure 5-7 illustrates the IP addresses that communicate with the Internet through HTTP, HTTPS, or SMTP protocols. The router has three dedicated IP addresses assigned to its external port. The internal port is directly connected to the firewall server. The firewall server is connected to the LAN with rules set to route all SMTP traffic coming into the LAN through the proxy server. All outgoing SMTP traffic goes directly through the firewall out into the Internet via the router (port 25). All outgoing HTTP/HTTPS traffic is filtered both ways through the proxy server (port 80 and port 443).

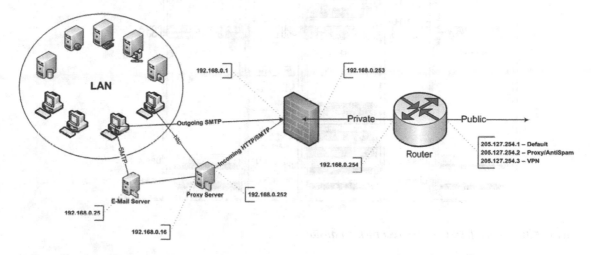

Figure 5-7. *Default route IP address scheme*

The router also provides an ability to log and manage data packets coming in and going out of the LAN. The log files grow quickly. The goal of managing those logs is to find a filtering scheme that lets you see what is important and ignore the mundane stuff.

Devising a filtering policy that works best for your organization takes time and requires updates as new potential dangers evolve. Studying the SANS institute[7] research will help you develop your policy. Periodicals such as *Information Security Magazine*[8] will give you up-to-date notifications of cyber defense information that can help you understand what might be happening to your network.

Saving and clearing log files will help you have a clean tablet to work with while keeping an archive of your router's use. Backing up routing tables, locking down the administrator's account (preventing remote administration), masking your public IP address, and disabling protocols such as ICMP will further remove possible modes of attack.

Using multiple layers of routing (such as a separate firewall, proxy server, threat management gateway, and other filtering technologies) will make it more difficult for hackers to gain access to your LAN.

---

[7]The SANS Institute home page: http://www.sans.org/
[8]*Information Security Magazine*: http://searchsecurity.techtarget.com/#

Looking at the server rack configuration, you can see that the DSU/CSU has been added to the router as an expansion card.

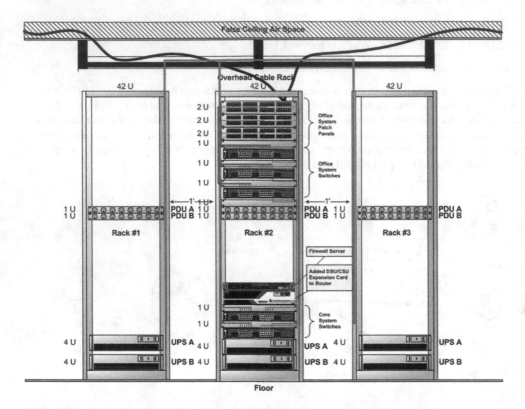

Figure 5-8. *Firewall, DSU/CSU server rack expansion*

The IP address scheme distributing into the network is descending from 192.168.0.254 down. This helps troubleshoot connectivity issues based on the IP address value. If you cannot access 192.168.0.254, you know there is a router access issue. If you cannot access 192.168.0.253, there is a firewall access issue. If you cannot access 192.168.0.253, you have a VPN access issue. If you cannot access 192.168.0.252, there is a proxy issue.

Core network services internal addresses (other than Ethernet switches) start from the bottom up. They represent the local network services and equipment. All of the 192.168.0.0/254 subnet can be defined as the network management subnet and should only be occupied by shared network services.

Network Security Plan

The foundation for a secure network has been intertwined with the design for Internet routing. But that is only a small part of the security plan. It provides a modicum of security and has many holes that need to be managed so that attacks from outside can be monitored and defended against.

There is also the issue of internal security attacks. These issues take on a wide range of potential problems that need to be addressed both with technology, organizational policy, education, and proper employee vetting.

Technical Security Mechanisms

Technical security mechanisms need to be in place in parallel to policies and procedures. Antivirus, intruder detection applications, centrally managed patch management, secure firewall settings, masked external IP addresses, etc.; they all work to minimize successful attacks. Installing operations management application servers, forced strong passwords with scheduled password changes further add to security. Blocking personal e-mail (Yahoo, Hotmail, Gmail) and personal instant messaging becomes essential when your organization's primary business is intellectual property. Limiting the size of attachments you can add to corporate e-mail also reduces the potential for information loss. Monitoring corporate e-mail activity may also be useful. Blocking or monitoring USB drive access, CD-ROM drives, or removable media may also help ensure the security of intellectual property.

With all of these security issues comes legal issues and employee behavioral education. Many technical security mechanisms require strong organizational policies that are enforced by the top down. There needs to be a clear understanding of how important these security practices are to the welfare of the organization and ultimately the employee.

It is also imperative to understand and produce policies for exceptions to the security policies that are enacted. There will always be special circumstances and users who require unique flexibility with security. These exceptions should be documented in a role-based permissions policy that provides for due diligence and oversight. This includes service accounts (not owned by users but services) that have no individual user associated with their use. One of the most unmonitored security risks rests with those service accounts and their maintenance.

Publishing a security policy login banner (vetted and approved by the legal department) ensures that everyone logging onto the system acknowledges and accepts those policies. Keeping the logon security policy message simple and easy to understand helps ensure that there is no confusion about what has been stated.

Breaking down some of these security technologies, the following list provides some options available to an organization:

- Centrally managed antivirus/antispyware solutions (for both servers and workstations)

- Intrusion detection systems (for monitoring access points and reporting possible attacks) installed between the firewall and the router to provide an early alert system. You may wish to have a second IDS installed between the firewall and the LAN to act as a secondary alert system.

- Centralized patch management (distribution security patches, hot fixes, and service packs to operating systems and applications) distributes and reports patch management compliance.

- Operations management applications (such as Microsoft's System Center Operations Manager 2007—SCOM, Microsoft's System Management Server 2003—SMS, SAS IT Management solutions, etc.) providing tools to manage systems, inventory, integration, and general operations tasks.

- Firewall technology (boundary protection for the LAN, proxy protection for e-mail and web services, and workstation personal firewalls centrally managed by group policy settings and supporting LAN based *IPsec*[9]) multi-layered using varied manufacturers to complicate defenses and slow down a hacker's attack.

---

[9]IPsec: http://technet.microsoft.com/en-us/network/bb531150.aspx

- Proxy server (used to filter and route data traffic) to help manage the information flow between the LAN and the rest of the world.

- Spam filter (used to extract spam mail from organizational communications) as part of the proxy server services.

- Web content filter (used to block access to unauthorized web sites and limit download content) as part of the proxy server services.

- Web load balancing (Used to minimize overloading of web server activity. Load balancing should be implemented along with monitoring activities and alerts.)

- Centralized account management (directory services, domain services, etc., used to create, delete, and manage user, printer, and computer accounts on the LAN) such as Microsoft Active Directory,[10] Apple Open Directory,[11] Oracle Directory Services,[12] Novell eDirectory,[13] etc.

- Removable media management (software that manages and monitors USB, CD/DVD-ROM, floppy disks, or other removable media devices such as Checkpoint's PointSec[14]) used to control data duplication and mobility.

- Fingerprint recognition (fingerprint readers[15] used to log on to a computer on or off a LAN) often used as an alternative to entering passwords to log in to an existing user account.

- Biometric readers (such as retinal scanners, hand scanners, etc.) often used to add security when entering a secured office or location.

- Smartcards/pass cards (ID cards that can be inserted into a smartcard reader to authenticate access) often used in conjunction with a pass key number to log in to a computer on or off a LAN and access secure rooms.

- Fiber/Fiberswitch network media (used in high-security networks as a replacement for CAT 5/CAT 6 networking cable) providing high-security media for LAN connections.

While there are more security technologies out there that can be used by organizations to secure their intellectual data, you probably will not find all of these in use at any one organization. The cost is prohibitive and the administration can be overwhelming. Selecting what is best for the organization should be balanced by the values of the data as well as the cost of administration over a given length of time to ensure value is added.

Operational Security

Operational security is everyone's business. But that in turn means that everyone is well educated on security measures, has access to the security policy and fully understands it, and has a stake in maintaining that security for their benefit as well as others. You can have all the technology in place and someone who does not want to follow your security policy will, in time, figure out how to get around it. That is human

---

[10]Microsoft Active Directory: http://www.microsoft.com/windowsserver2008/en/us/active-directory.aspx
[11]Apple Open Directory: http://training.apple.com/itpro/leopard301
[12]Oracle Directory Services: http://education.oracle.com/pls/web_prod-plq-dad/show_desc.redirect?dc=D46306GC10&p_org_id=1001&lang=US
[13]Novell's eDirectory: http://www.novell.com/products/edirectory
[14]Checkpoint PointSec: http://www.checkpoint.com/pointsec/
[15]Fingerprint Recognition: http://www.webopedia.com/DidYouKnow/Computer_Science/2004/fingerprint.asp

nature. It is also human nature to want to do something that offers benefit over something that does not. Operational security requires willingness on the part of the organization's membership to comply and support both policy and practice.

It is operational security that requires constant diligence, administration, and oversight to ensure compliance. Official security policies need to be posted appropriately. The login banner needs to clearly define those policies (and not just point to a link on the Intranet). Timely notices and security alerts need to let everyone know about current dangers on the Internet (viruses, phishing, etc.). The organization's security policy should be presented as a community awareness program for the preservation of employment and productivity.

With all of that in mind, and fully knowing the vast technologies available to employ security in an organization, security must be done seamlessly and as unobtrusively as possible. There are things that users must deal with every day (such as login banners, user accounts, and passwords). And there are things that can be done without the user noticing (such as firewalls, web filters, proxy servers, spam filters, etc.).

And then there are those security measures that can irritate users and make daily work seem unbearable (such as locking down the CD/DVD-ROM drives and USB ports and prohibiting personal e-mail). The more personal the impact a security policy has on a user, the more IT needs to focus on education and acceptance. Users will accept security, no matter how intense, as long as there is a reasonable policy that clearly defines the rules and obligations the organization's membership must follow.

But the security policy must come from the top down. It must be supported from the top with every layer of management supporting it completely. Homegrown policies are much more difficult to support and often ignored. Poorly implemented security policies can lead to more work for the IT staff. And the time wasted in supporting poorly implemented security policies is time taken away from the normal workload needed to maintain operational readiness.

DNS

DNS (Domain Name System[16]) is one of the most important services in networking today. Most users know something about DNS but few really understand it. While the fundamentals of DNS are fairly simple, the implementation and administration of DNS can be complex. There are books that cover only DNS and the topic can be extensive. This book will cover what you need to know in order to understand how DNS works in this example LAN and with Internet access.

Quite simply, DNS is a TCP/IP service that takes IP addresses and converts them into "user-friendly" names. It incorporates a hierarchal database that binds IP addresses to domains and advertises services. DNS is a fundamental technology used by directory services to simplify access to resources. It further aids to bind networks together so that they can share resources and communicate. If you have problems with DNS, you have problems with your LAN and everything it is connected to.

How do you know if you have a DNS problem? One way is to use the ping command, as shown in Figure 5-9.

---

[16]DNS RFCs: http://www.dns.net/dnsrd/rfc/

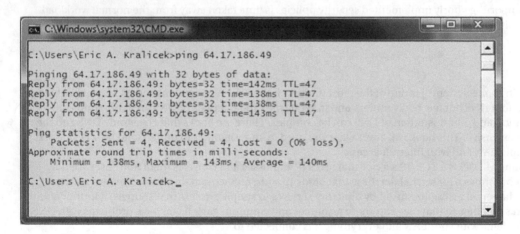

```
C:\Windows\system32\CMD.exe                                    _  □  X

C:\Users\Eric A. Kralicek>ping www.wiles-kralicek.com

Pinging www.wiles-kralicek.com [64.17.186.49] with 32 bytes of data:
Reply from 64.17.186.49: bytes=32 time=140ms TTL=47
Reply from 64.17.186.49: bytes=32 time=138ms TTL=47
Reply from 64.17.186.49: bytes=32 time=139ms TTL=47
Reply from 64.17.186.49: bytes=32 time=139ms TTL=47

Ping statistics for 64.17.186.49:
    Packets: Sent = 4, Received = 4, Lost = 0 (0% loss),
Approximate round trip times in milli-seconds:
    Minimum = 138ms, Maximum = 140ms, Average = 139ms

C:\Users\Eric A. Kralicek>_
```

Figure 5-9. *Ping command using user-friendly name*

You should select something that you know you'll get a reply to and then, in a CLI (a command-line interface; aka DOS prompt), try to ping it. If you don't get a response with the user-friendly name (as in our example) then try it again with the IP address associated with that user-friendly name (see Figure 5-10).

```
C:\Windows\system32\CMD.exe                                    _  □  X

C:\Users\Eric A. Kralicek>ping 64.17.186.49

Pinging 64.17.186.49 with 32 bytes of data:
Reply from 64.17.186.49: bytes=32 time=142ms TTL=47
Reply from 64.17.186.49: bytes=32 time=138ms TTL=47
Reply from 64.17.186.49: bytes=32 time=138ms TTL=47
Reply from 64.17.186.49: bytes=32 time=143ms TTL=47

Ping statistics for 64.17.186.49:
    Packets: Sent = 4, Received = 4, Lost = 0 (0% loss),
Approximate round trip times in milli-seconds:
    Minimum = 138ms, Maximum = 143ms, Average = 140ms

C:\Users\Eric A. Kralicek>_
```

Figure 5-10. *Ping command using IP address*

If you can ping the IP address and not the user friendly name then you most likely have a DNS problem. You can test your DNS further using the nslookup command, as shown in Figure 5-11.

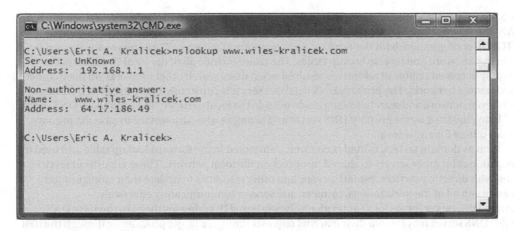

Figure 5-11. *The nslookup command*

In Figure 5-11 you get a non-authoritative acknowledgement because the responding DNS server is unknown. This is because in this example, there is no local DNS server. Had there been a local DNS server you would get the name of the DNS server.

ping and nslookup are used with Microsoft Windows, and all UNIX including Apple's OSX and all Linux. While ping is just a *test of life* tool to see if a host is available on the network using either TCP/IP or DNS, nslookup has several useful options[17] (called switches) that can verify DNS services (see Figure 5-12).

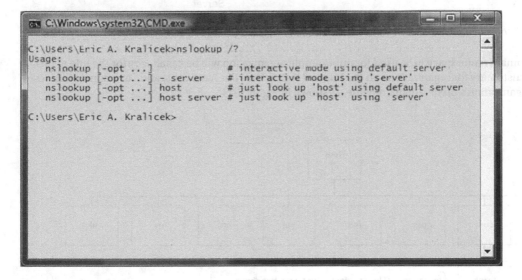

Figure 5-12. *nslookup options*

---

[17]Nslookup online Microsoft help: http://support.microsoft.com/default.aspx/kb/200525

If you are using UNIX, you can type man nslookup to get a full description of how to use nslookup.

On a LAN, the internal DNS service is one or more databases (primary and secondary DNS database servers). In TCP/IP configuration, both the primary and secondary DNS server IP addresses are entered to allow access to the foreword and reverse lookup tables. The tables include all of the local IP addresses as well as commonly accessed remote IP addresses resolved when users search other networks on the Internet or other linked remote networks. The primary DNS database server is constantly being updated by changes made to the internal network and searches being made outside the local network. The secondary DNS server is "read only" being updated by the primary DNS server and acting as a backup service in case the primary DNS server goes offline for any reason.

Services, such as domain servers, e-mail servers, etc., are stored in the forward lookup table and used to point to workstations and other servers to shared resources on the local network. These advertised services work in unison with directory services, e-mail servers, and other resources to update their configuration information and keep all of the workstations, printers, and servers communicating effectively.

The primary DNS server for the local network resolves external IP addresses through the ISP's DNS servers. The ISP DNS server may resolve their external requests through a larger provider or through the root Internet DNS servers (as seen in Figure 5-13).

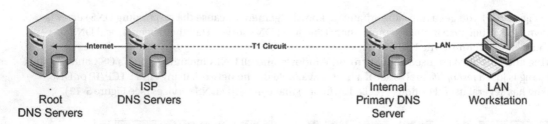

Figure 5-13. *Resolving a domain name space*

The domain name space to be used for our example organization will be tasah.com for the title of this book. It is customary for organizations on the Internet to purchase the .com, .net, and .org domain names with the organization's preface domain name, as shown in Figure 5-14.

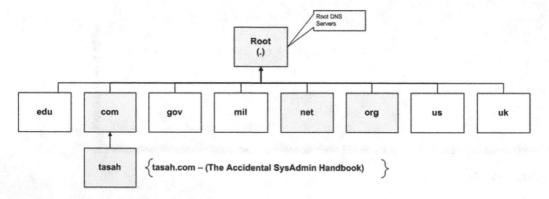

Figure 5-14. *Subset of the Internet domain naming tree*

In Figure 5-14, the fictitious organization owns the following *fully qualified domain names* (FQDN):

- `Tasah.com`

- `Tasah.net`

- `Tasah.org`

These FQDNs are then linked to resolve back to the primary domain name (`tasah.com`) to protect the organization's trademark on the Internet and to lead all search results to the main home page of the organization. This provides the Internet DNS presence for the organization and helps define the FQDN for the internal LAN DNS.

The internal DNS servers can have any FQDN. To help keep things easy to understand, our example will use the `.local` suffix to the domain name (`tasah.local`, as seen in Figure 5-15). This aids in the troubleshooting process by separating the external domain name space from the internal name space.

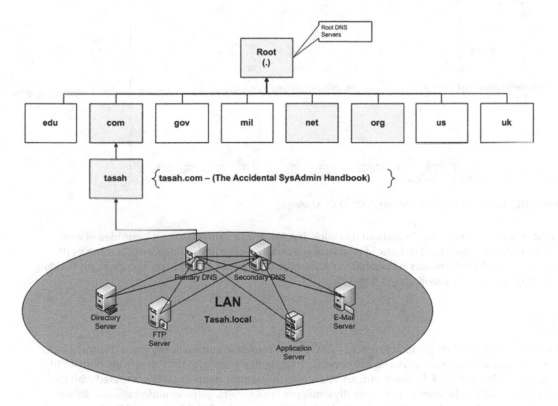

Figure 5-15. *Internal to external DNS*

Since all internal LAN hosts (workstations and servers) resolve their DNS information to the local DNS servers, the FQDN for a sample workstation might be `workstation01.tasah.local`, and a server might be `server01.tasah.local`. Since these names are not advertised to the Internet, they are not publically available (the same as their CIDR IP address).

In Figure 5-16 a Windows Server 2008 DNS database has been created for the `tasah.local` domain. As you can see, there is a forward lookup zone, a reverse lookup zone, and a conditional forwarders zone. Within the forward lookup zone, you find the `msdcs.tasah.local` tree that is used to advertise Microsoft Windows 2008 Active Directory services. The `tasah.local` tree is used to publish IP addresses in the local domain. The reverse lookup zone is used to define the reverse address listing and can be used to define active non-domain IP addresses that will use this DNS server but may not be a Microsoft operating system (such as UNIX, OSX, or Linux).

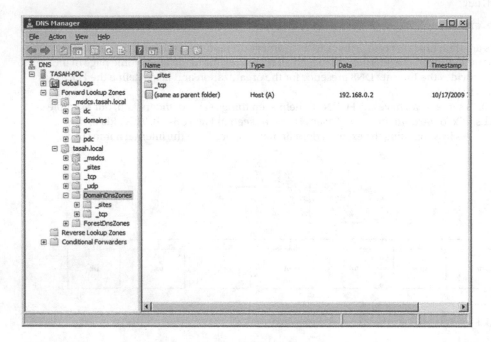

Figure 5-16. *Microsoft Windows Server 2008 DNS Manager*

DNS will be covered more throughout this book, but for now you should have a basic idea of what DNS is and what it is used for. The basic idea of having a domain name and a database that resolves IP addresses to user-friendly names is essential to the foundation of your LAN and how you go about building, maintaining, and troubleshooting your network.

DHCP

DHCP (Dynamic Host Configuration Protocol—RFC 2131[18]) is used to automatically grant IP addresses to new or existing computers or devices on the network. It works in unison with DNS to provide both an IP address and update the DNS database with an "A" record (the friendly name in DNS associated with the IP address). DHCP can be used to automatically configure DNS servers, gateway addresses, and subnet settings. It can also be used to configure detailed information regarding IP addresses and hostnames associated with services offered on the LAN.

Many organizations use DHCP for all of their workstations, laptops, and printers but not usually for servers (since servers usually require static IP addresses). DHCP is used in conjunction with BOOTP[19] to allow system administrators to build workstations remotely.

---

[18]DHCP RFC: http://www.faqs.org/rfcs/rfc2131.html
[19]Bootp: http://www.networksorcery.com/enp/protocol/bootp.htm

Our LAN DHCP will be used for dynamic hosts only (laptops and build images). DHCP is configured by scope and limiting the number of dynamic DHCP addresses will help limit the potential security problems that can arise from its misuse. Setting up reservations for those laptops will help to further minimize DHCP security holes.

In Figure 5-17 there are two DHCP scopes:

1. 192.168.1.100 through 192.168.1.110 for imaging computers.

2. 192.168.2.1 through 1.129.168.2.50 for laptop IP reservations.

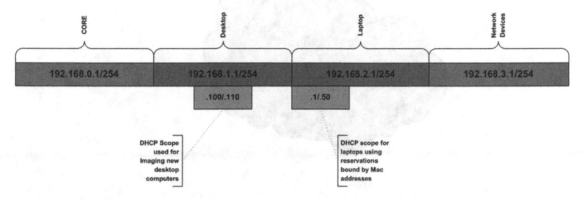

Figure 5-17. *DHCP scopes*

The imaging DHCP scope is active when computers are being built for deployment and inactive when computers are not being built. The laptop DHCP scope is active at all times and the scope is limited to the actual number of laptops to be deployed on the LAN. The laptop DHCP scope can be extended or retracted at any time based on the number of laptops deployed.

This approach to deploying DHCP is not common in most organizations. Many organizations use DHCP extensively. The problem with that approach is that DHCP can get out of hand and give unauthorized IP addresses automatically. DHCP often has problems releasing old addresses and requires occasional attention. Limiting scope and availability promotes control and aides in network security. Sloppy DHCP deployment often leads to unforeseen user problems and unnecessary additional work for the system administrators. Having a sound DHCP deployment strategy will help reduce IP issues and generate a streamlined approach to troubleshooting IP issues.

Later on in the book we will go further into DHCP and explain how it will be applied to the example LAN. For now, having a plan for implementation is the key thing to know about DHCP.

E-Mail Services

E-mail traffic has several aspects to plan for. You need to plan for who will provide the services, how they will be managed, and where the server will be located. All of this is important to think about prior to selecting the e-mail server technology and all of the rest that will become your main form of organizational communication 24x7x365.

E-mail Strategy – Option 1

Many organizations have a solution in mind even before planning starts. The option presented in Figure 5-18 is not common but provides a fault-tolerant solution that works with any internal e-mail solution that may be deployed in an organization.

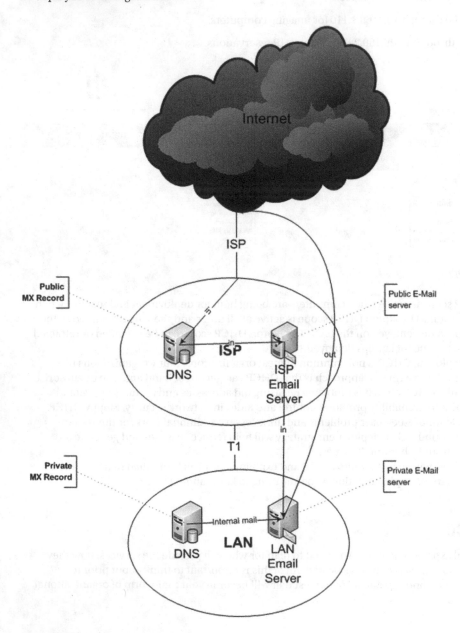

Figure 5-18. *Simple mail traffic diagram option #1*

In Figure 5-18, external e-mail addresses are managed through the ISP. All e-mail from the ISP e-mail server is forwarded to the internal e-mail server. Any outgoing e-mail bypasses the ISP e-mail server and goes directly to the recipient.

In this way, even when the T1 is unavailable, e-mail is staged on the ISP server and then transferred to the LAN e-mail server once the T1 connection is restored. The ISP e-mail account names are used for the "primary SMTP" e-mail names from the e-mail service on the LAN e-mail server and the forwarded ISP e-mail address is the secondary SMTP e-mail address. The LAN e-mail server will have two SMTP mail addresses for each user (an internal address such as @tasah.local) and an external address such as @tasah.com).

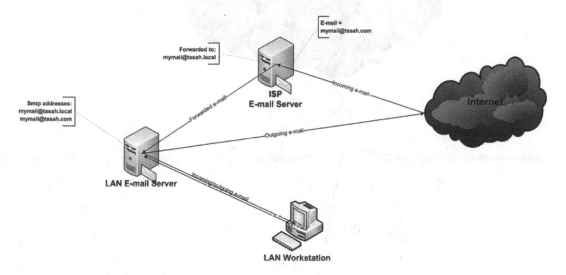

Figure 5-19. *Simple mail address routing option #1*

This also allows for two antispam/antivirus solutions to filter incoming e-mail and further helps the security model. This also allows for business travelers to access and use their e-mail accounts while on the road without opening SMTP ports into the LAN and exposing internal e-mail servers to potential attacks.

The ISP e-mail services are usually manned 24x7 and a contract helps ensure availability. The internal LAN e-mail server is managed internally and it's the responsibility of the organization's IT department to ensure availability and access.

E-mail Strategy – Option 2

Option number two is more common. Your organization manages all e-mail traffic through an internal e-mail server (such as Microsoft's Exchange Server) and the ISP provides an MX record in their DNS servers to publish public access to the Internet.

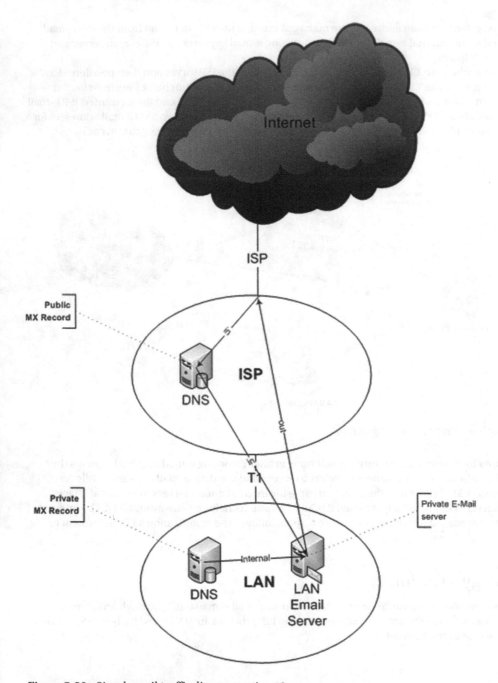

Figure 5-20. *Simple mail traffic diagram option #2*

As long as the T1 circuit is up and running, e-mail can be sent and received through the network. If the T1 circuit is down, external correspondence is unavailable. While some e-mail may be queued by the ISP, the retention and retransmission of messages may be limited or non-existent. There is little legal recourse for lost correspondence if mail is lost.

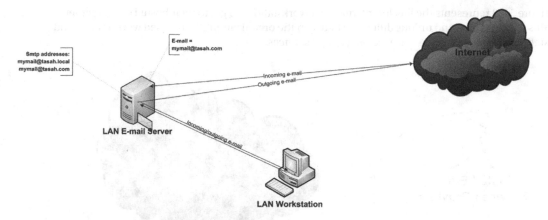

Figure 5-21. *Simple mail address routing option #2*

For all intents and purposes, e-mail services are the sole responsibility of the Internal IT department. This includes antispam/antivirus services along with all of the other security methodologies included in previous network diagrams (proxy servers, firewalls, etc.). Unless the Internal e-mail services provide for redundant e-mail servers, there are no failover or fault-tolerant solutions in place.

E-mail Strategy – Option Three

Option number three introduces a hosted e-mail service (either through an ISP or a hosted E-mail service) that provides a complete, professional e-mail service for your organization. The benefits of this option simplify the organization's IT support model for e-mail services, ensures that e-mail is available remotely, and offers legal liability for disaster recovery.

The pitfalls of this option are control and access. With a hosted e-mail service you have all of the operations for that service outside the organization. This limits your control over the operations and when your T1 circuit goes down so does your access to e-mail. There is the additional support model that enables you to continue laptop access to e-mail via a secondary business DSL linked to a wireless router but that does not enhance your ability to manage e-mail services.

Legal contracts help ensure ownership of the data and provide an SLA (service level agreement) to define operational roles and responsibility, but, as in all contracts, there is the fine print. There is an element of separation that needs to be observed and managed that would not be in place if your organization had options 1 and 2 in place. On the other hand, there is an option of security in place that would otherwise be time consuming for your IT department (such as spam mail, antivirus, maintenance, and disaster recovery).

There are two types of hosted e-mail services:

1. Software as a Service (SAAS)

2. O365 (cloud-based office application services)

Examples of hosted e-mail services available:

- Rackspace

- Zoho Mail

- FastMail

Figure 5-22 represents the link for internal LAN workstations to get to their hosted e-mail server. With this option there is no unique difference between the organization's LAN based workstations and workstations on the Internet when accessing e-mail services.

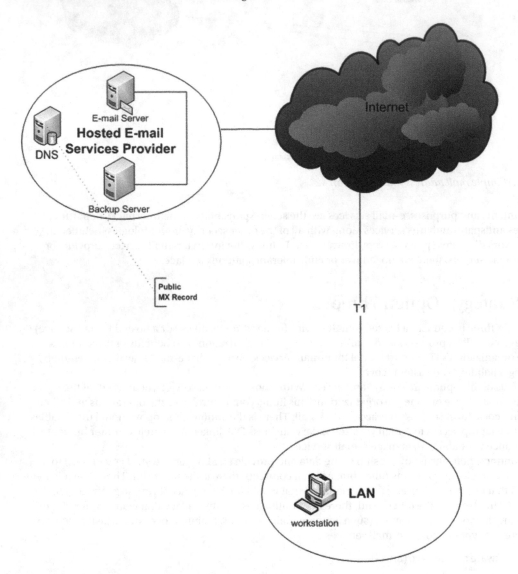

Figure 5-22. *Hosted e-mail services*

For organizations with limited IT staff, a great need for remote access, and a reasonable bank account, option three can provide substantial flexibility while maintaining a sound DRP solution.

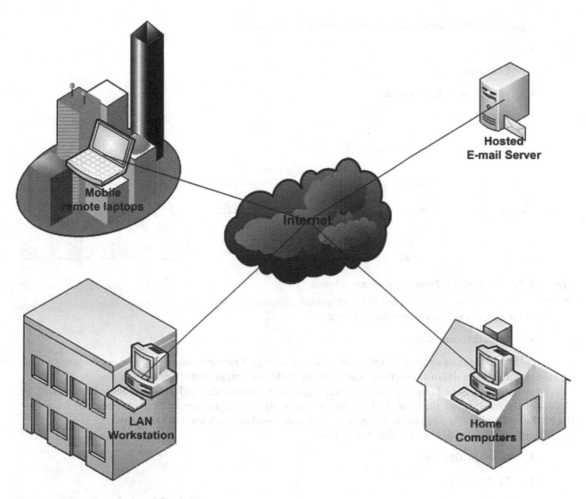

Figure 5-23. *Hosted e-mail flexibility*

Domain Services

An organizational network, as you have seen so far, is complicated. Domain and directory services try to contain services so that users and computer accounts can be centrally managed (not like home networks that maintain individual accounts on each computer). Along with managing user and computer accounts, there are additional resources (such as group policy objects —GPOs—found in Microsoft Active Directory). These GPOs allow system administrators the flexibility to centrally manage system security, application configurations, and many more things remotely and centrally. It can be argued that GPOs are one of the most powerful tools available to system administrators to manage and secure their network resources.

There are many ways to architect domain schemas. You can develop strategies for GPO aggregation, delegated authority, and tree structure. Architectural design should reflect operational logic before organizational representation. In other words, the schema tree should first follow the logical distribution of group policy objects and delegation of authority, and then follow a simple hierarchy based on organizational design.

In Figure 5-24 there are the default active directory containers:

- Builtin

- Computers

- ForeignSecurityPrinciples

- Users

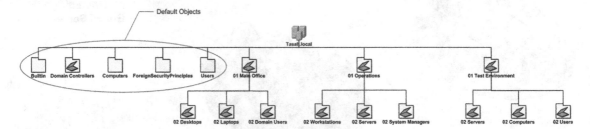

Figure 5-24. *Basic Active Directory domain schema*

There is also the default organizational unit:

- Domain controllers

Non-default (or user-defined) domain objects such as organizational units (OU) and containers should remain separate from default objects in order to simplify design and provide troubleshooting.

To make user-defined objects float to the top of the tree, the user defined OUs have been labeled with 01 (such as 01Main Office). Each sub-OU is incremented by its level in the tree, such as 02 Desktops found in the 01 Main Office OU. This helps separate the tree levels and builds a level of hierarchy.

There are three level 1 user-defined OU trees:

1. 01 Main Office

2. 01 Operations

3. 01 Test

The 01 Main Office OU can be considered the production tree. The 01 Operations OU will be used by the IT department. The 01 Test tree will be used to validate changes using virtual computers and servers.

The tree structure below each of these user-defined OU structures should be designed for policy implementation and delegation. If policies are applied at the top of a tree, they are inherited by all of the children OUs. While you can break inheritance, you also add complexity to the inheritance process. The first thing you should have in mind when deploying group policy objects is avoid breaking inheritance and keep it simple.

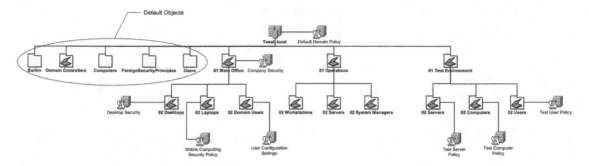

Figure 5-25. *Active Directory with GPOs*

There are three basic types of group policy objects:

1. Computer configuration

2. User configuration

3. Combined configuration

You can design group policy objects to only affect the computer or user (depending on the computer objects in the OU that you have applied the group policy and those in child OUs below that). If you apply a group policy object in a parent OU that has both computer and user objects, you can configure computer and user settings—the policy configuration settings will filter down to their respective objects. The key to group policies is to keep it simple, don't mix objects, and name your group policy object by what it is intended to do (for example, computer security policy would be a computer configuration that locks down the computer to meet a security requirement).

Always test your group policy objects before you deploy them. It seems obvious but often events overtake planning and you may find yourself rushed to push policies without the time to verify them and before you're sure they will do what was intended. Don't let that happen. You will notice that in Figure 5-25 there is a separate tree structure for testing. Use it as your first deployment stage to ensure that the policies you push will in fact do what you want them to.

Directory structure and documenting schema objects will be discussed later in this book. For now, having a basic architectural design and strategic concept down on paper will help control the building of the organization. This binding of architecture and strategy will help lay the foundation for supporting applications and help fine-tune the service business model and keep all of the service elements cohesive and simplified.

IT Services Administration

As you can see, the role of system administration touches all aspects of the information infrastructure—even those things that seem unlikely (such as electrical, fire prevention, and HVAC). Coordinating all of these vast elements and designing business processes to help design proactive responses and contain emergency reactions must be enforced from the top down. But, in turn, the details and daily experiences that system administrators face must also be the underlying fundamentals from which those business processes build. This is a give and take relationship that ensures your organization's "best practices" become sound enforceable policy that everyone can understand and support.

Figure 5-26 represents a role-based IT organization. Each of these roles can be combined or expanded into multiple people, depending on the size of your organization. The roles, however, are important and should be envisioned in the overall scheme of the organization. No two organizations are designed the same so you should be aware that this example is an abstract of what you might find in your organization.

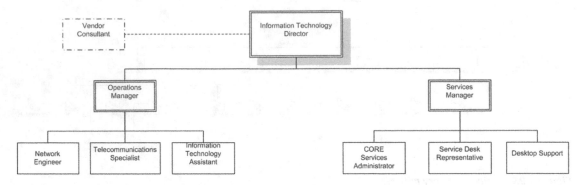

Figure 5-26. *IT organizational structure example*

The Information Technology Director (ITD) is responsible for overseeing all IT services and operations. The ITD develops a service level agreement (SLA[20]) in conjunction with other departments in order to set boundaries and expectations for how the IT department will work with other departments to maintain and evolve IT services delivered to other departments. This SLA should not incorporate internal IT service details but should be understood in a way that other departments can expect services to be delivered. The ITD has an overall responsibility for all of the OSI model levels.

The Operations Manager (ITOM) is responsible for all infrastructure and security. Network architecture, firewall management, DNS, DHCP, and telecommunications are driven and maintained by this role. The ITOM must have a sound understanding of internal network operations and Internetworking connectivity. He or she should have a reasonable understanding of directory services and desktop management. They work hand in hand with the Service Manager (ITSM) to maintain and tweak operations to provide existing operations and seamlessly incorporate changes to the network. They may have subordinate roles (such as network engineers, telecommunication specialists, and information technology assistants) to effectively manage operations. The ITOM supports all lower-level OSI model levels.

The Services Manager (ITSM) is responsible for overseeing all software services, excluding DNS and DHCP. The ITSM manages all subordinate roles that maintain domain/directory services, information management, and collaboration technologies. This person is responsible for what goes on servers, workstations, laptops, and the intranet. He or she also manages the service desk, which is the single point of contact between internal customers (other department members) for issue resolution and change management. He or she maintains software licenses and application purchase approvals. The ITSM supports all upper OSI model levels.

The Vendor Consultant is the contact point for vendor-related issues (such as manufacturer of technology support and purchases). While this person has no internal relationship with your organization, he or she plays an important role. There is usually one contact person for each manufacturer and could also be a repackaging agent that provides a variety of products from many vendors (such as a consultancy firm).

Based on the size and complexity of your organization, the number of persons supporting the IT roles can be either small (as small as one person for the whole job) or extensive (as many as hundreds for a large corporation, government organization, or educational institution). There is a balance to how many people should be in a given IT department. The fewer the number, the fewer services that can be successfully managed. If your IT department becomes too large, it can ultimately be overwhelmed by bureaucracy.

---

[20]Service Level Agreement Toolkit: http://www.service-level-agreement.net/

Summary

Planning network architecture before it is built will help set the foundation for more in-depth planning and documentation as the network is deployed. Designing the basis for IP and routing strategy before implementing it will lead to better questions about what you are doing and why. Defining your e-mail strategy and exploring all of your options prior to installation will help ensure that what you end up with will be well thought out. Sketching out your domain schema before you run your dcpromo[21] command for the first time will help answer all of the questions during the directory build. Documentation of all of the concepts considered and those tossed out (and why) will help build the next stage of building the organizational IT environment. Understanding the IT organizational roles before dividing responsibilities to those in the department will help define strengths and weaknesses in the department. All of this leads not only to how you will move forward in building the organization's IT, but where future developments should be concentrated.

---

[21]DCPROMO: http://technet.microsoft.com/en-us/library/cc732887(WS.10).aspx

CHAPTER 6

■ ■ ■

Network Support Plan

Given the organizational roles represented in Figure 6-1, this book's example organization IT personnel will be required to support multiple roles. The quality of support will be limited by the number of hats each individual is required to wear.

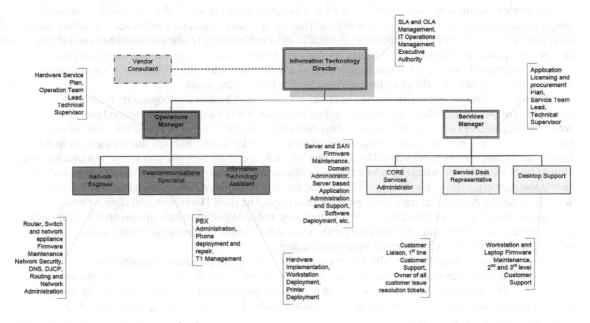

Figure 6-1. IT organization and roles

In an ever-tightening IT budget, these tradeoffs can be made randomly with mixed results. By diagramming the basic functions as seen in Figure 6-1, it is somewhat easier to match multiple roles to the personnel currently employed to help mitigate the potential problems that would result.

By coupling roles with priorities, the organization can balance the workload and still provide a strong IT support presence. The following is a list of priorities that may help in planning for an understaffed IT team:

1. Service Desk Support

2. Core Services Support

3. Communications Support

4. Inventory and Maintenance Support

5. Disaster Recovery

The service desk provides real-time IT support for the organization members and customers (either directly or indirectly). This is a number one priority for the organization and IT staff because it is the primary liaison between the IT staff and everyone else. As long as the service desk presents a confident and reliable IT presence, all other services will be seen positively. If the service desk looks chaotic and dysfunctional, even though you have a crack team working the rest of IT, IT will appear to be in disarray. Too many organizations fail to put the proper people in service desk roles and suffer because of that decision.

Core services (AD, DNS, DHCP, e-mail, file services, etc.) must be operational at all times. These services are important to the organization's ability to make money and provide the services required to keep operational. These services are second only to the service desk in priority.

Communications support (routers, switches, and network appliances) usually require less frequent maintenance and therefore take lower priority based solely on a sound, generally unchanging maintenance plan that can take less time to manage than that of core services or the service desk. Communications, of course, is essential to the overall operations of IT in the organization, but it requires less hands-on work to maintain a reliable service.

Inventory and maintenance is third on the list. The maintenance referred to in this instance is not the daily maintenance (as in front-line service support) but the planned maintenance (firmware updates, BIOS upgrades, and overall tuning maintenance) generally neglected by many IT organizations but essential to the proper operations lifecycle. These inventory and maintenance services are quarterly and sometimes annually performed to ensure that equipment is up to date and accounted for. While these are important services, they are not time critical to the daily operations of the organization.

Disaster recovery is last on the list but not least in importance. Proper development of a disaster recovery plan should include an automated backup process as well as an organized archival process whereby backup tapes are stored offsite based on the value of the data and the backup schedule. In many cases, archival tapes can be gathered and stored offsite on a weekly basis, although many larger companies have taken offsite on a daily schedule. However this schedule is maintained, the process (when automated) should be managed with as little human interaction as possible. There should be weekly, monthly, and yearly test restoration of archived data to ensure that the data being stored offsite is usable, but the overall service should be designed to have the least amount of impact on daily IT services and support staff.

Organizing IT roles and assigning responsibilities for available personnel in support should be thought through very carefully so that roles with the greatest immediate impact to the organization are covered. All other IT services should be supported as soon as possible.

Too many businesses disregard disaster recovery. It is easy to ignore disaster recovery because of cost and the impact of maintaining and testing on IT department assets. While it is true that a proper disaster recovery implementation takes time and requires dedication to keep from failing, a well-planned and maintained disaster recovery solution can be the difference between surviving a catastrophe and disappearing as a business overnight.

Hardware Services Plan

The hardware service plan should be in place prior to deploying hardware. The plan needs to be integrated with daily operations, policies, and technical mechanisms used to manage and maintain network services. The hardware service plan needs to be embraced from the top down and integrated with the service desk toolset.

Hardware purchases should be made with the thought of maintaining a standardized configuration and should focus on vendor support. Hardware inventory mechanisms and support history need to be integrated with the service desk trouble ticket application. A policy dictating configuration changes and lifecycle maintenance needs to be clearly defined and promoted from the top down.

The hardware procurement and deployment process starts prior to the employee being hired. Equipment needs to be in place and readied so that when an employee comes on their first day of work, everything is in place and working correctly. All too often employees come to work and find nothing to work with, or find equipment that was used by a former employee and not reconditioned for them. This first impression sticks with new employees and makes the IT department look bad. The hardware service process begins with the preparation for hiring employees or services and not when the employee or service is intended to start.

The employee's first day is step nine in the hardware lifecycle (Figure 6-2). By the time a new employee starts, purchasing, manufacturing, receiving, warehousing, inventory, imaging, QA testing, and deployment should have been completed. If the hiring process is a week, that can be an impossible task.

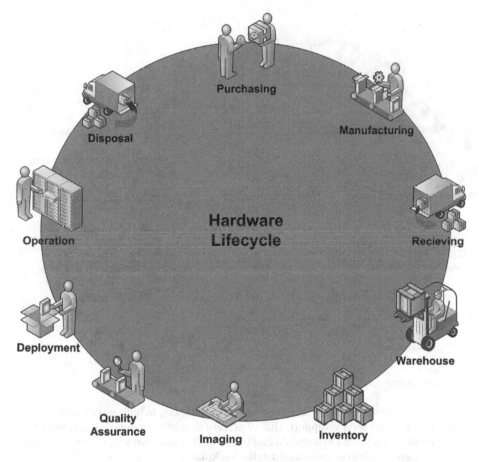

Figure 6-2. *The hardware lifecycle*

Many companies develop a trickle-down distribution of hardware based on the importance of an employee's role and the dependability of equipment in inventory. This trickle-down method usually ensures that members of the organization who have a vital need for cutting edge technology always get the newest and greatest equipment. Their old equipment is refurbished and given to others in the organization who have the oldest equipment and are in need of better working machines. This, of course, requires a sound evaluation process ensuring that the equipment trickled down is both functional and able to support the new owner's needs. In any event, the trickle down process assumes that a pool of older working machines is maintained (both for new users and for emergency replacement).

Figure 6-3 displays the hardware point of view for lifecycle maintenance and does not fully reflect the repurposing phase described in the trickle down process. The average life expectancy of a given workstation can vary based on the original quality and technology of the hardware. However, you can assume that most equipment outlives its usefulness over a period of three to four years (which is the given amortization period of most accounting practices for such equipment). Servers have a longer lifecycle due to the ruggedness of the equipment and the difficulty in replacing both hardware and services.

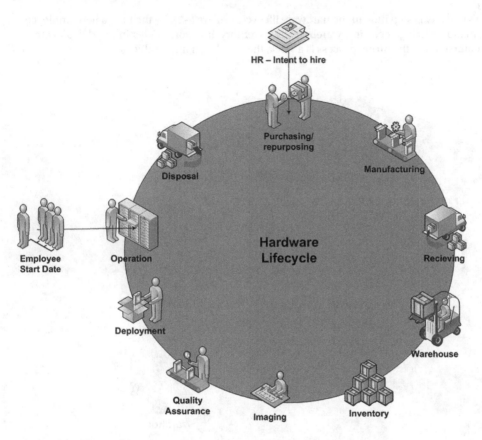

Figure 6-3. *Time to hire, time to buy*

If you are deploying all new equipment, the organization will most likely buy in bulk and should have at least a 10 percent excess for growth and service support. This 10 percent should be maintained and any use of that excess should be immediately replaced to maintain that balance. This also works for printers, servers, and any other essential equipment that is to be maintained in the workplace.

Firmware/BIOS Maintenance

No hardware should be deployed prior to updating BIOS and firmware in conjunction with the hardware matrix defined by subsystem requirements (such as SAN technologies). All too often systems are deployed out of the box and without thought of firmware and BIOS versions. But the value in maintaining firmware and BIOS versions is obvious. Just as hot fixes and service packs for operating systems shore up security holes and make the operating system more stable, firmware updates and BIOS revisions help make the hardware more secure and can operate more seamlessly with newer operating systems and third-party hardware.

Many vendors (such as Dell,[1] Hewlett Packard,[2] and IBM[3]) have online inventory maintenance agreements that will either automatically update firmware and BIOS versions or provide you with notifications as to when updates have been made available. It is never a good idea to automatically update firmware or BIOS versions; however, having automated notifications is priceless. This gives you the ability to schedule updates when your IT staff has the time and maintenance cycle to perform those updates. More often than not, the update process will require downtime and you will need to assess the time for delivery (if it is a single system or multiple of systems that will be affected by the upgrade).

Just as you would with all hot fixes and service packs, you will need to have a failback strategy in case something unexpected happens. Keeping archives up and installing firmware and BIOS updates can be a lifesaver and does not usually require a lot of storage to support.

As stated earlier in this chapter, this is not a full time job, but it is essential to the proper operations of IT hardware. This process should be applied to all IT hardware (servers, routers, switches, printers, laptops, workstations, etc.), basically anything that has firmware or BIOS versions that can be updated. Of course, it is necessary to look at the whole picture when developing your update strategy. If your server is connected to a SAN, you need to coordinate the firmware and BIOS versions with the SAN host support matrix (such as the EMC Support Matrix[4] or the HP StorageWorks hardware and Software Compatibility Matrix,[5] as two examples).

Hardware Implementation

Implementing hardware is more than just loading software and configuring systems to work on the network; there needs to be a process for inventory, baseline settings to manage growth, and security. Remember, having physical access to hardware is the greatest step forward in gaining access to data.

Mounting hardware and dressing up cables are important aspects of properly managing IT systems. You can tell a lot about an IT department by how clean their cabling is and how well mounted their rack equipment is. Properly dressed cabling includes labels that keep track of what is connected to what and indicate how important that cabling is to network operations. They also allow technicians to remove and upgrade cabling and rack mounted systems more quickly.

Adding cable protectors to workstation cables that run across the floor helps protect against damage to both the cable and the pedestrian crossing that cable. Of course, the best solution is to avoid running cables across walkways and having them underneath workspace legroom areas.

User Services

There are four key living documents that manage user services:

1. The Service Level Agreement (SLA)

2. The Operational Level Agreement (OLA)

3. The Change Management Database (CMDB)

4. Underpinning Agreements (UA)

---

[1]http://www.dell.com/

[2]http://www.hp.com/

[3]http://www.ibm.com/us/en/

[4]http://developer.emc.com/developer/devcenters/storage/snia/smi-s/downloads/EMC_Providers_SMI-S_Only.pdf

[5]http://h18000.www1.hp.com/products/storage/software/XPcompatibility.html

These four living documents provide both an understanding of services to be offered and what timeline has been established to resolve service issues. These are industry standards found in the ITIL version 3 framework.[6] Each organization defines these documents uniquely. They can all be maintained online through service desk applications (such as BMC's Service Desk Express[7]). Service Desk Express can integrate with popular system management software (such as Microsoft's SCCM[8]) to help automate the inventory lifecycle. Service Desk Express can also be configured to apply SLA requirements to ensure automatic and proper application of the SLA.

Integrating of the four service management documents into the service desk application saves time.

SLA

The SLA (Service Level Agreement) is the contract between IT and all other internal departments describing the level of service that will be offered, timelines for resolution, and quality of IT equipment and maintenance that is required for the organization to conduct business effectively. It should be simple to understand, allow for adequate time in which IT can provide services, and leave no grey area for misunderstandings. It should be prominently displayed on the IT Intranet web site for all to review. The SLA needs to be properly renegotiated on a timely basis to keep content up to date and relevant.

OLA

The OLA (Operation Level Agreement) defines the internal IT roles, responsibilities, and expectations. Reviewing the roles presented in the IT organizational chart, you can begin to picture the responsibilities and expectations for each role:

- Information Technology Director (SLA/OLA management, executive authority)

- Operations Manager (hardware service plan, operations team leader, technical supervisor)

  - Network Engineer (routers, switches, network appliances, firmware maintenance, network security, DNS, DHCP, and network administration)

  - Telecommunications Specialist (PBX, phone maintenance, and T1 management)

  - Information Technology Assistant (hardware implementation, workstation deployment, and printer deployment)

- Services Manager (application requisition/licensing service team leader, technical supervisor)

  - Core Services Administrator (server, SAN administrations and firmware maintenance, domain, database, and application administration and support, software deployment, etc.)

  - Service Desk Representative (user liaison, customer support, issue tracking and resolution manager, and first- and second-level technical support)

  - Desktop Support (workstation and laptop firmware maintenance, and second-and third-level technical support)

---

[6]http://www.itilv3.net/
[7]http://www.bmc.com/products/offering/Incident-and-Problem-Management.html
[8]http://www.microsoft.com/systemcenter/configurationmanager/en/us/default.aspx

Expectations are driven by what members in each role are capable of supporting (their training, experience, and overall skillset). This should be documented in an IT training evaluation for members of the IT team.

CMDB

The Configuration Management Database (CMDB) can be one or many integrated databases depending on the complexity and size of the organization. Usually the CMDB is integrated with the service desk trouble ticket software, operations management software, system management software, directory services, change management front end software, and inventory. The purpose of the CMDB is to maintain a comprehensive database that tracks all IT changes within the organization so as to provide an up-to-date picture of IT operations, changing trends in IT services and equipment, and help guide IT operations in developing future services, roles, and system assets.

UA

Underpinning agreements (UA) are contracts between the internal IT organization and outside support organizations (vendors). UAs extend internal IT services by providing vendor support for hardware and software (warrantees, support plans, automatic licensing upgrades, and in-depth specialized engineering support). In many cases, UAs shore up internal IT training shortfalls and outsource the more complicated time-consuming tasks to vendor support teams. This allows the internal IT staff to focus on the daily issues that need the quickest resolution.

Workstation Deployment

Workstation deployment can be complicated in so many ways. There is licensing assurance, quality assurance, time-to-life processes for deploying workstations effectively, and inventory maintenance. Security is always important—devising the best method for securing hardware issuance, return ability, and maintaining proper antivirus/software updates. There are many ways a workstation can be prepped for deployment (remote installation, imaging, single instance installations, etc.). The goal is to standardize on one method for deployment, provide adequate support for that method, and ensure that the method works as envisioned.

Deployment options (in least to best order):

1. Individual workstation deployment (building each workstation manually)

2. Imaging (building static images)

3. Remote installation (building images and deploying those images over the network)

4. Virtual workstations/VDI clients

Individual Workstation Deployment

Deploying workstations individually is time consuming, unstructured, and prone to human error. It is hard to maintain tight control over software media and leads to poor license management. However, many IT organizations do install software manually and build each workstation from scratch. Most IT organizations do not deploy systems straight out of the box with prefabricated vendor images mainly because of the "bloatware"[9] preinstalled and the varied versioning and licenses of applications that come with boxed images.

---

[9]http://www.webopedia.com/TERM/B/bloatware.html

The basic concept requires building computers from CD or DVD media, first the operation system and then the applications. Following that process, you need to install with the original software media or copies of that media time and time again. CDs and DVDs scratch over time and often get lost when they are used often enough. The process (even when written down) is open to interpretation and almost never identically duplicated by one or more technicians.

While this is often the starting point for most new IT organizations to build their workstations and laptops, most IT organizations quickly move toward imaging and remote workstation deployment for cost savings and to standardize their systems.

Imaging

Creating an image is most often the best solution for small, medium, and large-scale IT organizations. You still have to build the original workstation image, but then you clone that image onto many systems. There are many imaging applications out there (Symantec Altiris,[10] Microsoft SCCM,[11] Norton Ghost,[12] etc.). Windows Vista and Windows Seven, along with many Linux and UNIX versions, come with imaging built into the operating system. The value of imaging and cloning workstations and laptops has been well known for many years in the IT industry. Many organizations create images and have their vendors pre-image their workstations and laptops prior to having them delivered (at a small cost). Some organizations have the vendor custom design images for them (at a more significant cost).

There are a variety of ways in which images can be created. The goal is to make one image for each type of hardware platform that needs not change. This becomes difficult to achieve when applications are constantly changing along with service packs and hot fixes being updated.

Static Images

Many organizations create full workstation images (including the operating system, most recent service packs, all standard applications, and hardware drivers) also known as static images. These take time to create and need to be tested thoroughly. They are deployed with minimal inventory management and quite often are out of date by the time they are fully tested. They consume large amounts of bandwidth to deploy. There is a significant investment in time by the IT staff to produce them and you need one image for every type of workstation and laptop in your network.

The main benefit to a static image is the time it takes in deploying a workstation. With the static image you install everything once. You are assured that every workstation of any given hardware type has the exact same set of applications and services.

But over time as the diversity of workstations sets in, the burden of maintaining independent custom static images uses up staff resources and disk space. Each static image can take up tens of gigabytes of disk space. There may be need to have multiple images for each hardware type. You'll need upgraded images to keep current with newer applications and licensing and a dedicated image librarian to keep up with the creation, deployment, and maintenance of images.

Dynamic Images

Creating raw operating system images with baseline hardware drivers reduces the time for creation and the size of the image to store and deploy. Dynamic images provide the raw operating system with hardware drivers deployed to a workstation. Service packs and hot fixes can be slipstreamed into that image to keep

---

[10]http://www.symantec.com/business/deployment-solution
[11]http://www.microsoft.com/systemcenter/configurationmanager/en/us/default.aspx
[12]http://www.symantec.com/norton/ghost

it current without requiring the need to rebuild another image later on. Applications would be installed remotely after the image has been deployed. This allows for Microsoft Active Directory and/or SCCM, Symantec's Altiris, or another third-party packaging tool to deploy applications remotely.

The benefits of this approach are that you can centrally manage the installation and removal of applications modularly and maintain a current inventory of application deployment. You can also fine tune the distribution of applications and upgrade those applications remotely.

The disadvantage of this approach is that the deployment phase of the workstation will take longer to complete.

Remote Installation

Pushing the workstation image remotely helps secure software media and limits the distribution of applications and operating systems. It helps prevent the unauthorized copying of licensed software and promotes consistency in the distribution of those applications where needed.

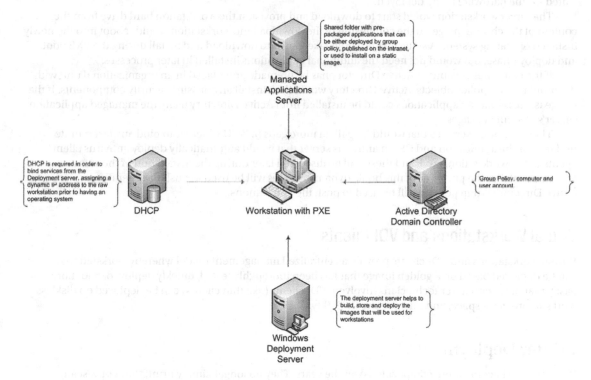

Figure 6-4. *Remote installation components*

There are five basic components found in a Microsoft remote installation scenario:

1. WDS (Windows Deployment Server)

2. AD (Active Directory Domain Controllers and DNS)

3. MAS (Managed Applications Server)

4. DHCP (Dynamic Host Configuration Protocol server)

5. Target (the raw workstation)

While many of these components (excluding the target workstation) can be combined onto one physical server, performance-wise it is better to separate the components onto individual physical servers. UNIX, Linux, and other remote installations follow a similar design but don't share the same naming convention.

Remote Installation Process

The DHCP broadcasts availability of services to the local network (in this case, DHCP broadcasts that WDS is available to workstations with PXE[13] NICs booting from the network). The PXE (or pre-boot execution environment enabled network interface card) can obtain an IP address without requiring the workstation to have an operating system installed.

There is a WDS menu (generated from the WDS server) advertising premade images. These images can be the *static* image with a full workstation OS and application suite preinstalled or a *dynamic* image with only the OS and hardware drives preinstalled. In either case, the technician would select the image best suited for the hardware being deployed.

The target workstation would start to download and provision the workstation hard drive from the content of the chosen image. At the conclusion of the download the workstation would reboot into the newly installed operating system. A static image would take longer to download and install during the PXE boot and deploy phase, but would not need the additional applications installed in later processes.

If the computer account in Active Directory has be premade and placed in an organizational unit with the proper group policy objects, Active Directory would then install any missing security components. If the image is a *dynamic*, all applications could be installed from Active Directory using the managed application server's custom packages.

There are other services that would help fill in more gaps (a WSUS[14] server to bind any last minute updates for the application and OS, an antivirus server that would automatically deploy antivirus client agents to the workstation, etc.), and these will be discussed later during the installation of the software environment. For the purposes of this book, dynamic images will be used to push the operating system and Active Directory group policies will be used to push the applications.

Virtual Workstations and VDI Clients

Virtual workstations and VDI clients provide a centralized management model whereby workstations can be deployed based on a golden image that has been thoroughly tested, quickly deployed, and more easily managed with fewer technicians involved. VDI clients (aka thin clients) can be deployed on diskless workstations, save space, and offer greater flexibility.

Printer Deployment

Printers have become more complicated over the years. They no longer simply print; they copy, scan, e-mail, and collate. They print on both sides and in color. Printers can store and retrieve print jobs. With the complexity of printing services (multipurpose devices) comes a host of third-party software and ways in which the device can fail. People rely on printing; they expect printers to work every time they use them. But printers are mechanical devices prone to failure and often abused by those who use them. Printers require endless amounts of fairly expensive supplies (tones and paper and replacement fusing devices). Many times problems with printers are related to running out of supplies or people not knowing how to properly maintain the supplies for a given printer.

---

[13]http://www.pxe.ca/
[14]http://technet.microsoft.com/en-us/wsus/default.aspx

Designing a remote monitoring service (web pages on the intranet or e-mail notifications when a printer is out of supplies or is malfunctioning) can help minimize the user-related issues that come from printer problems. If the IT department can show up minutes after a printer runs out of paper or malfunctions, users will feel assured that they are responsive and have everything in hand. The trick is to have a quick response monitoring process that will notify the right people immediately when an issue crops up.

Obviously having spare printers is also a good thing. Having and maintaining proper supplies at all times is also important. If the printer is a multipurpose device, it should have a handbook easily accessible for users to refer to so that they can learn how to use everything the device is capable of providing them.

Truly the best way to manage multipurpose devices is through support contracts with trained professionals. If you are renting the devices and have a service/support contract with an outside vendor (also known as an underpinning agreement), you can lighten the load and responsibility of the IT department to manage devices known to be high maintenance.

File System Plan

The concept of a single file system to store all of the organizations data is a very difficult proposition. The fact that a network is by definition a distributed computing environment opens many avenues for data to be stored in different ways and at different locations. Quite often users have no idea where their data is stored or why. And just as often, applications may have obscure default file locations for the user's data.

Data stored on local workstation hard drives is difficult to back up and lost when the hard drive fails. There are two methods available in Active Directory to minimize that:

1. Roaming profiles

2. Folder redirection

Roaming Profiles

Roaming profiles synchronize data stored on the local hard drive with a network share. This usually is done when a user first logs on to the network and when a user logs off. The first time a roaming profile is established the logon time takes longer. This is because all of the profile data is synchronized. From that point on, each logon using that workstation and user will take less time. Only the data that has changed during the logon session is copied to the network drive. Every time the user logs on to a new workstation the synchronization process starts over synchronizing with the new workstation.

Roaming profiles are bandwidth intensive and can become corrupted when users log on to workstations of varying hardware configurations. Roaming profiles also have the potential to leave personal data on every machine the user logs on to. In environments where workstations are identical and group policies delete duplicate data when a user logs off a machine, roaming profiles can be very useful. Roaming profiles ensure that users get the same desktop and access to their files no matter where they log in as long as they are part of the organization's domain.

Folder Redirection

Folder redirection binds the user's profile storage to network file storage. It is less bandwidth intensive and oblivious to the user. Users get the same personal folder content no matter what workstation they log on to and can access their Internet Explorer favorites as well. Folder redirection works as long as the network share is available. If the network share is not available, users cannot work successfully on any workstation on the domain.

The benefits of folder redirection is speed, agility to access data anywhere, and assurance that if the workstation is stolen or damaged the personal data created on that workstation is not lost or accessed by unauthorized persons. The disadvantage is that the network file storage (where the personal data really resides) must be available for users to use their workstations properly.

Laptops versus Desktops

Given the unique options available for roaming profiles, laptops can benefit most from their use. The profile on the laptop can be updated when the laptop is connected to the domain and maintain the profile configuration while traveling. Data that is generated while traveling will automatically upload to network storage when reconnected to the domain and be stored while away. Data is fairly safe while traveling since the profile is protected.

Desktop computers benefit most using folder redirection. The boot up is quicker and the data is automatically stored on the network share. If a desktop computer hard drive fails or there is a total desktop failure, simply replacing that desktop will get the user back up and running in no time at all and they will have not lost any data previously saved.

Some organizations mix roaming profiles with folder redirection. This can be complicated and needs to be thought out very carefully. Some companies use folder redirection with folder synchronization; that too needs to be thought out very carefully and fully tested.

In any case, there should be a well-planned decision over what method is used to ensure organizational data is stored on network shares so that it can be backed up automatically. All of the IT staff should be fully versed in the method used and why it was chosen. An educated IT staff is invaluable and this is something that should be first on their mind when dealing with user data and distribution practice.

Mobile Devices

As mobile devices (such as smart phones and tablets) become more common network access devices, there is a greater need for IT to secure and manage their implementation. Applying the same security application suite, locking down configuration access, and monitoring and managing potential theft becomes more difficult. Encryption, poison pill applications, and low jacking traceability all play a part in securing the mobile business communications model.

Intranet Deployment

Figure 6-5 displays a simple IT home page designed with user support in mind.

Figure 6-5. *IT intranet home page*

There are six web page parts:

1. The Navigation Bar—Accesses additional web pages (MAIN, OPERATIONS, SERVICES, and SUPPORT DESK).

2. Operations Status—Gives an immediate update on the general operational status of the network services.

3. Information Technology Updates—Provides the phone extension for service desk assistance, an update on current patches and hot fixes, and an announcement of when the next maintenance cycle will be performed.

4. Service/change request and documentation links—Submits the service requests and change configuration requests, views the status of all requests, and accesses all internal information technology documentation.

5. Security Software Download buttons—Provides manual download options for antivirus/antispam and operating system updates.

6. Quality assurance statement—A statement requesting comments and suggestions for improving services. An e-mail link is added to ensure the right people get those comments and suggestions along with an additional e-mail link for users to recommend support staff for awards in performing above and beyond the job requirements.

For the IT staff this web site acts as a portal into their world. The Navigation Bar links sections to their specific web sites where they can find detailed support documents, drivers, and additional information to management their daily workload. They can also go to the main internal organization web page by selecting MAIN from the Navigation Bar options list.

At a glance, user and IT staff can easily have a global picture of the status of the network, note upcoming maintenance times, ensure the security their system, and communicate issues they need to have addressed. This simplicity in design helps users, IT staff, and everyone who needs IT support address their needs quickly and without confusion. Many web designs start out simple and work their way to a complexity that confuses even the most technology savvy user. This page should only change to make things simpler and more readable.

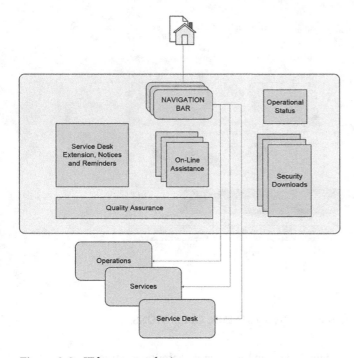

Figure 6-6. *IT home page logic*

Service Desk and User Support

User support encompasses everything that the IT department is contracted to provide. User support provides operational health and performance. It is the fundamental services the IT team manages. The service desk is the front end to user support, and all other IT staff members act in direct support of the service desk, providing in-depth knowledge and experience.

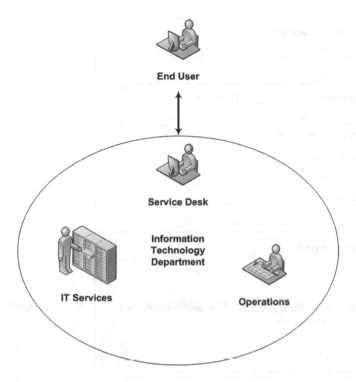

Figure 6-7. User support protocol

When a trouble ticket is opened, the service desk takes full responsibility. This responsibility is maintained throughout the life of the ticket. The content of the ticket is essential to the performance of the team to resolve that ticket quickly and professionally. A trouble ticket should contain all of the pertinent information for evaluating the issue. It should tag inventory not only to define replacement components (when needed), but also to build a history of defective parts.

The trouble ticket should define if the issue is security related, and/or if the problem has a potential to spread to other systems. You need to define location and user information, and try to gather any historical data that may have led to the issue. All of this sounds rather difficult to gather, especially when the user is in the middle of a work stoppage and wants to get back up and running quickly, but it is essential to building the knowledge base that will help minimize and resolve the issue.

In Figure 6-8, there are five main areas of the form:

1. Title

2. Incident Information

3. Client Information

4. Description

5. Resolution

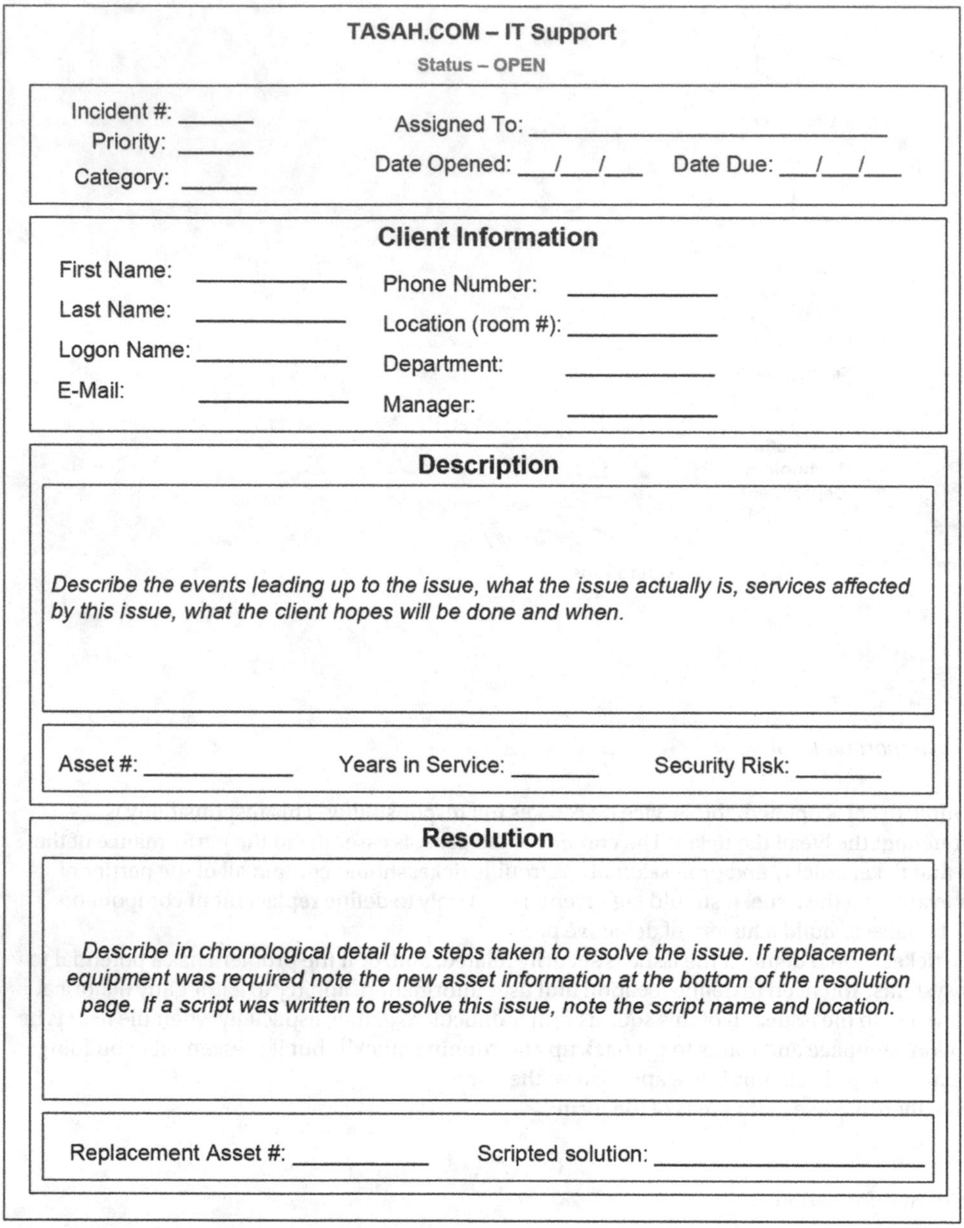

TASAH.COM – IT Support
Status – OPEN

Incident #: _____

Priority: _____

Category: _____

Assigned To: _____

Date Opened: ___/___/___   Date Due: ___/___/___

Client Information

First Name: _____

Last Name: _____

Logon Name: _____

E-Mail: _____

Phone Number: _____

Location (room #): _____

Department: _____

Manager: _____

Description

Describe the events leading up to the issue, what the issue actually is, services affected by this issue, what the client hopes will be done and when.

Asset #: _____   Years in Service: _____   Security Risk: _____

Resolution

Describe in chronological detail the steps taken to resolve the issue. If replacement equipment was required note the new asset information at the bottom of the resolution page. If a script was written to resolve this issue, note the script name and location.

Replacement Asset #: _____   Scripted solution: _____

Figure 6-8. *Sample trouble ticket information form*

Figure 6-8 is a simple form that, if manually entered, might take more time than actually resolving the issue would. This is where having the proper supporting system management software in place will aid in making things go faster:

- Incident number, status, date opened, and date due can automatically be entered based on system information and SLA data from the category information.

- All client information can be obtained automatically from the directory services database. Once the person requests assistance, the service desk support personnel would enter in the client's last name and the service desk application would fill in the rest of the client's data from the uploaded directory services data.

- Asset description data can be managed by system management software that's maintained the inventory.

The only things that the service desk personnel should have to enter is the client's last name, category of the issue, who the ticket will be assigned to, and the description. If the ticket can be resolved by the service desk personnel without escalation to higher levels of support, then the service desk personnel should assign the ticket to themselves.

Of course, there are SLA guidelines that restrict the amount of time a ticket can be resolved by (this should be part of the category time resolution data). There should also be business rules that send an e-mail out to the clients notifying them that the ticket has been opened and when it is closed. A lot of supporting management software interacts with the service desk data to streamline all of the data input processed and ensure that data is synchronized across the board.

Once the ticket is resolved, it should be returned to the service desk for closure. This falls in line with ITIL best practices where the service desk owns the trouble ticket even when it is assigned to other sections for resolution. The service desk opens the ticket and closes it; all other support groups work for the service desk while the ticket is open.

Figure 6-9 displays a simple flow diagram depicting the life of a trouble ticket and the information interface. Once the ticket is opened, client information is retrieved from directory services, asset information is retrieved from system management services, and the service desk manually enters the description.

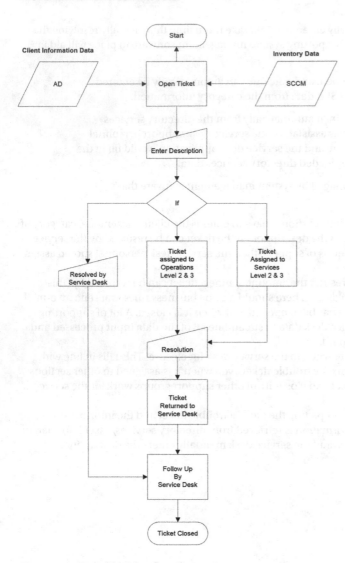

Figure 6-9. *Trouble ticket flowchart*

If the service desk can resolve the ticket, that resolution is recorded internally. If the ticket needs to go outside the service desk (to other services administrators or operation administrators), then the ticket is assigned to them for resolution.

Once the resolution is completed and recorded, the ticket is returned to the service desk. The service desk follows up by contacting the clients to evaluate their appraisal of the resolution process. Once everyone is satisfied with the resolution, the service desk closes the ticket.

Summary

Having a plan to build on at the beginning is the optimal way in which to design your organization's IT services strategy. Usually there is some idea of how things should work and what the IT department will do in case things happen, but often that's about it. While this chapter is by no means a comprehensive depiction of what should be in place, it does offer a sound fundamental to start with.

While the IT department envisioned in this book is small, it shares many of the same fundamentals with larger IT organizations. The need to lay down the roles, responsibilities, and general workflow helps define the type of skillsets your organization needs and the level of experience employees should have.

Having a strong ITIL-based framework with well-defined SLAs, OLAs, UAs, and CMDB concepts will help ensure professional services are rendered. If the agreements are based on mutual arbitration between the client base and IT management, everyone should know what to expect.

There is an excellent online article written by Malcolm Fry titled "Top Ten Reasons Organizations Are Unsuccessful Implementing ITIL,"[15] where Mr. Fry details the need for continuous improvement in implementing IT infrastructure and the dangers of overdesigning your ITIL-based IT organization. Each IT organization is different. Each IT organization has its commonalities. Take the time to fully evaluate the level of complexity your organization needs to provide the best networking service plan and be ready to change when the time comes. Realize there is no cookie-cutter template that fits every organization's service plan.

---

[15] http://costkiller.net/tribune/Tribu-PDF/Top-Ten-Reasons-Organizations-are-Unsuccessful-Implementing-ITIL.htm

CHAPTER 7

■ ■ ■

Server Hardware Strategy

Servers tend to last longer than laptops and desktop computers. Server hardware is built to take a lot of punishment. Servers come preloaded with redundant devices so they don't need to go offline as often as workstations would. Servers are generally noisy and consume a lot of power. Servers require additional air conditioning and cost more because they do more. Most servers share basic configuration characteristics:

- Redundant power supplies

- Dual Ethernet ports

- Multiple 64-bit high performance central processing units

- Front and back end KVM ports

- Extensive cooling fan placement

- Ultra SCSI or SATA RAID disk controllers

- Hot swappable hard drives

- CD/DVD drives for installation

- Setup disk

- Rack mountable

- Nine-pin serial or USB ports

- Multiple PCI-E /16 full length/full height expansion slots

Depending on the environment in which your servers are deployed, there are many variants on the culmination of configurations characteristics to be applied. The decision over having a physical or virtual server infrastructure will play an important role in formulating the server configuration and storage design.

Servers come in many sizes depending on what the server will do and if it will be connected to remote storage (such as a SAN). Whatever configuration decisions are made, they should be made based on the value added to the organization and its goals.

Servers come in the following types:

- Tower systems

- Rack-mounted systems

- Frame-mounted systems

Figure 7-1. *Dell tower server*

Tower servers can be a variant of low-end servers found under desks or in other places where desktop workstations would be deployed. They are usually referred to as workgroup servers and provide a local service to a workgroup or small business. Tower servers can come with the same operating system as rack-mounted servers or (in the case of Microsoft) a small business server OS.

Figure 7-2. *HP rack-mounted server*

Rack-mounted servers are used in some small businesses but usually are designed for medium to large organizations. They require expensive racks to mount them, proper environmental conditioning (air conditioning, air filtering, etc.), and rack-mounted UPS/PDU and KVM equipment.

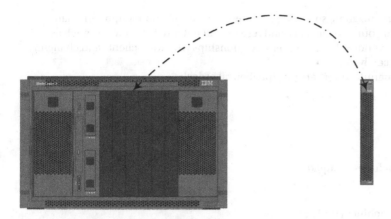

Figure 7-3. *IBM frame-mounted servers*

A frame-mounted server (more commonly known as a *blade server*) requires everything the rack-mounted servers do and some sort of remote storage as well. The rack-mounted frame provides a backbone for blade servers. The blade servers are inserted into the frame (much like an expansion card is inserted), allowing for many servers to share a single backbone. This reduces space and simplifies the network cabling scheme.

Choosing the right platform for your organization is important. Cost of ownership, vendor support, subsystem support, and supported services are just some of the variables that make the server hardware equation. The most obvious variable is workload. Gauge the server's size and performance on the workload, the type of server (tower, rack, or frame) on the vendor, the expected server lifecycle, and the internal components in support of the services and subsystems that the server will support. Microsoft and other manufacturers have downloadable tools you can use to help estimate the size and performance of the systems you will need for specific applications and services given a predetermined number of clients and workload. It is always a good idea to use these tools prior to talking to hardware vendors.

Vendors

There are a variety of manufacturers out there that make exceptional servers. The market has stabilized over the years and most offer similar products at fairly equivalent prices. The difference in most cases is the support level offered by the vendor. Some of the most important questions to consider when selecting a vendor are:

- How dependable is this vendor?

- How long have they been providing server products to the market?

- What type of clients do they support?

- Are the reviews about either the products they sell or their support positive?

- How has their stock faired in relationship to other potential vendors selling similar products?

- Do you like how the vendor treats you?

Depending on the size of your organization, some of these questions may be more important than others. Needless to say, you should do your due diligence and research all potential vendors as much as possible prior to selecting one. Server vendors have long-term relationships with their clients and changing from one vendor to another can be a costly decision.

Some of the best known server manufacturers are (in alphabetical order):

- Apple Computers

- Asus International

- Dell Computers

- Hewlett Packard (HP); includes Compaq

- Intel Corporation

- International Business Machines (IBM)

- Oracle (formerly Sun Microsystems—SUN)

Buying directly from the manufacturer is not always possible, nor is it always the best solution. Vendors often add value to the product in terms of contracted support and in-house inventory. Vendors are usually tied to one or more manufacturers' products. Usually they avoid conflicts in product market share and focus their inventory on products that complement one another. Dell, HP, Apple, and IBM provide direct sales and support but also work through local vendors to sell and support their products. It is wise to understand the relationship of your vendor with the manufacturer so that you are not caught off guard by any conflicts of interest down the road.

Remember, buying a server is not the same as buying workstations or laptops. Workstation and laptops can have mixed manufacturers when it comes to support and replacement. Servers should come from a single source and you should have a solid relationship with your vendor and therefore can rely on a quick response when hardware fails. While it is always better to use as few vendors as possible (for servers, laptops, and workstations), it is by far more critical to keep your server base the same.

When buying servers, you should try to buy in bulk. This gives you more leverage on the price and contractual benefits. The more servers you purchase at once, the better the contractual agreement and price. Having competing bids will help improve your odds at getting the best bang for the buck.

Extended Warrantees

Paying more for extended warrantees where server hardware is concerned is a no-brainer. You should determine how important a server is to your organization, determine how long your organization can function without it, and base your warrantee requirements on that information. If the server is redundant, the replacement time can be estimated in days or weeks. If the server is unique and your organization depends on it to make a profit or perform essential services to your customers or clients, then you most likely will want a quick turnaround with an on-site support contract.

Balancing the cost of downtime with the overall cost of purchasing an extended warrantee is essential. Using warrantee technicians to perform emergency tasks reduces the immediate need to provide internal staff or support technicians. This in turn reduces the impact that job would have on the day-to-day operations your IT staff can perform. It is essential that any extended warrantee be well documented in a DRP (Disaster Recovery Plan) that is both easy to read and well organized. All documentation should be easily available, in both hard and soft copies, so that IT professionals can quickly find the documentation and the specific content they need to best evaluate their next steps in resolving issues.

All warrantee information should be reviewed annually to determine if there is a need to extend current warrantees or schedule replacement equipment. Warrantee information should be part of the service desk support software and inventory data found in the CMDB.

Server Hardware Support Library

Each server manufacturer provides support software to help you install operating systems and drivers so that your server will run at maximum potential. All too often, these CDs (or DVDs) are discarded or lost after the installation is completed. It is important to save these disks in an easy-to-retrieve library. Servers often go through reincarnations during their usefulness. They may start out as a mail exchange server, get replaced as organizational needs require, and be repurposed for another use. Having the support disks available when old servers are repurposed makes life much easier.

A lot of time is lost trying to recreate the original disk set to repurpose servers. This can lead to hours of research (trial and error), until the server finally gets provisioned correctly. Sometimes servers end up configured in less than optimal shape due to the inability to find all of the correct support disks. One of the marks of an efficient IT group is their organization of support software and checklists regarding its use.

Online Vendor Inventory Support

Some manufacturers provide an online inventory support web site (like Dell) where the systems you maintain are documented with hardware information, firmware update information, and downloadable media. They even offer automated notifications as well as automated updates to keep your systems current. This type of support benefits the customer and the manufacturer by ensuring that equipment is maintained at its peak. It also allows the manufacturer to keep data on how well the systems their customers own are performing.

As stated previously in this book, automated server updates are not the best thing to ensure uptime, but having updated notification is. Keeping track of firmware and BIOS updates gets harder as time goes on and having an automated reminder can prevent that.

Redundancy Outside the Box

As presented in this chapter's introduction, redundancy inside each server is an engineered default. But redundancy of services is just as crucial. Prioritize your organization's services in terms of ensuring uptime for both productivity and client-side support. Using clustered servers for critical servers will help ensure uptime and provide a methodology for leap-frogging system upgrades.

Here is a list of common critical services:

1. Domain services

2. DNS/DHCP

3. E-mail services

4. Database services

5. Web services (internal and external)

6. Print services

7. Firewall and boundary protection devices

Having more than one domain server is essential. This helps both balance out the load and provides failover in case a domain controller fails. In the case of Microsoft Active Directory (which uses FSMO[1] roles to distribute domain server functions), reliability is shared between two or more systems that distribute

---

[1]http://support.microsoft.com/kb/324801

services when all servers are functioning correctly and allows for one or more servers to seize the roles of incapacitated servers when necessary. This keeps everything going even when a critical server fails. Of course, DNS is an important function embedded into most Microsoft Active Directory domain controllers and each domain controller should have DNS installed.

Having redundant DHCP servers is essential to any DRP. While you cannot cluster DHCP services, you can distribute them. Backing up DHCP scopes to a third server so that those scopes can be migrated to one or another DHCP server when a system fails will help get things back up more quickly. These backups should be automated and tested on a regular basis to ensure that the methodology works and that IT personnel can react quickly and effectively.

Clustering

Both e-mail and SQL (database) servers can be clustered. Figure 7-4 represents a simple two-node logical diagram of a two-node e-mail cluster. There must be at least two physical servers and a shared storage with two or more specific volumes (quorum and data). You must have a heartbeat Ethernet connection between both physical servers and a second Ethernet connection to the LAN. The physical servers use the heartbeat network to notify each other when one of the servers is incapacitated. The cluster creates a virtual server to act as the public IP address and cluster hostnames for users to access services.

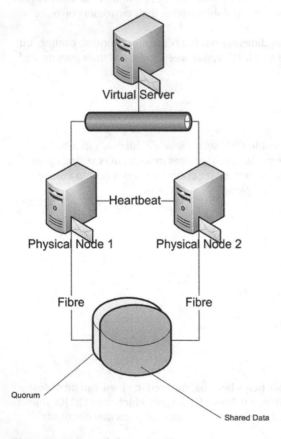

Figure 7-4. *E-mail cluster logical diagram*

The users on the LAN see a single server (the virtual server) and communicate with that. On the cluster side there are two physical servers configured as an "active/passive" or "active/active" cluster. In an active/passive cluster, one server is working while the other server is waiting. When the active server becomes incapacitated (either the system crashes or goes through an update process where it is required to reboot), the passive server becomes active and takes over the responsibilities of the active node. This ensures that services continue even when nodes are being patched or repaired.

Clustering can be expensive and requires more technical ability by the IT staff to maintain. It also requires greater planning, testing, and documentation to ensure everything works according to plan. The benefits are obvious. There can be more than two nodes in a cluster. The more nodes the higher the cost. In Microsoft Clusters, you must use special server versions to build clusters, which further adds to the cost. It is also essential that all physical nodes in a cluster be as identical as possible to ensure seamless failover of cluster resources.

Web Farms

Web servers become redundant when they are placed in web farms. Web farms are groups of physical web servers with shared storage and a single point of access, as shown in Figure 7-5.

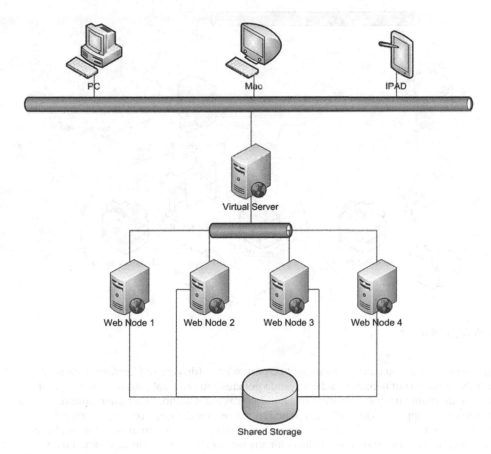

Figure 7-5. *Simple web farm*

Figure 7-5 displays a four-node web farm where connections are made through the virtual server entry point and then maintained by one of the physical web nodes (most often done through a round-robin process). This balances the load and allows for one or more servers to fail while maintaining overall service access. If a connection is broke due to a malfunctioning physical node, then the connection must be re-established by the user.

While there can be a loss of service to some, there is no loss of service overall. This approach can also act as a front end to SQL clusters offering an additional layer of redundancy.

Standby Servers

Print servers can be duplicated and distributed, thereby providing a primary print server and backup print server for each printer on the LAN, as shown in Figure 7-6.

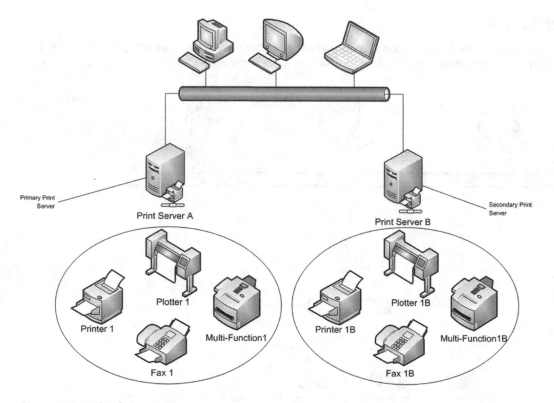

Figure 7-6. *Redundant print servers*

By duplicating the print pool, you can update individual print servers (drivers, hot fixes, etc.) without downtime. This is fairly simple to put together, and with group policies you can pool your resources so that the process of selecting alternative print spoolers in done automatically and without user intervention.

The same concept can be applied to firewalls and boundary protection devices, creating an active/ passive relationship between two or more physical servers providing those services. In most cases you have the technical capacity to provide redundancy and failover for any service. It is the cost analysis and business criteria that enables IT departments to ensure uptime. Having the facts at hand when presenting fault-tolerant technology will increase the willingness of organizational leaders to accept the expense.

If you are successful in gaining funds to build a fault-tolerant solution and you are successful in implementing a sound strategy, very few people will notice. This is the good and bad side of DRP solutions. People only notice when things break, not when they work as they should.

Footprint Strategy

Choosing the type of servers you will place in the server room is critical to how you view your server hardware's lifecycle. Your server's footprint (tower, rack, or frame) will be chosen based on the size of your business, the environment the hardware will live in, and the skillset of your IT staff. It will also be based on how much money you're allotted to purchase the physical equipment. This is not something you can cut corners on, but you do have many alternatives available to reduce costs and fine-tune your IT assets.

Blade Servers

Blade servers have the benefit of reducing space and cables that connect servers. They also allow you to start relatively inexpensively by purchasing the frame and one or more servers and build from there. Almost all major server manufacturers offer blade servers.

The major upsides to blade servers are a reduction in power consumption, standardization of system components, and less rack space. Server blades can be replaced fairly quickly when problems occur and new systems can be added quickly as long as open ports remain in the frame.

The major downsides to blade servers are the limitation placed on what type of servers can be added to the frame, the need to buy more frames if you expand your server set beyond the initial frame, the projected lifecycle of a frame, and the manufacturer's support for all components supporting frame expansion.

Traditional Servers

Traditional servers (physical servers either tower or rack) provide redundancy, defined power, and versatility that go beyond a single blade server. Tower and rack servers are designed to last. They provide all of the basic requirements to house most services internally and can be repurposed quickly. As described in this chapter's introduction, rack-mounted servers have redundant power supplies, as well as many other internal components. They come in all sizes (1U,[2] 2U, 4U, 6U, and 8U) and fit in any 19-inch rack frame. They can have terabytes of internal hard disk space, multiple quad core processors, and plenty of RAM.

The major upside to traditional servers is that you generally know how far you can push the hardware and evaluating software specifications is a snap. Traditional servers often come with predefined installation applications that support most of the popular operating systems and can be made to automate further installations through system preparation scripts. Rack-mounted servers can easily outlast their original intent and serve individual and clustered services.

The downside to traditional servers is that they usually end up over-purposed (meaning that they may have started out as a single service server but ended up supporting other services through time). It is difficult to say how traditional servers should be purchased (minimum specs or maximum). If you purchase a server with minimum specs and repurpose it later, you may need to purchase additional hardware (ending up disposing of older bits of RAM, hard drives, etc.). If you purchase a server with maximum specifications, you will most likely end up expanding its role in IT, causing more and more services to be supported on a single server. This could result in unbalancing the distribution of services across the server base.

---

[2]http://www.sizes.com/units/rack_unit.htm

Virtual Servers[3]

Virtual servers have come a long way from their infancy. Up until recently, virtual servers were seen as something less than physical servers. They ran slowly and were something difficult to provision properly (technicians following the default installation usually under-provisioned virtual servers). It was also hard to explain to upper management the cost associated with each virtual server. Host servers (those physical servers hosting virtual server instances) needed to be big and extra powerful. Until recently they needed to be provisioned by the manufacturer.

Today, virtual servers have become a workhorse for the IT industry, supporting almost every service available. They work in production networks and lab networks, on laptops (as marketing environments), basically everywhere you find physical servers and more.

The major benefits are reduced server footprint, less power consumption, less space, fewer HVAC requirements, reduced hardware costs, etc. Three well defined virtual server hosts could easily support a small organization with extensive services available. Those three hosts could also provide redundancy, failover services, clustering services, rapid deployment services, etc.

The major downside to virtualization is technology obscurity. People are used to seeing a physical device providing services. Virtual infrastructures require virtual networks, servers, and services to perform functions normally done by physical devices. This can complicate the overall network strategy and require advanced thinking in order to enact a virtual solution and maintain its operability.

Operating Systems

Choosing the right operating system for server platforms in order to support essential services can be complicated. Usually an organization focuses on one primary server operating system and enhances its capabilities with specialized operating systems. For instance, in office environments Microsoft Windows server operating systems are most common. Alternatives may include Apple OSX, Linux, and Solaris for specialized purposes. In scientific environments, Solaris is often the production operating system of choice. An ever-growing interest in Linux operating systems has made a dent in office environments, but can be most often seen as the base operating system of network appliances (such as firewalls, boundary protection devices, etc.).

Cost is often the major factor in choosing the right operating system for your organization. Not just the cost of acquiring the operating system, but the cost of maintaining, updating, and training personnel. These are all key issues. Often though, you find that the product drives the solution, even though it is a given that the solution should drive the product selection. If the business is new (like the example LAN in this book), there needs to be a thorough evaluation of what services are essential to the operation of the organization and what is most often the best solution providing optimal value added at the lowest possible cost (or return on investment).

It is important to note that when you choose the base solution, most operating systems work best with applications made by the same vendor. The Microsoft Windows environment works best with Microsoft products and cost can be reduced when buying packaged solutions (i.e., Microsoft Exchange, SQL server, System Center solutions, etc.). While almost every vendor will insist that their solution works seamlessly with Microsoft Windows Server, they cannot always ensure that their product is more seamless than Microsoft's when implemented. Sun Solaris operating system will work best with other Sun products; Apple OSX will work best with other Apple products. Quite often, the operating system choice is dependent on the service vendor's choice. When evaluating the best choice, take a holistic approach and evaluate all of the possible solutions prior to selecting a vendor.

---

[3]See Chapter 8 for more detailed information on virtualization.

Hosting Applications

Hosting applications (databases, e-mail servers, web servers, etc.) involves a layered separation of operating system and application in terms of administration. While system administrators usually are responsible for the operating system of a given server (and may also be responsible for the networking and hardware side), application managers are often responsible for the hosted applications administration. This requires a sound separation of responsibilities and administrative accounts, along with access permissions and maintenance cycles.

A database server is an excellent example of layered administration. The system administrator is responsible for the server's operating system while the DBA (database administrator) is responsible for the database operations and maintenance. Operating system patches, updates, and hot fixes would be done by the system administrator while the database patches, updates, and hot fixes would be done by the DBA. Both would have access to the server but on different levels. The system administrator would be able to schedule server reboots while the DBA would be responsible for stopping and restarting database services. There needs to be coordination between the two administrative layers when any service is performed in order to not cause unforeseen outages.

Designing a symbiosis between each administrative layer that reflects both the responsibilities and administration and hardware maintenance lifecycle is a must to prevent miscommunication and unplanned outages. Taking the time to diagram this relationship in an easy-to-understand flowchart will save valuable hours later on. These are often referred to as *dependencies*.

Summary

The server hardware strategy of any organization will have a profound impact on the IT environment, training strategy, and interdepartmental distribution of IT responsibilities. Mapping out what is essential for the organization, designing your strategy based primarily on requirements, and deciding on a specific solution only after all of the organizations requirements are well understood will save time and money in the long run. It will help develop training scenarios, functional awareness, and service support plans. The more detailed the plan, the greater the odds of having a sound solution in place. Even the best plans will need to be adjusted as the organization puts its IT in place. The goal is to minimize those changes and be aware of the potential options available when those changes are needed. You do your planning not simply to provide a solution, but also to understand the options that are available when the plan needs modifying.

CHAPTER 8

■ ■ ■

Physical vs. Virtual Server Environments

Chapter 7 touched on physical and virtual server solutions and hinted at the varied benefits of both technologies for IT organizations. One of the best ways to start evaluating which solution fits best with any particular organization is to plan both solutions on paper and analyze which is more cost effective. Key points in making the decision rest on what type of funding your organization has, how flexible your organization wants to make their IT infrastructure, and what will be the expected growth rate for your proposed server farm. Other considerations include the type of operating systems at hand, the physical building limitations, and the communications infrastructure outside your organization's IT operations.

This chapter will build two models:

- One based on the physical server technology with traditional server roles and hardware

- The second based on virtual server hosts using a shared storage solution

Figure 8-1 is the baseline (rack diagram prior to adding servers) of rack content prior to implementing each solution.

Both models will take the liberty of providing redundancy, failover, and DRP solutions while trying to minimize hardware costs. Using the example server rack diagrams presented earlier (represented in Figure 8-1), each solution will be detailed with sample hardware to help display its physical elements. The following services will be provided in each solution:

- Directory services/DNS/DHCP

- E-mail/electronic collaboration

- VoIP/teleconferencing

- Intranet services

- Internet services

- Print services

- File storage/shared storage

- Database services

- Antivirus/antispyware/junk mail filtering

- System management services/application and image deployment

- System update solutions (WSUS)

- Inventory/CMDB/Service Desk applications

- Backup services/DRP

- Engineering environment/test LAN

- Financial services applications (payroll, accounting)

- Sales applications

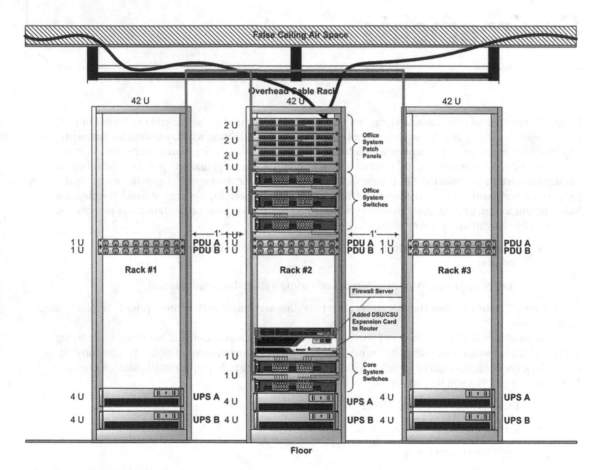

Figure 8-1. *Server rack without server options*

Physical

The basic rule of thumb when estimating the number of physical servers an organization needs is to minimize the number of services per server (grouping like or interdependent services) and provide redundancy where possible. Smaller organizations find themselves in the precarious position of stacking many of their most important services on one or two servers. There is actually a market for this. Microsoft provides a line of servers called "Small Business Server" packages that cram all the most essential services a small business may need on to one server. In an effort to minimize expansion, Microsoft limits their Small Business Server packages so that it becomes almost impossible for those services to merge with a larger domain or group of servers providing enterprise solutions.

It isn't just the cost of hardware, it's the cost of software, user licenses, and installation that forces small businesses to put all of their eggs into one basket. If the organization is not going to grow to more than five or eight personnel at most, this may be the best solution for the company. But if that organization plans further expansion down the road they must take into consideration that any investment in the Small Business Package will ultimately be thrown out the window and the data has to be migrated to enterprise solutions.

The example organization in this book reflects growth and the options defined in this chapter are based on flexibility. Each solution presented in this chapter is costly and time consuming to put in place. But the end result is that the solutions presented will provide a high level of performance and disaster preparedness.

There are two physical server solutions presented in this chapter:

1. Blade servers

2. Traditional rack servers

Blade Server Solution

The blade servers chosen[1] for this solution provide up to 16 individual blades per frame. Each frame has been fitted with 15 G6 blade servers[2] and a SAN gateway. A tape backup library has been added to rack number 2 to support disaster recovery and provide data archival processes.

---

[1]HP c7000 blade enclosure: http://h18000.www1.hp.com/products/quickspecs/12810_div/12810_div.pdf.
[2]HP BL280c G6: http://h10010.www1.hp.com/wwpc/us/en/sm/WF02a/3709945-3709945-3328410.html.

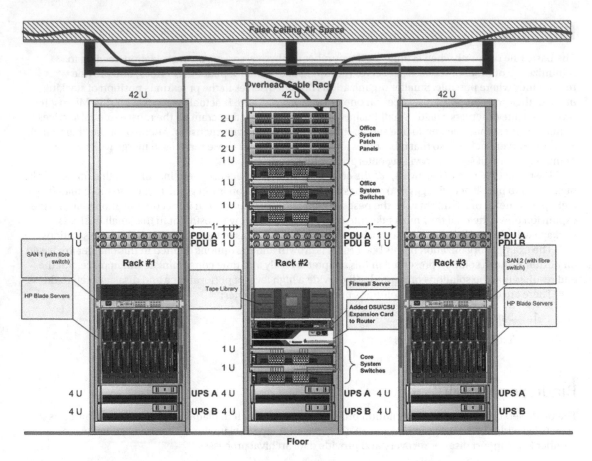

Figure 8-2. *Blade server solution*

Two SAN storage units (MSA2000fcs) have been added to provide 24TB of shared disk storage that can be used for clustering, data, system drives, etc. SAN storage will also be used for server boot drives so as to make each blade server independent from its boot source and provide quick replacement when blades fail. All system and data files will be stored on the SAN.

Traditional Server Solution

Traditional rack servers take up space, consume power, and generate heat. Each server requires at least IU (or more) of rack space and can weigh up to 60 pounds.

Figure 8-3 represents the same server base that Figure 8-2 provided using traditional rack mounted servers. There are 12 HP DL360 G5s[3] in each rack along with three DL380 G5s.[4] The benefit of having traditional servers lies in the flexibility to replace individual servers without having to replace expensive server frames.

---

[3]http://h18000.www1.hp.com/products/servers/proliantdl360/
[4]http://h10010.www1.hp.com/wwpc/ca/en/sm/WF05a/15351-15351-3328412-241475-241475-1121516.html.

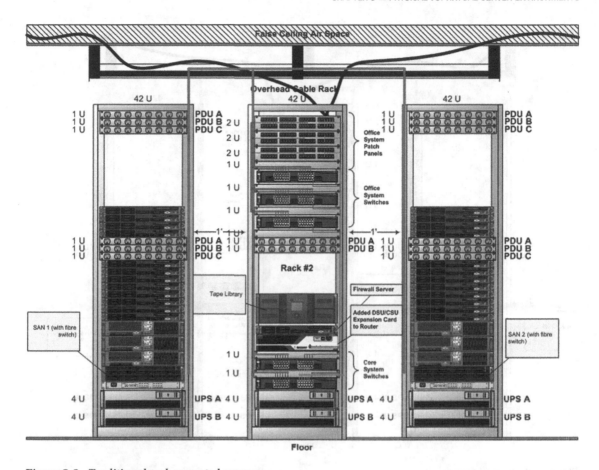

Figure 8-3. *Traditional rack-mounted servers*

Virtual Solution

Virtual server hosts allow a minimal number of powerful physical servers to present virtual servers capable of doing what many servers would normally be required to do. In fact, the six servers presented in Figure 8-4 could provide as many as 80 or more virtual servers when configured correctly (which would more than fill available rack space in the example server room if they were all physical hardware).

The choice of four virtual server hosts and four physical servers may be more psychologically driven than technically required. Technically, three of the four virtual server hosts would provide ample virtual servers for this organization along with adding redundancy for disaster recovery and a playground for technicians to test potential changes to the network. The fourth server is insurance against one or more virtual hosts failing. The four physical servers provide a graceful recovery in case the virtual servers behave badly after an outage (power or otherwise).

Given cost reductions, Figure 8-4 could easily be downsized to two or three servers without affecting the operational performance of the LAN. It would, however, increase the likelihood that the LAN may not recover easily from an outage and that recovery time may be an outage that could substantially affect revenue. It is wise to balance cost with the potential downside to not having a robust disaster recovery option at hand.

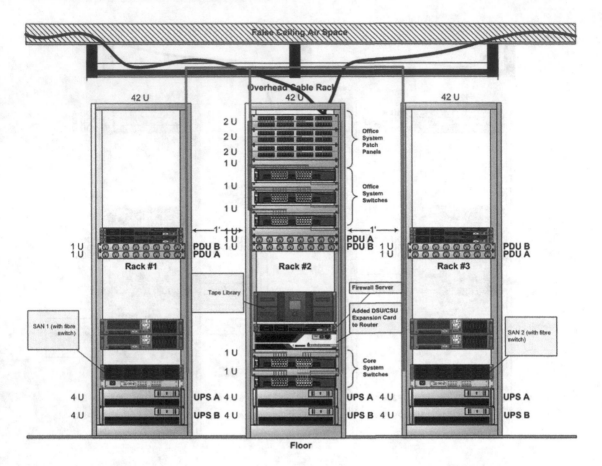

Figure 8-4. *Virtual servers*

The Unseen Network

But virtual servers require a virtual network. The unseen network inside each virtual server host can be simple or complex. With newer versions of virtual server systems (such as VMware Vsphere and Microsoft's Hyper-V), many options can be designed into the virtual networks that emulate high-end network devices.

The best solutions are the simplest when dealing with intangible network devices. The most basic configuration is one where there are two separate networks (public and management). Where one network supports all of the virtual management network traffic and a separate "public" network supports office network traffic. Additional networks can be added later on to support a test LAN, an engineering LAN, etc. You should have at least one physical network interface card per virtual network in order to isolate and optimize bandwidth and network performance. The more physical network interfaces per virtual LAN, the better the performance and failover capability.

Figure 8-5 represents the most basic virtual network design. It is wise to draw out what you intend to build prior to building it. Always separate the virtual network management functions from the public network; it not only improves performance but also increases security.

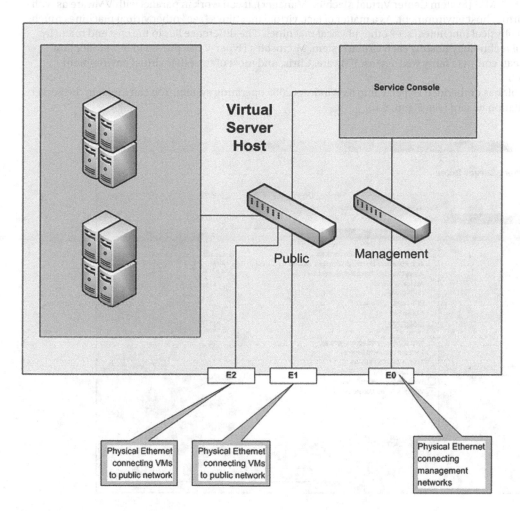

Figure 8-5. *VMware ESX host server*

It is also important to create VLANs on the physical network switches and mark the network ports (management, public, test and engineering, etc.) to make troubleshooting simpler. You might also choose to color-code the cabling scheme so that you can easily see the separation of networks without dragging out a network diagram.

It is also a good idea to have a folder attached to each virtual server host that has a basic diagram of the virtual environment (along with virtual hostnames, virtual IP addresses, and virtual switch design). If your system loses power completely you may have to refer to hard copy configuration data to get things back up quickly. This is referred to as a "continuity guide". You must make changes to this guide as you make changes to each virtual host (better yet, use your planning data to update the continuity guide before you make changes).

Hyper-V

Microsoft's Hyper-V comes with Windows 2008 and can be clustered, combined, and managed using Microsoft's SCVMM (System Center Virtual Machine Manager). It can work in parallel with VMware as with any other virtual host environment. As a matter of fact, virtual machines "see" other virtual machines much the same as physical machines "see" other physical machines. The difference lies in the cost and maturity of the virtual technology hosting each virtual system. Microsoft's Hyper-V has proven to be "production ready" and can compete fairly well against VMware, Citrix, and most of the other virtual environment manufacturers.

Microsoft has embedded Hyper-V into its Windows 2008 operating system. You can find it in the Server Roles Installation wizard (see Figure 8-6).

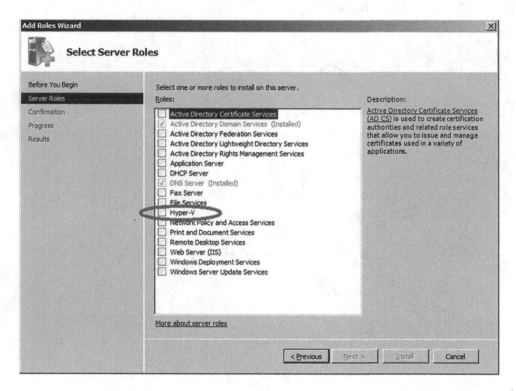

Figure 8-6. *Windows 2008 roles*

Since Microsoft's Hyper-V is a server role in Windows 2008, its hypervisor consumes a larger footprint. In other words, Windows 2008 consumes a larger portion of hardware resources that could be part of the virtual environment, leaving fewer resources to build virtual servers from. Of course, you can help minimize this footprint by installing Windows 2008 with a minimum of installed services, but the bottom line will always be a significant chunk of what could have been used to build virtual systems.

VMware

Unlike Microsoft's Hyper-V, VMware's Vsphere (aka ESX server 4 and 4i) requires dedicated virtual hosts. The virtual environment is accessed either through a RDP client (Microsoft uses the *mstsc*— Microsoft Terminal Services Client) that's part of the Windows operating system components, or through a special graphic interface that can be downloaded from the virtual host. You download the Virtual Infrastructure Client (VIC) from the VMware host using an Internet browser (entering in the host IP address). The VIC presents basic administrative tools to build virtual machines, manage storage, configure security, and design the virtual network environment. Once the VIC is downloaded, it is used mainly for virtual environment administration, virtual machine creation/maintenance, and capturing images. You should not use the VIC to access virtual machines for normal virtual machine operating system administrative activities.

The hypervisor in VMware has a small footprint and allows for a more flexible use of host resources. It provides a more secure platform for virtual systems. Based on a hardened version of Linux, the VMware hypervisor does not require an antivirus solution nor most of the basic security applications, as would Windows 2008 and Hyper-V. You do have to update patches from time to time, but not quite as often.

Figure 8-7 represents the management network for this book's office system. There are many ways that this network can be designed, but this is the simplest way in which four virtual hosts could be connected. It allows for all virtual administration to be conducted on a separate network that interlinks all service consoles together. It supports the heartbeat between servers, internal protocols, and failover services.

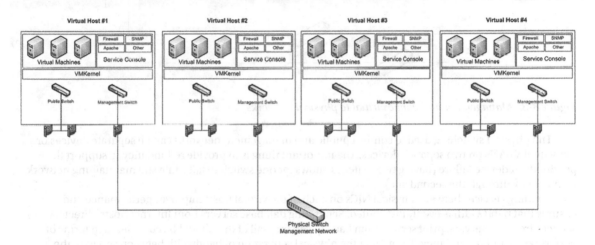

Figure 8-7. *Virtual environment management network*

Figure 8-8 presents the management and public network interface. More often than not, you will find more than two NICs per virtual host for the public network for two main reasons (redundancy and performance).

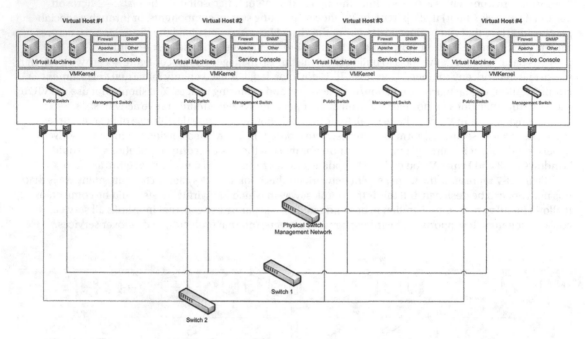

Figure 8-8. *Management and public virtual to physical networks*

The physical switching used to connect public and management networks can be separate devices or individual VLANs on two separate devices. The important thing is to provide redundancy to support the possibility of device failure (having two switches allows for one switch to fail while still maintaining network connectivity through the second one).

Dividing services between physical NICs on each of the virtual hosts improves performance and ensures that bandwidth is evenly distributed. Separating database servers from Internet hosts, directory services from file servers, print servers from backup servers—all of this should be considered in terms of performance and redundancy. The greater the physical separation of bandwidth between services, the better the performance and reliability.

Additionally, there needs to be physical and logical separation between the types of networks you have in place. The production network should use separate NICs from the engineering and test networks to ensure isolation. All of this should be well documented and explicitly labeled (both in naming conventions and port allocation). When possible, for all physical devices, color-code port assignments so that their importance to operations can clearly be seen when troubleshooting conflicts or upgrading services.

Balance the load. Make sure that the number of virtual machines per virtual host can be failed over to other virtual hosts without over-taxing the capacity of those other hosts. A rule of thumb is to not exceed 50 percent of a given virtual host's capacity so that it can perform efficiently and failover without overtaxing its target virtual host.

Shared Storage

Shared storage in a virtual environment is essential. While any virtual host can use internal storage (the virtual servers local hard drives), it cannot failover virtual machines when configured that way. There must be a shared storage that all virtual hosts can access to allow virtual machines to failover and share a common disk space. Shared storage can be in the form of iSCSI[5] or SAN[6] storage depending on the available finances. Whatever shared storage solution your organization chooses, it must be easily expandable, provide dynamic partitioning, and fall in line with potential business impact caused by foreseeable growth. Overcoming a maxed out SAN solution can prove almost impossible.

In a NAS shared storage environment, all the data goes over the same network as public data (as seen in Figure 8-8). This minimizes cabling and reduces cost. NAS technology can share the same switching technology used to connect servers and does not require expensive connectors (such as GBics and fiber optic cabling found in the more expensive SAN solution). As with the storage solution chosen for this book's SAN solution example, the storage can support either NAS or SAN technology so upgrading from one storage solution to another can be done after the fact if you plan your solution accordingly. The downside to NAS storage is performance. Since all data goes across the same network bandwidth, the performance of both data access and network communications is reduced and the overall result is less than what you would expect from a SAN solution.

Figure 8-9 represents the same storage solution but in a SAN solution. It requires special fiber switching technology that includes GBics[7] and special fiber optic cabling. The performance increases dramatically (from 1GB shared bandwidth in a NAS solution to a 8GB dedicated bandwidth in a SAN solution). The cost of fiber, GBics, HBAs,[8] and redundant fiber switches is a large investment but it can greatly expand both the performance and extensibility of the storage solution. Storage becomes operating system independent and can be expanded over time without affecting the operational integrity of the virtual host environment. It can support the virtual environment and physical servers independently without degradation of performance.

---

[5]http://searchstorage.techtarget.com/sDefinition/0,,sid5_gci750136,00.html.
[6]http://compnetworking.about.com/od/networkstorage/g/storage_san.htm.
[7]Gigabit interface converter: http://www.webopedia.com/TERM/G/GBIC.html.
[8]Host bus adapter: http://searchstorage.techtarget.com/sDefinition/0,,sid5_gci1083748,00.html.

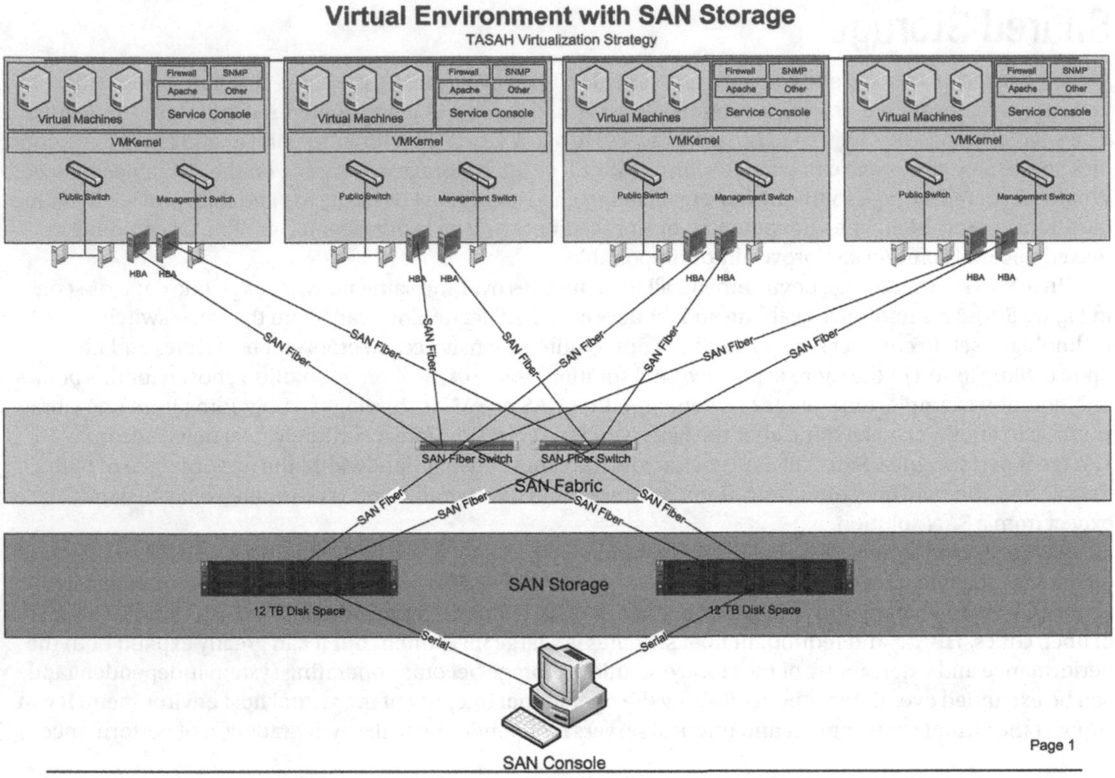

Figure 8-9. *Virtual environment with SAN storage*

SAN and NAS storage can be carved up so that specific servers have dedicated storage solutions in various RAID configurations (including virtual RAID arrays) so that data stored on disks are less susceptible to physical hardware failure and improved security. Generally speaking, SAN technology can offer better performance for hosting virtual operating systems than local hard drives (the bandwidth available on a SAN can exceed that of local SCSI storage adapters).

Carving up disk space is an important decision that requires a detailed understanding of both the current needs of the systems connected as well as future requirements that may have an impact on storage. You should always allow for more storage per virtual solution than you may think you need. You should separate streaming data from random IO. This will allow you to fine-tune data flow so that faster RAID sets are geared to streaming data, and more reliable but slower RAID sets are dedicated to data stored on databases, or randomly accessed data sources.

In Figure 8-10, both storage arrays are carved into six separate drive sets (none exceeding the 2TB in size). The first drive set is made available for virtual machines (mirrored system drives with one drive per storage array). The second drive set uses RAID 0 to provide high performance. The RAID 0 drive set is mirrored with the second SAN storage array to allow for redundancy. The next three drive sets are designed as RAID 5 drive sets and act as independent drive sets with built-in redundancy. The last drive is unused. It is automatically assigned to any given drive set that has a physical drive failure. Once a failure occurs, the SAN administrator is alerted via e-mail to replace the failing drive.

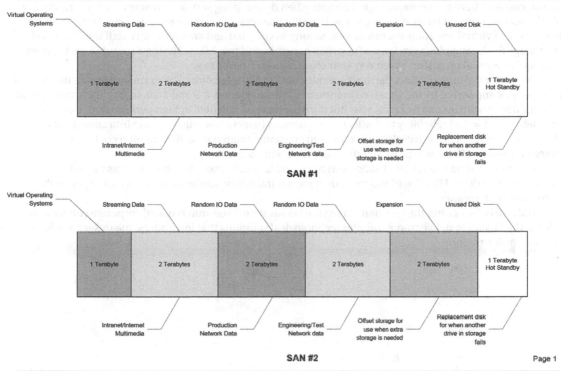

Figure 8-10. *SAN disk partitioning*

Given this scenario, each virtual server (30 virtual servers per virtual host) could have a 30GB system drive mirrored for redundancy and failover. The production storage would total 4TB (as would the engineering and test environment). And there would be an additional 4TB of disk space allocated for expansion for both production and engineering/test. The expansion disk set can be automatically set to upgrade other disk sets if a threshold is met, adding to the stability and adaptability of the storage solution. Additional SAN storage arrays can be added as needs require without having to add more fiber switches.

It should be noted that RAID and redundant storage solutions are not a practical replacement for backup solutions. It is essential for data to be backed up and stored offsite in order to protect your organization's intellectual property. Redundant SAN solutions (and/or NAS solutions) protect against physical hardware failures only.

It is also essential to have a well-trained SAN manager to care for the organization's data. Both NAS and SAN solutions require maintenance and administration. Left to their own devices, storage arrays can get corrupted and become unmanageable. This leaves your data prone to self-inflicted disaster.

Summary

As you can see, there are many things to consider when determining server hardware and strategy. Buying all physical servers can be wise as long as you have the finances to cover the environmental overhead. Buying into a virtual environment can be wise as long as you plan and ensure your IT staff is well trained to manage the intangibles associated with virtual networks and machines. Having a sound shared storage strategy is essential no matter which way your organization chooses to go.

The larger the organization, the more complex both options become. The example network in this book can easily be supported by the virtual environment shown in Figures 8-9 and 8-10. In fact, this environment is overkill for organizations twice the size. But thinking this way will deliver high performance, extensive scalability, and sound reliability that will ensure customer (user) satisfaction. Taking into consideration the cost of downtime, a disgruntled user base, and constant maintenance, this solution could easily be described as cost effective. It provides due diligence in a proactive strategy.

There was a time when virtualization was not ready for production, but that time has passed. The savings on electricity, HVAC, etc., will more than pay for the robust hardware solution that supports the virtual host environment.

The real issue behind the question of physical versus virtual solution is one of corporate culture and faith in the IT staff to deliver more complex technological solutions that incorporate the unseen world of virtual administration.

CHAPTER 9

■■■

Data Storage Technologies and User Data Strategy

Data storage technologies have grown exponentially over the years. Average hard drives found in personal computers are now at the terabyte range and beyond. Portable USB hard drives are much the same. With so much disk space available on the average home computer, office systems are expected to share those characteristics. Everyone tends to be a bit lazy in housekeeping their disk space and this is natural. As space becomes cluttered and data becomes bloated, storage becomes unmanageable. In the end, it affects the overall performance of each system. However, the reality is that in the office data belongs on server-based drive sets and not on local workstation hard drives. Local disk storage on workstations becomes more of a liability in office settings—it's difficult to back up data, workstation drives are less reliable than server based storage disk sets, and larger local drives make it harder to control where data ends up.

At home the smart PC owners realize that everything is on their local hard drives and they back that data up to a USB disk regularly and store that portable drive in a fireproof safe. If they lose a hard drive, they can retrieve their data from the portable disk and only lose the *delta* data (information written between the time of the failure and the last time they backed up). They still have to reload the operating system and all of the applications they previously had, which takes a lot of time and effort.

Since workstation hard drives are generally a single point of failure they should be used to store things that are easily and quickly replaced without losing any intellectual property. Having the option to store information locally can jeopardize the security of intellectual property and lead to complications in managing data. Limiting the options presented to users in storing data will make their data more secure and controllable. Automatically redirecting the storage of information created on workstations in the office without requiring users to manually select storage locations is more natural for users. It eliminates the need to train users to store their data on special networked drives.

There are a host of options available for system administrators to automate and optimize their storage strategy. Each has its pros and cons. One important thing to keep in mind—it's best to select one file storage strategy and stick with it. The more options a user has, the greater the risk of losing control of data.

These options include the following:

- UNC drive mapping (also known as folder redirection)

- Roaming profiles

- Public folders

- Intranet portal

- Boot from SAN

In addition to these options, system administrators should have portable storage devices available to retrieve data from systems that no longer connect to the network and are difficult to move. This chapter looks at all of these options and provides the solution to be used in the example organization's storage strategy.

Local Workstation Hard Drives

The strategy for local hard drives is somewhat controversial. Talk to any hardware vendor and they will tell you to buy the largest drive you can for each workstation so that your system can grow with the business. But if you only place an operating system and applications on the local drive, how big does it really need to be? If, in fact most of your applications are provided by some sort of remote application strategy, the size requirements of the local drive decrease even more. If your local boot strategy includes booting from SAN, the local hard drive becomes irrelevant all together.

Having lots of local disk space leads users to fill that space. Most users have the belief that what's on the local drive is theirs. This is not the best perception for an employee to have. Locking down the local hard drive is difficult. Backing up the data on local hard drives is an expensive and error-prone process. The bigger the local drive, the greater the threat to data management.

One strategy suggests that you should have a hard drive large enough to hold the operating system and basic applications. It should also have enough room to download and incorporate any potential service packs, hot fixes, and log files and still have 10 percent free disk space to perform adequately. While no exact size can be given without evaluating your business needs and potential for growth, a ballpark figure of 60GB is a reasonable starting point.

This takes into account the following:

1. Windows Operating System at 20GB

2. Swap file space, which should be up to four times the physical RAM onboard (4GB physical ram x 4 = 16GB swap space)

3. Office Suite at 10GB

4. 10 percent disk space set aside for optimization

The total disk space would be 56GB of dedicated disk space with 4GB set aside for service packs, hotfixes, and partitioning allocation. With this scenario, there is little room left for users to store their data locally.

Best practices have each local drive mirrored in a RAID 1 set so that if one of the local drives fails, the users can continue working and the failed drive could be replaced after working hours to minimize downtime.

Best Practice

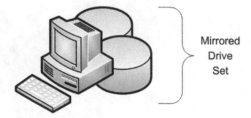
Mirrored
Drive
Set

Figure 9-1. Mirrored workstation SATA hard drives

Partitioning a single drive and mirroring is not a good option. If the drive fails, both partitions fail. Mirroring drives does not constitute a backup strategy, it only offers the ability to survive a physical drive failure. If data becomes corrupt on one of the drives in the mirrored set, both drives share that corrupted data. In any case, if you plan to mirror drives, use a hardware RAID solution and avoid software RAID solutions. This ensures the best performance and provides the easiest recovery method. Most modern workstations have SATA RAID controllers by default; it's worth exploiting their benefits.

Booting from SAN, while a great idea, is expensive and comes with added administrative overhead. Each workstation has an HBA installed with dedicated SAN fiber and a disk set configured to act as its boot drive. Since all storage exists on the SAN, none of the data created is saved to a local disk inside the workstation. To the employees using the workstation, they would see it much differently. They would see their SAN boot disk as local storage. This option can provide better performance, greater security, and improved backup capabilities. It ensures that when a workstation fails, you can replace that workstation with another one and be back up in the time it takes to configure BIOS to boot from SAN. But the cost can be three times the original cost of the workstation and is limited to the extent of the SAN fiber connectors. Most organizations don't boot workstations from SAN.

While the most common type of workstation hard drive is mechanical (SATA, Ultra-SCSI, etc.), alternatives such as SSD and USB thumb drives offer an alternative that can both outperform and outlast the conventional technology. SSD (or Solid State Drives) are expensive in comparison to mechanical drives, but they offer greater performance and use less power to operate.

The inexpensive alternative (USB thumb drives) is large enough (64GB) to act as the primary workstation hard drive and can outperform the conventional mechanical drives as well. The major benefit to using USB thumb drives is their portability and speed at which they can be replaced (you don't have to open the workstation case to change them when they go bad). Since they are solid state, there are no moving parts that can break over time. They also use less power to operate and produce less heat.

Roaming Profiles

Roaming profiles do exactly what they imply—every workstation a user logs on to downloads and updates a copy of the user's profile. This allows for every workstation to have the same look and feel. Users get the same desktop, access to their personal folders, the same menus, etc. Each desktop gets a copy of the user's profile the first time they log on. After that, users get synchronized updates of the delta data. The more desktops the user logs on to, the more copies of their profile are proliferated. The master copy remains on the server drive set and gets updated every time users change their personal settings.

Figure 9-2 represents the basic concept where a server-stored user profile is downloaded to three workstations. This process can consume a large amount of bandwidth every time the user logs on to a new workstation. Bandwidth utilization goes down dramatically after that (only delta data is replicated when the user logs on or off). The local user profiles remain stagnant until the user logs on again. Each workstation can end up with multiple copies of personal data and is only accessible when the user owning the profile logs on again. There are options to have the profile removed when the user logs off, but this adds time to the log on and off processes.

Roaming Profiles
TASAH

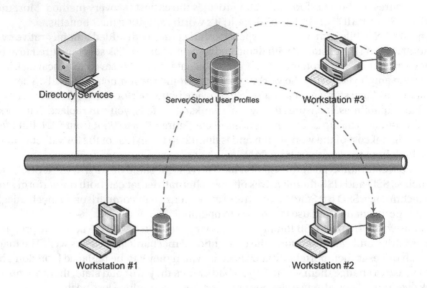

Directory Services

Server/Stored User Profiles

Workstation #3

Workstation #1

Workstation #2

Page 1

Figure 9-2. *Distributed profiles*

Roaming profiles are hardware dependent, in that the differences in hardware from one workstation to another is recorded in the master profile and can cause user profiles to act in unexpected ways. This can lead to corrupted profiles or lost data as well as application or operating systems malfunctions.

Before deploying roaming profiles, you should test the solution to ensure that any foreseen changes in hardware and software are taken into consideration to minimize the potential for problems down the road. Roaming profiles work very well for users who travel (having their laptop as their primary workstation in and out of the office). Roaming profiles allow users to continue working even when the network is down (the local profile copy will automatically re-synchronize when the network becomes available).

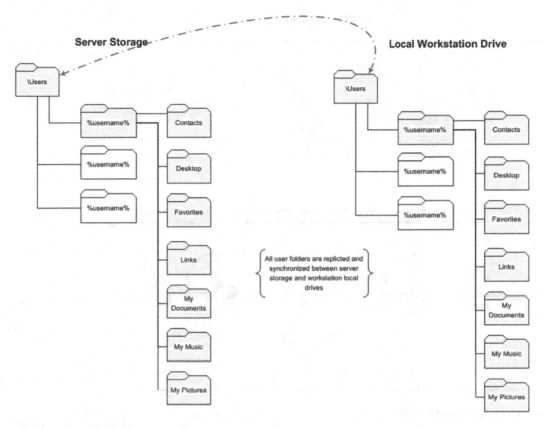

Figure 9-3. Roaming profile folder replication

Since the data is only visible to the user who owns the profile, if the hard drive is lost or stolen, it will be more difficult for anyone to stumble upon intellectual property stored on the local hard drive. Of course anyone who is deliberately absconding with a laptop or hard drive for the purpose of stealing intellectual property can find ways to access locally stored roaming profile data (even if its encrypted). This of course would require a certain level of technical skills not common in the public sector.

Folder Redirection

Folder redirection is the process of redirecting personal folders away from the local hard drive's default location.

Figure 9-4 displays three users' workstation data being relocated to a server-based storage drive set. The actual personal folders that can be redirected are fully configurable but the basic concept is shown in Figure 9-5.

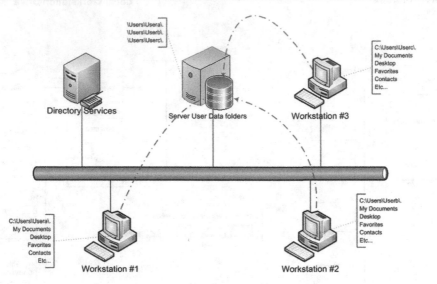

Figure 9-4. *Microsoft's folder redirection*

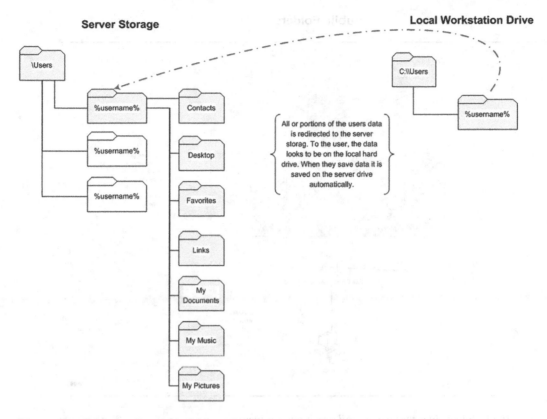

Figure 9-5. *Folders redirected in folder redirection*

Unlike with roaming profiles, the logon/logoff time for users is not affected. The whole process is transparent to the users. Users can access all of their redirected files from any workstation that has access to the server storage share and recognizes the users' logon credentials. Also unlike roaming profiles, folder redirection is hardware independent as long as you can access the folders with your user account.

The downside to folder redirection is that when the network is unavailable, so is the user's data. Having a sound network infrastructure with clustered data storage is a must if you plan to keep the users busy.

Public Folders

Public folders are generally available through Microsoft Exchange Server. Users access and save documents through Microsoft's Outlook e-mail thin client or through the OWA (Outlook Web Access). This has the advantage of providing a single point of collaboration (both e-mail and organization documentation (and business intelligence). You can build forms and model your business collaboration with less training while promoting a controlled file storage strategy.

But public folders are not as natural as folder redirection. It requires the users to know that files are to be stored through the e-mail service and it takes an extra step in saving files.

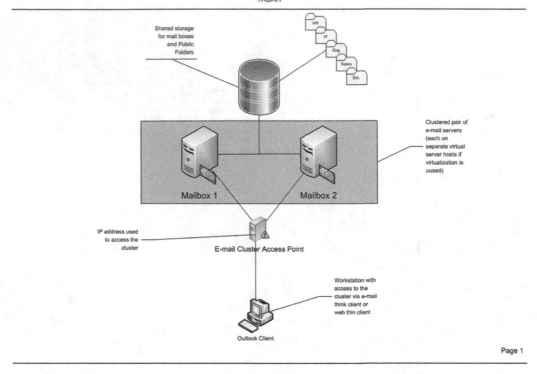

Figure 9-6. *Public folders in a clustered e-mail server environment*

Public folders add more functionality to the collaboration suite. It allows remote users to access the organization's business data through the e-mail client. Public folders support security, easy access (two things that don't normally go together), and complex forms. These forms can be managed through macros defined in the public folder environment. Users can reference folder items without requiring attachments.

The clustering of e-mail servers provides fault tolerance (not only for public folders but for e-mail as well). With a clustered environment system administrators can perform maintenance without taking down the service or losing access to folder data. This strategy is independent on the desktop or workstation operating system. However, once again, all business documents require access to the network, as well as to the e-mail services.

Folder Synchronization

Folder synchronization is much like roaming profiles but it is linked to a workstation and not the user account. In roaming profiles, your data moves with you, from workstation to workstation. In folder synchronization, data that is generated on that workstation will make a working mobile copy of the network data on the local hard drive.

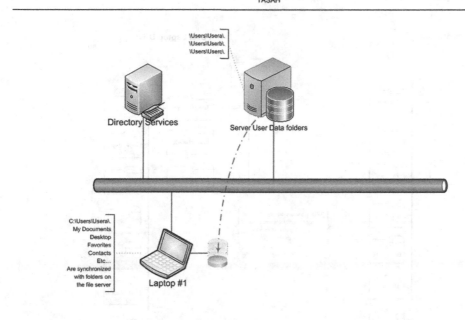

Folder Synchronization
TASAH

\Users\Usera\
\Users\Userb\
\Users\Userc\

Directory Services

Server User Data folders

C:\Users\Usera\
My Documents
Desktop
Favorites
Contacts
Etc...
Are synchronized
with folders on
the file server

Laptop #1

Page 1

Figure 9-7. Laptop folder synchronization

Each person using the laptop will only see the files they create and synchronize with the file server. This helps protect personally generated data from being accessed inappropriately. You can configure the synchronization process to occur at startup (connecting to the network file server) or when shutting down. You can also have synchronization occur both during startup and shutdown. The synchronization policy is dependent on the organization's needs and the users' patience.

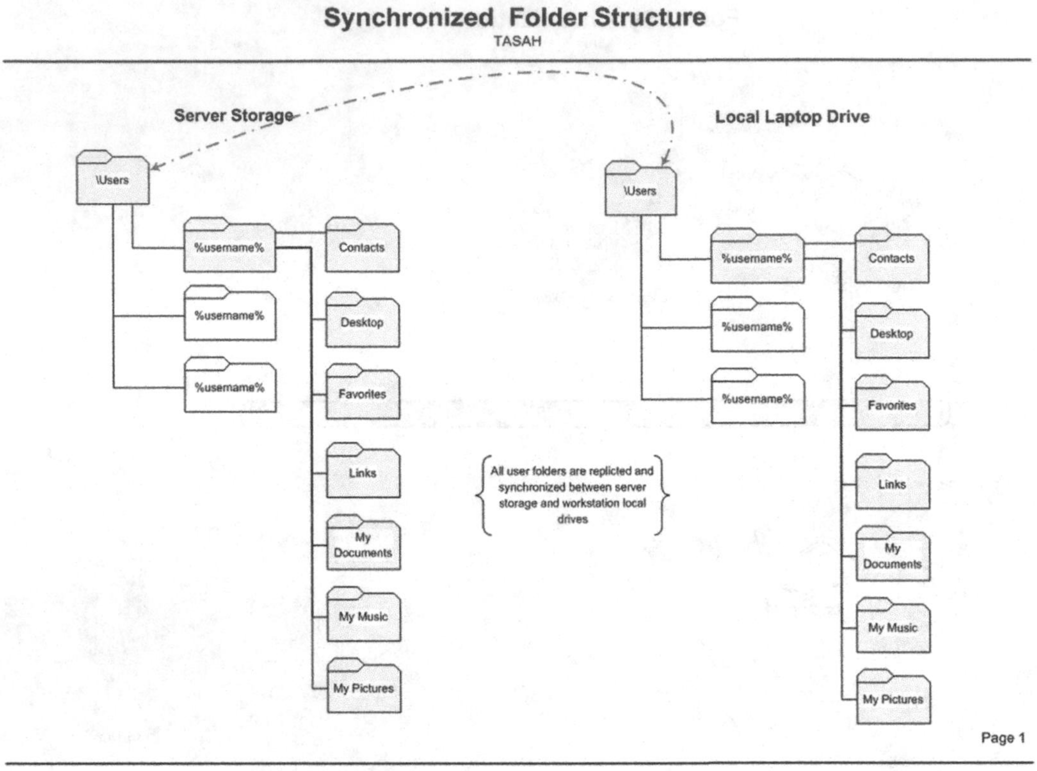

Figure 9-8. *Folder structure in folder synchronization*

Disk quotas are usually created on the file server to limit the amount of data that can be synchronized (disk quotas are usually set based on the file server user storage drives). This not only ensures a defined amount of synchronization, but also minimizes the time to synchronize. There are two ways in which disk quotas are applied to user data:

1.   Warning users when they get close to their limits but not stopping users from exceeding their limit. This approach lets users continue to exceed their disk quota but continually sends annoying warnings that the users have exceeded their disk quota.

2.   Warning users when they get close to their limit and not allowing them to go over that limit. This approach requires users to remove data once a quota has been reached before they can save more data.

Most data in the personal storage is considered RAW and pre-collaborative. Having an organizational data repository for all collaborative data is essential. Once data matures from the personal thought process to organizational collaboration, it needs to have some sort of document-handling system in place that maintains versioning, editing, and the overall lifecycle of that document or data. This process will be discussed in the "Portal Storage Strategy" section of this chapter.

The overall goal of synchronization is to maintain the synchronization of user files found on the file server while allowing the mobility of that data to go with network users who travel. Many organizations also use folder synchronization as a tool to allow users to continue working on their data and documents when the network is experiencing outages. There is much debate over the merits of this, but it is clearly an option if an organization finds its network somewhat unstable and needs to enforce the added redundancy. If that is the case, then there should also be a clear disaster recovery process that incorporates uninterrupted power supplies and clearly written policies to detail what users should do in that event.

Thin Clients

The concept of "thin clients" is not new. In reality it is an option to take the distributed computing environment (that grew from the PC network world) out of the PC network calculation. Previous to (and throughout) the growth of the personal computer network technology, mainframes, mini systems, and specialized computer environments built a centralized computer platform that maintained the gross CPU power, storage, etc. that was shared by users through VTs (video terminals), teletypes, and other data entry points.

Sun Micro Systems Inc., Digital Equipment Corporation (DEC), and other large-scale computer manufacturers created diskless clients that distributed CPU power to "smart desktops" but maintained most (if not all) of the storage- and data-sharing technology on larger systems like servers.

Thin clients follow the approach that Sun Microsystems, DEC, and other large computer manufacturers had built up in the late 1970s, 80s, and 90s. This approach works well for many organizations, but not for all.

The two types of thin clients represented in Figure 9-9 are the most common. They represent two different ways to look at thin client provisioning. But they both have the single dependency of a working network in order to function properly.

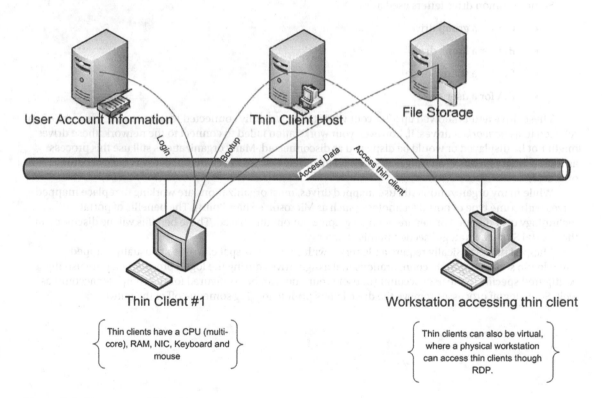

Figure 9-9. *Two types of thin clients*

The thin client #1 (also known as Virtual Desktop Infrastructure clients, or VDI[1]) in Figure 9-9 is the traditional thin client where a small box has a CPU, RAM, video card, network interface, etc., but boots from the network to a thin client host server. If the network is down, the thin client is unusable. It is completely dependent on the network to function and for its overall performance. If the network bandwidth is saturated with requests from other clients or network processes, the performance of the thin client is affected.

The second type—where a PC accesses a thin client (or Terminal Services[2]) through the Remote Desktop Protocol (RDP)—only the thin client is affected by the performance and availability of the network. If the network is down and the workstation has local applications and an OS installed, then some remote work can continue.

In both cases, special thin client provisioning licenses must be bought and maintained along with the normal licensing required for OS, applications, etc. Thin clients usually don't propose to reduce computing costs, but they do purport to contain data management, standardization, and data security. There is a lot of additional hardware and software related to thin clients and it is wise to spend extra time evaluating the pros and cons given your business model to ensure you are making the best technology choice.

Mapped Drives

Drive mapping has been part of personal computer networking from the very beginning. It was, in fact, the fundamental file sharing methodology used to post files in a place where everyone could get to it.

Some common drive letters used are:

- G:\ for a group drive

- H:\ for a home drive

- S:\ for a shared drive

- U:\ for a user drive

These drive letters showed up after your workstation was fully connected to the network. They are often referred to as *networked* drives. If, however, your workstation failed to connect to the network, these drives might not be displayed or would be displayed as disconnected. Many organizations still use this process as their primary means of sharing disk space on their network. However, mapped drives have become outdated.

While many organizations still use mapped drives, most organizations are working to replace mapped drives with some type of portal technology (such as Microsoft's SharePoint). The benefits of portal technology over mapped drives are not only graphic but options-based. These benefits will be discussed in the "Portal Storage Strategy" section in this chapter.

Mapped drives basically require a file server with shared disk space. Drives are usually mapped using logon scripts or profile configurations that assign drives during the logon process. They are usually configured specific to the user account (or user group) but can be configured for the computer account as well. Some logoff processes remove the drive letters prior to logging someone off of the network.

---

[1]VDI: http://searchservervirtualization.techtarget.com/sDefinition/0,,sid94_gci1250545,00.html
[2]Terminal services: http://technet.microsoft.com/en-us/library/cc755399(WS.10).aspx

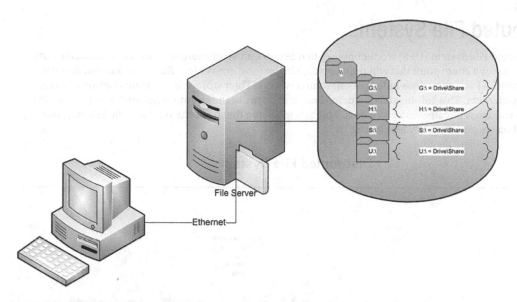

Figure 9-10. *Simple drive mapping*

Here is a sample CLI-based[3] drive mapping script:

```
@echo off
Cls
Net use G: /delete
Net use H: /delete
Net use S: /delete
Net use U: /delete
Net use G: \\server\shareG
Net use H: \\server\shareH
Net use S: \\server\shareS
Net use U: \\server\shareU
exit
```

In place of server, you must give the NetBIOS name of the file server where the share is located. In place of shareG, you must provide the actual share name. You might want to clear the drive mappings prior to remapping the drives so that there is no confusion (that's the purpose of the net use G: /delete command[4]). You can also give a description of what the drive letter represents.

The users accessing the mapped drives must have their access defined in the security of the shared folder as well as the access point on the server. Whatever the user rights are (read, write, modify, etc.) defines what the user can do on the mapped drive. There is a host of options that can be defined (both as a user and as part of a group). It is always best to define rights and permissions based on groups whenever possible.

---

[3]CLI (Command Line Interface): http://www.webopedia.com/TERM/C/CLI.html
[4]Net use syntax: http://www.microsoft.com/resources/documentation/windows/xp/all/proddocs/en-us/net_use.mspx?mfr=true

Distributed File Systems

The Distributed File System (DFS) is a technology that allows for two or more files servers to replicate data. The user accesses a share point that will populate data in the most convenient file server nearest that user (on the network). Each server has independent shared storage. Their storage is replicated between servers mirroring each other. This solution has a storage limit and does use the common network to replicate data.

DFS is used to replicate remote site data. This acts to ensure that each site has local data storage but allows for data created remotely replicating.

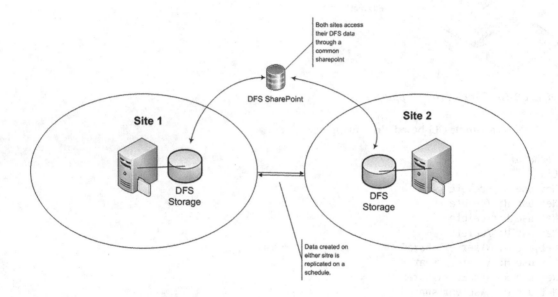

Figure 9-11. *DFS site-to-site replication*

While not exactly real-time replication, given a programmable schedule, all data from one site is mirrored to the other. The replication is usually scheduled outside of business hours to have the lowest impact on network bandwidth. You can also manually force replication when the need arises. This can be a reasonably inexpensive way to provide fault tolerance for data from site to site. As stated previously, the size of the data store is limited (and the actual amount of data that can be replicated is directly related to the versioning of the server software used on both file servers).

The main benefits of DFS are the ability to move personnel from one site to another and keeping their data local to the site they log on to. This increases both data access performance and collaboration between sites. While DFS can be used in one location to mirror data, other technical solutions to mirror storage will provide better continuity and duplication. The failure of replication cycles will result in issues that need to be addressed as quickly as possible to protect against data corruption.

148

Clustered File Servers

Clustering server technology is used for fault tolerance, load balancing, and managed service maintenance cycles. It ensures that the service remains available as long as one or more of the cluster partners remains available and the data storage (SAN for instance) connected to the cluster is also available. Clustering can support filer servers, database servers (SQL), e-mail servers (Microsoft's Exchange), and any other service that is provisioned to work in a clustered environment. Clustering is supported in a virtual world (VMware, Hyper-V, etc.).

Clustering is referred to as a back end solution, in that most users don't see the cluster nodes or know that they are using a clustered solution. The users see the front end (the clustered share point or the application server services that are supported by the clustered solution, i.e., Microsoft's Exchange, Microsoft's SharePoint, and Microsoft's SQL Server).

Clustering physical servers is expensive (in the procurement of hardware/software, power requirements, additional space, and added administrational overhead). Each cluster node needs two HBAs, additional Ethernet port, and advanced server software. The SAN solution needs to provide added fiber ports, GBICs, fiber cables, etc. Figure 9-12 represents a four-node file server cluster. As you can see in Figure 9-12, there are five physical layers:

1. Shared storage (SAN storage)

2. Storage connectivity (SAN Fabric)

3. Physical servers (cluster nodes)

4. Heartbeat network (cluster private network)

5. Access for users (public network interface)

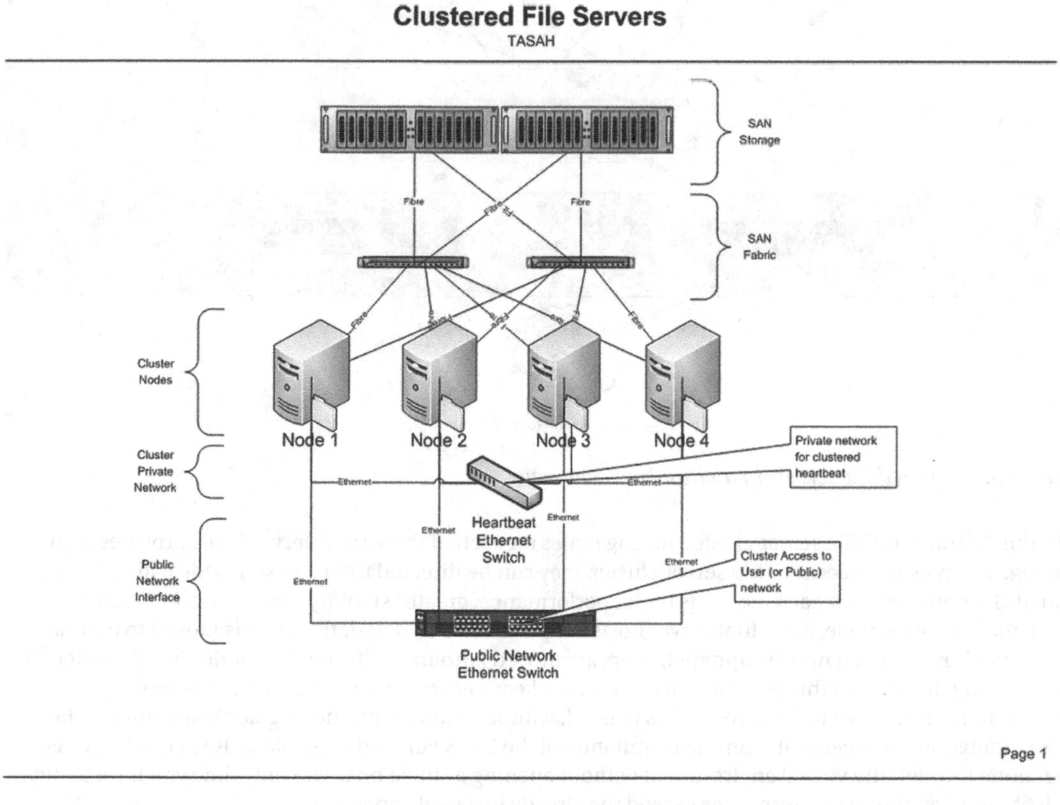

Figure 9-12. *Four-node physical file server cluster*

Each of the cluster nodes should be as identical as possible to ensure that when failover occurs, there is no unforeseen issue that may cause downtime. The more alike each device is, the less confusing it is to move services from one node to another.

In a virtual world (the one to be used in the example network for this book), clustering has many cost-saving benefits. Figure 9-13 presents one option for disbursing a file server cluster in a virtual environment. Each virtual server host would have a cluster node that could be failed over to another virtual server host when necessary. The virtual management switch would support the cluster's private heartbeat network. The virtual public switch would support the cluster's user access to shared data. The built-in virtual connectivity to the SAN would resolve the need for additional HBAs, GBICs, fiber cabling, etc. Using virtual cluster nodes would help standardize node hardware architecture and reduce the cost (eliminating hardware costs all together). The only added cost for implementing a clustered file server environment in the virtual environment ends up being the cluster node operating systems.

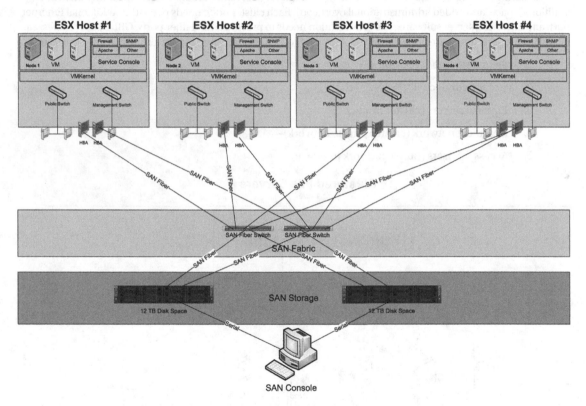

Figure 9-13. *Clustered file servers in a virtual environment*

In this "virtualized" file server cluster, having nodes on each of the virtual server hosts provides load balancing. When users access the file server cluster, they can be directed to the cluster node with the least workload. This ensures that each user gets better performance, greater stability, and access independent from the maintenance cycle. As virtual server hosts are patched or updated, the node is moved to another virtual server host. As each node is updated, users are moved automatically to other nodes in the cluster. The workload being distributed through the cluster resource keeps each virtual server host balanced.

SAN storage can be added and resized as needed, without adding or removing hardware (unless the need for storage space exceeds the physical limitation of the 24TB currently installed). RAM can be added to each node through the virtual environment without opening a single box. The only time you have to buy more RAM is when the virtual resources exceed the already installed capacity.

This clustered strategy can work for database servers and e-mail servers. Again, the cost is limited to the node's operating system and application software. This clustered environment supports the 99.999 percent availability[5] option by using rollover maintenance (bringing down one node at a time to update patches, hotfixes, and service packs).

Portal Storage Strategy

It is important for portal technology to be useful to the seasoned professional and the new employee. Often this is lost over time as the company matures and more content is added to the portal to make things more available to the staff. As more features are added, the site becomes more cluttered and less user friendly. Figure 9-14 presents a clear and easy-to-use portal profile.

Figure 9-14. Intranet Document and Services Portal

---

[5]Five nines availability: http://searchcio.techtarget.com/definition/99999

Everything a new and seasoned user needs is found on this "home page". There are five main working areas:

1. The navigation bar provides access to the Operations, Services, and Service Desk.

2. The Department Libraries are where each department can manage their documents.

3. Internal user documentation helps users find business strategies and support.

4. The operational status is provided for IT services.

5. Security download options include antivirus, antispam, and system updates.

The navigation bar helps users find quick support options for resolving internal network and operations issues as well as getting individual help when things aren't working right. The main consideration here is to make getting help as easy and quick as possible without having to search through the portal to find answers.

Within each of the department libraries can be found individual department working documents, the department home page, and other useful content pertinent to the department. Within each department library, users can post the work they have fine-tuned for the business. Within each department library is the content they share with others in their department to refine and prep for finalization.

The Internal Resources section is where final documents can be found. Documents finalized in the department libraries are reviewed by the Portal Documents Manager through an evaluation process that includes department managers and business strategists and then placed in there as business intelligence products.

The Operational Status section presents a quick reference to the state of the network so that users can see when services are degraded. Having this section on each page ensures that all users are kept up to date about any potential network issues that may impede their work process.

The security download options section is a way to ensure that users have direct access to updating the security of their workstations without hassle and remind them that there is a constant threat that they need to be aware of.

Many organizations also have a section that keeps users of abreast of current events that affect their organization. In any case, it is important to make the portal's home page simple to use and quick to find the things users need to do their work effectively.

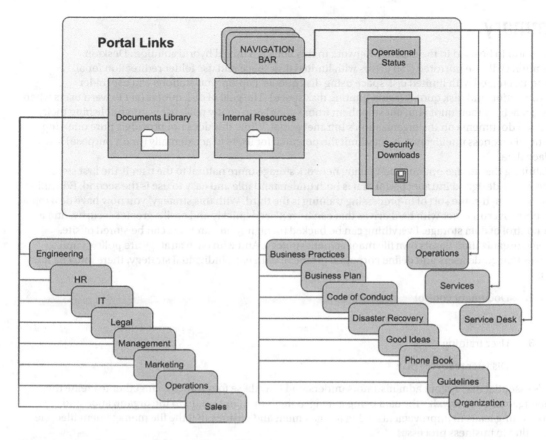

Figure 9-15. *Portal home page substructure*

All categories are alphabetically indexed to dissuade priority. This ensures that no one department or resource is more important than another. The substructure of the documents library can be further indexes with subsections that best describe content value and design for each individual department.

Each organization has its methodology for implementing portal technology. Having a strategy is essential to maintaining standards and best practices that everyone in the organization can abide by. Some organizations may wish to incorporate operational calendars on the portal's home page to keep their personnel attuned to deadlines and upcoming events. There are a host of things that can be displayed, which leads to the main problem of *super saturation*.

Keeping things simple and well organized with every page looking the same leads to a friendlier user environment. Having a PAB[6] to manage changes will help maintain consistency, interoperability, and conformance to design.

---

[6]PAB (Portal Users Board): Evaluates major changes in the structure, content, and complexity of the portal design.

Summary

The solution to be used in the example network in this book is a mixed hybrid solution. Desktop workstations will use mirrored USB drives with limited disk space and use folder redirection for all documents created with limited disk space using disk quotas. Laptop workstations will use folder synchronization and disk quotas (again limiting disk space). The goal of disk quotas (set to warn users when they are reaching their quota but not stop them from saving) is to gently push users into publishing their completed documents on the organization's Intranet portal. While this does not provide a pure one-stop shop for all business intelligence, it does limit the potential for users to accidentally (or on purpose) lose or misplace data.

Limiting the storage options and making network storage more natural to the user is the first step. Having a well-designed Intranet portal that is both understandable and easy to use is the second. Educating the users through some sort of in-processing training is the third. With this strategy, you now have desktop computers that run faster with hard drives that can be replaced quickly and easily, greater security, and a better control of data storage. Everything can be backed up nightly and archives can be stored offsite.

Each organization has its own file management strategy. And with each strategy are policies and directives that guide users and define corporate protocol. With each individual strategy, there must be four things:

1. Document control

2. Security

3. User training

4. Disaster recovery plan

It's essential that system administrators understand how these four things go together to create the file management strategy. It's the data being managed that's most important to the organization and understanding leads to improvements in file management and ensures that the file management lifecycle brings value to business processes.

CHAPTER 10

▪▪▪

Directory Services and Central Account Management

Directory Services provide centralized management for accounts used on the local network. These accounts support users and computers. The directory is a database of all logical components that construct the local network and, being based on a logical construct, can be managed through remote configuration of attributes associated with those account objects. The examples in this book use Microsoft Active Directory, which is an industry standard used widely in business and government.

In previous chapters of this book, Active Directory was mentioned. This chapter explores fundamental aspects of Directory Services from a working perspective and explains what you may encounter in supporting an Active Directory environment. There are several domain-specific icons used for Active Directory, as shown in Figure 10-1.

Active Directory Design Objects

 Domain

 Container

 Organizational Unit

 Site link

 Volume

 Domain

 Storage Group

 Policy

 Group

 User

 Print Queue

Figure 10-1. Active Directory design objects

There are many more used in the industry, but for this chapter, these will be used most extensively. For simplicity, the example Active Directory will be built on the Windows 2008 R2 technology.

Active Directory provides a centralized technology for managing network accounts (both user and computer). It acts to provide resilience and redundancy using FSMO[1] roles. FSMO roles have not changed from Server 2003 to 2008. For FSMO roles to be exploited, there must be multiple domain controllers[2] available. By having more than one domain controller available on your organization's network, you ensure that services remain available while maintenance is performed. Multiple domain controllers also ensure that when one domain controller fails, operations can continue while you repair or replace the disabled server. It also acts to balance the load, distributing services across multiple servers to minimize the account management overhead.

But what exactly is Microsoft Active Directory, and why would you need it? A directory service (in this case, Microsoft Active Directory) is a database consisting of a schema with objects that have attributes. The schema is the structure of the database (how it can be presented to the system administrator providing flexibility and usability). Objects are those things in the schema that represent users, computers, network connections, etc. (tangible things). The attributes are the things in an object that can be configured through directory services. Microsoft Active Directory provides a graphic management console that helps system administrators understand how all of the objects and attributes are combined to provide a working environment for the organization.

While this is a simple explanation, it is also something to keep in mind while designing and updating your organization's directory services. Some organizations develop their schema to reflect the organization's structure. Other organizations look at geographic structure and hierarchical substructures. The bottom line is that the schema must support objects and their attributes in ways in which the system administrator can best do their job and that does not always reflect either the organization's structure or geographic locations.

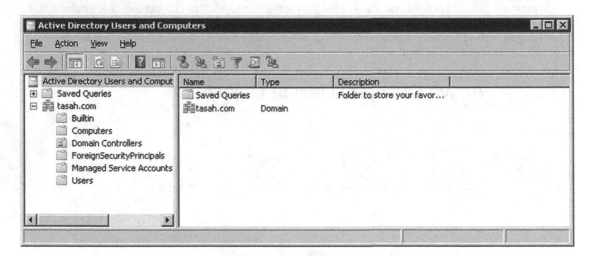

Figure 10-2. *Default Active Directory*

This chapter is focused on system administrator's usability over organizational design. The primary goal is to make a directory schema that is easy to maintain and flexible. Far too often the directory service design outlives its usefulness.

---

[1]http://www.petri.co.il/understanding_fsmo_roles_in_ad.htm
[2]http://technet.microsoft.com/en-us/library/cc786438(WS.10).aspx

One option is to place user accounts into Organization Units (OU) that reflect their department and then add the account to a Security Group (SG)as well. When the user is promoted to another department, you must move that account, remove it from the original group, and add it to another group.

Some system administrators simply move user accounts from OU to OU and don't add that account to any SG. While this may look to make things simple at first, it is not sustainable over time. SGs are used not only for grouping user and computer accounts. It is the basis for deploying Group Policy Objects[3] (GPOs) and is likely the most powerful function Active Directory provides.

While the next option may not seem the obvious choice, it does make sense for small to medium size organizations,[4] and that is putting users into one OU and adding each user to a department group. In other words, all users will be located in a single OU. But their user account will be added to the department SG that reflects their membership (see Figure 10-3). When a GPO is applied to the user OU, it is filtered by the associated SG.

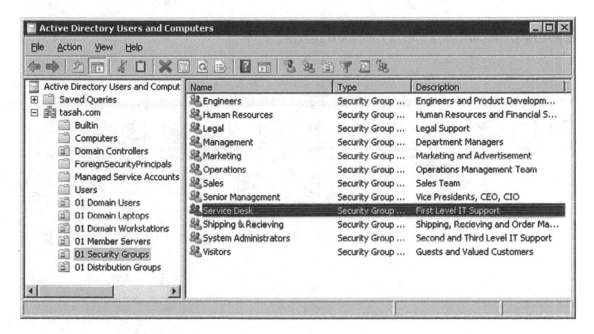

Figure 10-3. *Departmental Security Groups (SG)*

This not only works for departmental association but also for unique attributes that may be configured through GPOs for various reasons.

You should establish sub-OUs to make directory administration easier, not more complicated. Each sub-OU (or sub-tier) makes finding objects in the directory schema a bit harder. While that may not seem to be much of a problem with either Figures 10-4 or 10-5, many production sites have tier structures up to ten deep.

---

[3]http://technet.microsoft.com/en-us/windowsserver/bb310732.aspx

[4]Reference to maximum numbers of objects and object relationships in Active Directory: http://technet.microsoft.com/en-us/library/active-directory-maximum-limits-scalability(WS.10).aspx#BKMK_Objects

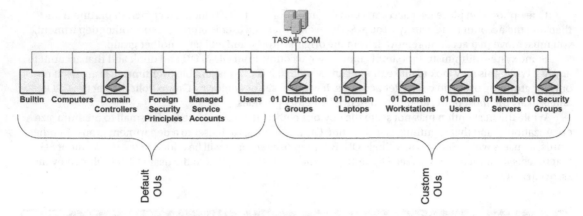

Figure 10-4. *Tier one Active Directory containers and OUs*

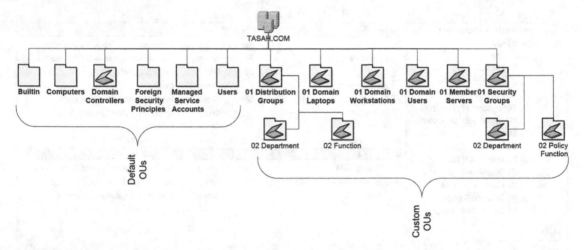

Figure 10-5. *Tier two Active Directory OUs*

Naming each custom OU—first by tier then by object type—helps simplify the administration process and remind the system administrators how deep each of the groups of objects are in the directory tree. While Microsoft defines limits based on the number of characters in a given OU name (256 maximum), many system administrators (and if fact Microsoft Certified trainers) have noted that once you build a sub-tree beyond three tiers deep, group policies may not work as planned.

For purposes of this book's directory example, the directory OU structure will not exceed three levels deep to ensure the best environment for group policy objects to optimally perform. It should be emphasized that group policy objects are applied to OUs with accounts. Group policies are only filtered by group membership.

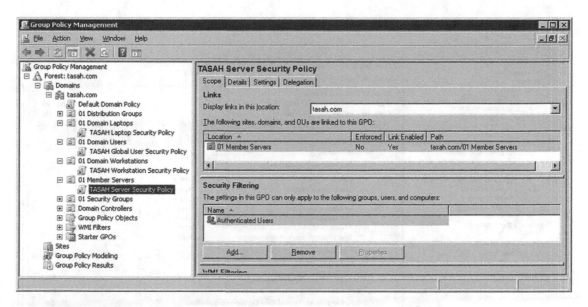

Figure 10-6. *Group Policy Manager*

In the TASAH directory tree, there are four custom OUs you need to push group policies to:

1. Domain laptops

2. Domain users

3. Domain workstations

4. Member servers

There are two other places where group policies are applied by default:

1. The root (`tasah.com`)

2. Domain controllers

In the root of the domain tree you will find the Default Domain Policy. Figure 10-7 presents a macro view of what is affected in the Default Domain Policy. By default, only computer configuration settings are configured. Changes made to the Default Domain Policy will affect all objects in the domain. Make changes to the Default Domain Policy with great care and be sure to document all changes.

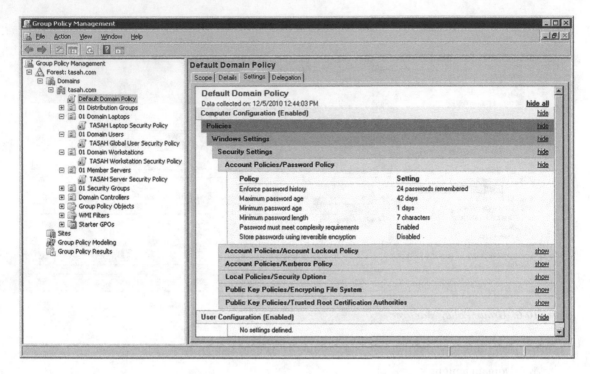

Figure 10-7. *Default Domain Policy*

The Default Domain Controllers Policy manages all things that are associated with the domain. This includes default user rights assignment (see Figure 10-8). Often that fact is not taken into consideration when troubleshooting user rights in group policy objects. In TASAH.com, there are three main locations where user rights can be affected through group policies:

1.   Default Domain Policy

2.   Default Domain Controller Policy

3.   Domain Users OU

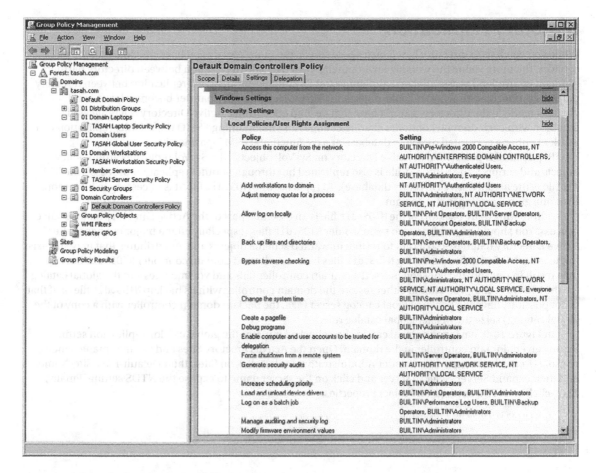

Figure 10-8. *Default Domain Controllers Policy*

The troubleshooting process for computers is a bit more complicated:

1. Default Domain Policy—Can affect *all* workstations, laptops, domain controllers, and member servers.

2. Default Domain Controller Policy—Can affect *all* workstations, laptops, domain controllers, and member servers.

3. Domain Laptops OU—Affects only those laptops that are objects in the Domain Laptop OU.

4. Domain Workstations OU—Affects only those workstations that are objects in the Domain Workstation OU.

5. Domain Member Servers—Affects only those servers that are objects in the Domain Member Servers OU.

The fewer the administrative variables, the quicker you will be at resolving directory-specific issues.

Directory Replication

While you can have a directory based on a single server, the more servers you have providing directory services, the more stable the working environment. With that said, replication between directory partners (domain controllers) is essential to maintaining stability and performance. If replication between directory partners is not consistent and reliable, objects shared by each directory partner become skewed and changes made to the directory may not have that desired effect. Since Active Directory is a replicated database with each domain controller sharing changes and maintaining FSMO roles, faulty replication can result in either a corrupted directory database or a dysfunctional FSMO partnership.

Replication is performed in Active Directory on SysVol[5] objects. The SysVol replicates group policy objects and scripts.[6] The NTDS.dit file is also replicated but through another replication process[7] (the NTDS.dit file is the actual Active Directory database). To replicate the NTDS.dit file, it is necessary to have more than one global catalog in the domain.

Automating daily backups of the NTDS.dit file is an essential part of the Active Directory maintenance process. You should be careful not to restore older NTDS.dit files (especially after a major change in the Active Directory database) so as not to restore unwanted schema objects and/or attributes that may still exist in the older NTDS.dit file. Restoring NTDS.dit files from a replicated domain controller NTDS.dit backup may result in unexpected consequences. If a domain controller fails and you must restore the global catalog (or the NTDS.dit file), you should either restore the domain controller with its backup NTDS.dit file or, if that is not possible, have the backup global catalog server (aka, the backup domain controller with a copy of the global catalog) seize the master global catalog role.

In Figure 10-9, having the global catalog box checked initiates the global catalog replication setting for any given domain controller in the domain. Open the Active Directory Sites and Settings management console (found in the start menu under Administrative Tools), click on Sites, then Default-First-Site-Name, and then expand Server. Select a server and click on the server name to expose the NTDS setting. Finally, right-click on NTDS Settings and select Properties.

---

[5]SysVol replication: http://www.windowsnetworking.com/kbase/WindowsTips/WindowsServer2008/AdminTips/ActiveDirectory/SYSVOLReplicationNotes.html

[6]http://msdn.microsoft.com/en-us/library/cc507518(v=vs.85).aspx

[7]How the Active Directory replication model works: http://technet.microsoft.com/en-us/library/cc772726(WS.10).aspx

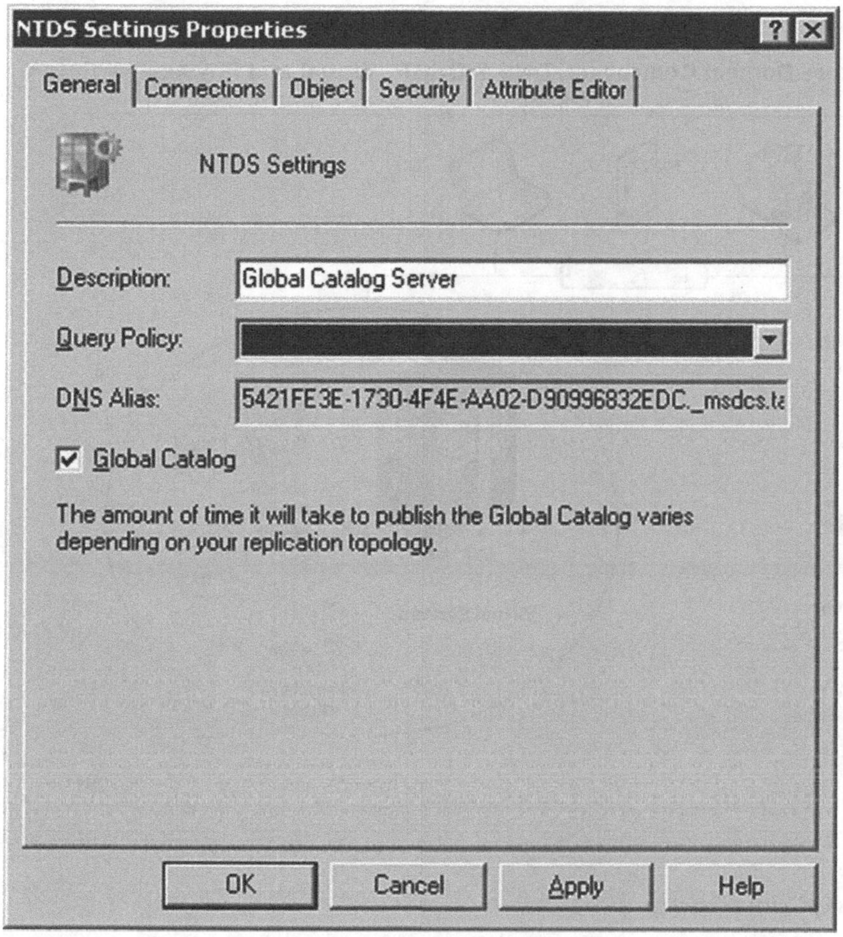

Figure 10-9. *Setting the global catalog replication*

It is suggested that your PDC Emulator role be supported by a physical server with a backup copy of the global catalog. That physical server should also manage the "secondary DNS" server role. This ensures that when you are restoring the virtual environment from a major power failure or system malfunction, you have the basic tools to get the virtual domain back up and running quickly and effectively.

In Figure 10-10, the PDC server has a backup copy of the global catalog along with the secondary DNS. Bringing this server online first ensures that all of the other servers, when brought online, will have enough services available to reestablish the domain services quickly and efficiently, without having to search through the virtual server hosts to initiate primary domain functions. The major benefit of this is that it gives system administrators more time to resolve virtual environment issues while reestablishing basic network services. There is no guessing as to which server should be restated after a major crash, causing less confusion and quicker response time. If directory partners are geographically dispersed across long distances and connected through disparate bandwidth links, the replication model can be impacted and cause extended delays in completing the replication cycle. While local systems and servers may perform optimally, replication delays can have a substantial effect on user perception and integrated IT services.

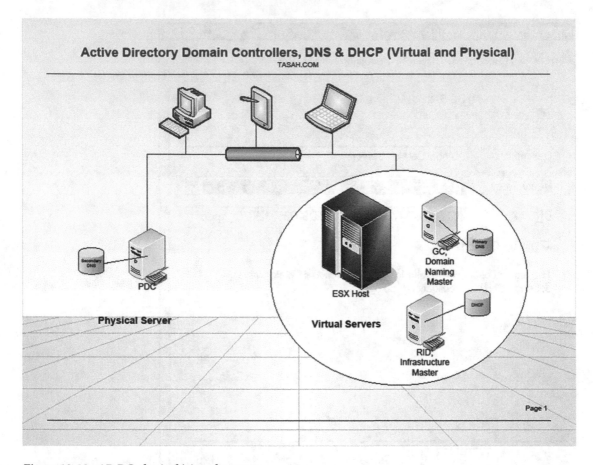

Figure 10-10. *AD DC physical/virtual strategy*

Directory Architecture

Designing your Directory Architecture should be based on current needs as well as potential for growth (both in house and across site boundaries). Previously in this chapter the design for OUs and containers was discussed. In keeping with the concept of "less is more," the directory architecture will be based on sites and subdomains (if needed).

The primary office site would be the root domain (simply because no other domains exist at this time). There needs to be guidance as to what constitutes the need for sites and/or subdomains. There also needs to be a predefined concept of when to use a forest of trees. While the business model would be the basis for most organizational site boundaries and forest of trees, there is a simple rule of thumb:

- **Root Domain**—Originating domain and site (the first instance of an Active Directory Domain installation).

- **Remote Site**—A remote network (office or group of offices) where the connection between the root site is limited in bandwidth.

- **Subdomain**—A child domain that shares a root domain name (subdomain\tasah. com). Subdomains are normally used to provide a separation of domain security.

- **Forest of Trees**—A forest of trees are used to bind multiple domain names under one root domain. This is very useful in binding merged companies or when an organization branches out into multiple domain names but wants a single federated IT organization.

Every Active Directory domain belongs to a forest. Every forest has at least one tree. And every tree has at least one domain. Every domain has at least one site. A site does not have to be a domain, but it must be part of a domain. So with that in mind, a single domain can be a site, a tree, and a forest. And in fact, when you promote your first domain controller for a new installation, you choose to build a new forest. Knowing how all of this goes together can help you project growth and determine what the best approach to designing the organization's network architecture.

Figure 10-11 is a simple diagram of what is created with the first domain of a forest. You'll note that the Enterprise groups live here. All modifications to the forest (schema extensions, added domains, and trees) must be authorized by members of the enterprise security groups from this domain.

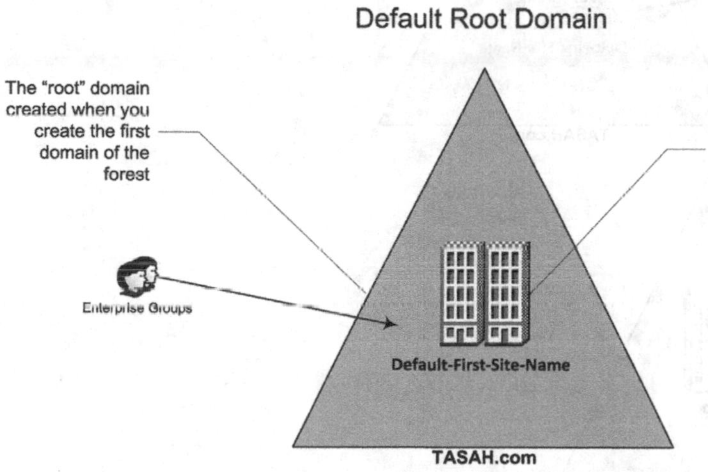

Figure 10-11. Default domain architecture

The NTDS.dit (aka global catalog) file is separated into four partitions:

1. Domain partition

2. Schema partition

3. Configuration partition

4. Application partition

The global catalog contains a partial copy of every domain partition in each of the domains in the forest. This acts as an index for all objects in AD. Every domain in the forest replicates global catalog data. This means that if you have a multiple domain forest, your account can be validated on any local global catalog without touching the home domain's global catalog.

Figure 10-12 represents one possibility whereby the TASAH organization plans to expand to Europe and will build a child domain there. By building a child domain, the root domain maintains enterprise authority over any major changes to the forest while allowing the Europe.TASAH.com domain to build its internal domain infrastructure. This allows for growth in Europe while maintaining control over all objects and attributes that affect the forest level. An alternative to this would be to build a second tree in the forest or a second site in the root domain.

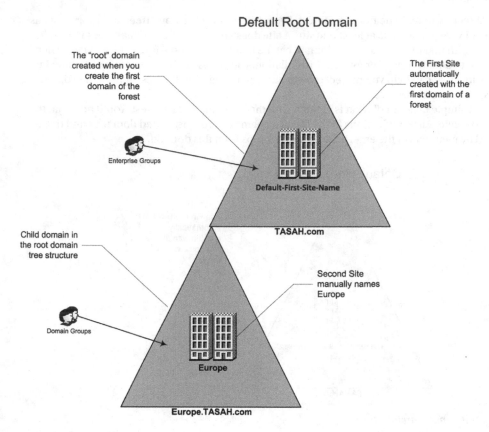

Figure 10-12. *Root domain tree*

The example network in this book will build a single tree forest with the possible expansion into Europe with a child domain. For more information on domains and trusts, see the Microsoft TechNet library: http://technet.microsoft.com/en-us/library/cc770299.aspx.

Accounts and Groups

Accounts and groups are in fact the essence of directory services. They are the authentication mechanism and authorization tool for all users and computers in the domain. It is important to look at account authorization in terms of roles people play in their daily business. Never create a single user account with unique permissions not granted through a group. If one person requires specific permissions, then maybe someone else will need the same later on down the road. Configuring accounts one at a time is time consuming and counterproductive. You quickly lose control of what users are able to do and that could lead to security problems later. Before creating a single user account, you must build the security groups that will authorize permissions based on the role an individual plays within the organization.

In defining your role-based group permissions, you should first consult your organizational tree and then the specific job descriptions associated with each position in that organizational structure. You should define the groups, grant permissions, build a template account, and test those permissions using the template account. Only after you are sure that the template account does exactly what you want it to do can you copy the template into actual user accounts. If a template requires additional permissions, you should make changes to the associated "role-based" security group and not the individual user account.

The naming convention your organization uses for groups is important. It should convey role, purpose, and permissions. The TASAH.com domain naming convention (having a subdomain associated with it) will need to also define the originating authority. Microsoft associates groups based on their architectural security principles (groups that have permissions granted only on a local level, groups that have permissions granted on a tree level, and groups that have permissions granted on a forest level).

Groups

There are three types of security groups in Active Directory[8]:

1. Global groups

2. Domain local groups

3. Universal groups

There is a common practice Microsoft proposes that system administrators adhere to when choosing how to use these three groups—it's commonly referred to as AGUDLP and it goes like this:

A – **A**ccounts

G – **G**lobal groups

U – **U**niversal groups

DL – **D**omain **L**ocal groups

P – **P**ermissions

Accounts go into Global groups. Global groups go into Universal groups. Universal groups go into Domain Local groups and Permissions are applied only to Domain Local groups. To use this practice correctly, you should do a little diagramming first.

Let's take a department security group. We know that it will have user accounts associated with it, so we will start off with a Global group. Let's say that department is "Sales". We also know that everyone in the Sales department requires specific permissions to the Sales catalog database, cold calling database, special printers, and the Customer database. They also need access to the Inventory database. They are regionally hired (meaning that they only work in a given location), so they will not need access to any other domain in the forest. So the following groups will be created for the Sales department:

- G US Sales Department Members—All sales user accounts for the root domain

- DL US Sales Catalog Users—All global groups who have rights to access the US sales catalog

- DL US Cold Call Users—All global groups who have rights to access the US cold call database

---

[8]http://www.southampton.ac.uk/isolutions/computing/auth/activedirectory/model.html

- DL US Customers Database Users—All global groups who have rights to access the US customers database

- DL US Inventory Database Users—All global groups who have rights to access the US inventory database

- DL US High Resolution Printer Access Pool—All global groups who have rights to access the US-based high-resolution restricted printer pool

The "G US Sales Department Members security group" is a member of the following Domain Local groups granting special permissions:

- DL US Sales Catalog Users

- DL US Cold Call Users

- DL US Customers Database Users

- DL US Inventory Database Users

- DL US High Resolution Printer Access Pool

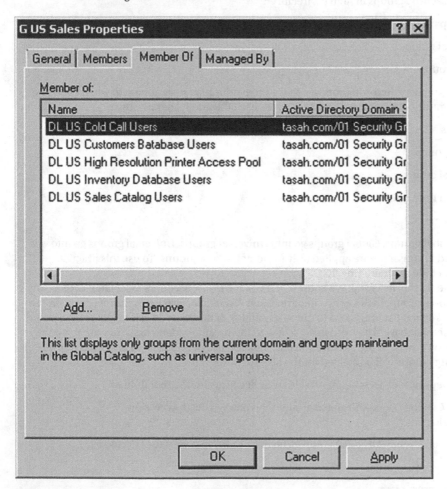

Figure 10-13. *G US Sales is a member of...*

This makes anyone who is a member of the G US Sales Department Members Security Group permission to anything on the groups it is a member of. A member of the G US Sales Department Members Security Group can access the sales catalog, the cold call user database, the customer database, the inventory database, and the high-resolution printer access pool. And since other departments may also need access to some of the same resources, their departments can become a member of the appropriate domain local group as needed.

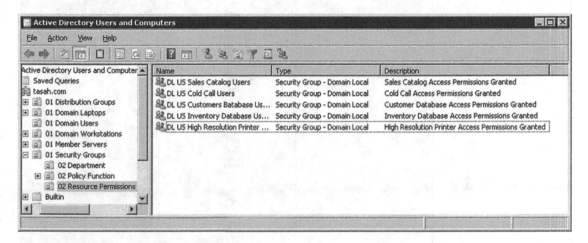

Figure 10-14. Resource permissions groups

It's all in a name really. By looking at the names of the OUs and the names of their content, you can quickly see exactly what's associated with each object. If you're looking for department personnel, you can go to the Department Security groups and expand the department global group members' properties. If you're looking to see who has access to a resource, you can open the Resource Permissions security group and expand the resource domain local groups member properties. If you're looking to see what group policies affect who, simply go to the Policy Function security group and expand the Policy Users Domain Local group's member properties.

While not a Microsoft definition of security group types, the following can be deduced by the types used in the example directory:

- Global groups are groups of accounts

- Domain local groups have global groups associated with access to resources or policies

- Universal groups have global groups that have forest-wide membership association

Keeping the group associations simple will make administration of domain resource allocation easier to troubleshoot.

By charting out the nesting of users, groups, and resources, you can build a clear picture of what each user in a department will expect. Figure 10-15 is a good example of how to plan the nesting of users, groups, and resources. You know who, what, how, and why each account gets its access. Keeping a journal of these relationships will help you not only build your group nesting but also manage changes as they are needed. These are the relationships that users may not see but they will know when it isn't right. You may also wish to make a similar chart for group policy relationships as well, as it will help you to visualize all of the things that must be in place to deploy a policy successfully the first time. Each department should have its own set of charts.

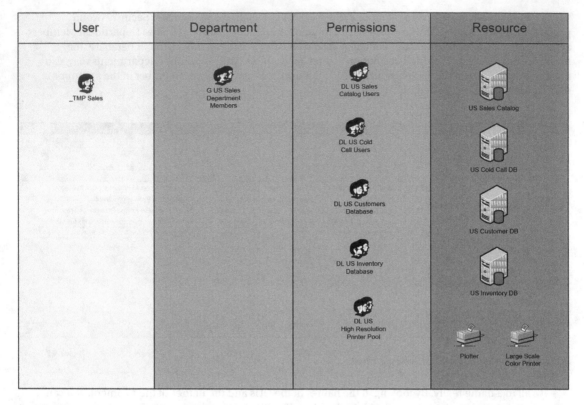

Figure 10-15. *Groups to resource chart*

Accounts

User Accounts

Accounts should be generic, only customized for permissions through their group association. Detailed information owned by an account should be user-centric (name, e-mail address, office, phone number, etc.). These details can be searched (using the Search option in the Start menu) by any authenticated user in the forest and make for a nice simple way to build an internal organization directory. Having this data up to date is extremely important. Not only can users access this data but it can also be pushed to applications that require it (like Human Resource databases, service desk toolsets, etc.). It becomes a one-stop shop for managing an organization's personnel location, title, and contact information.

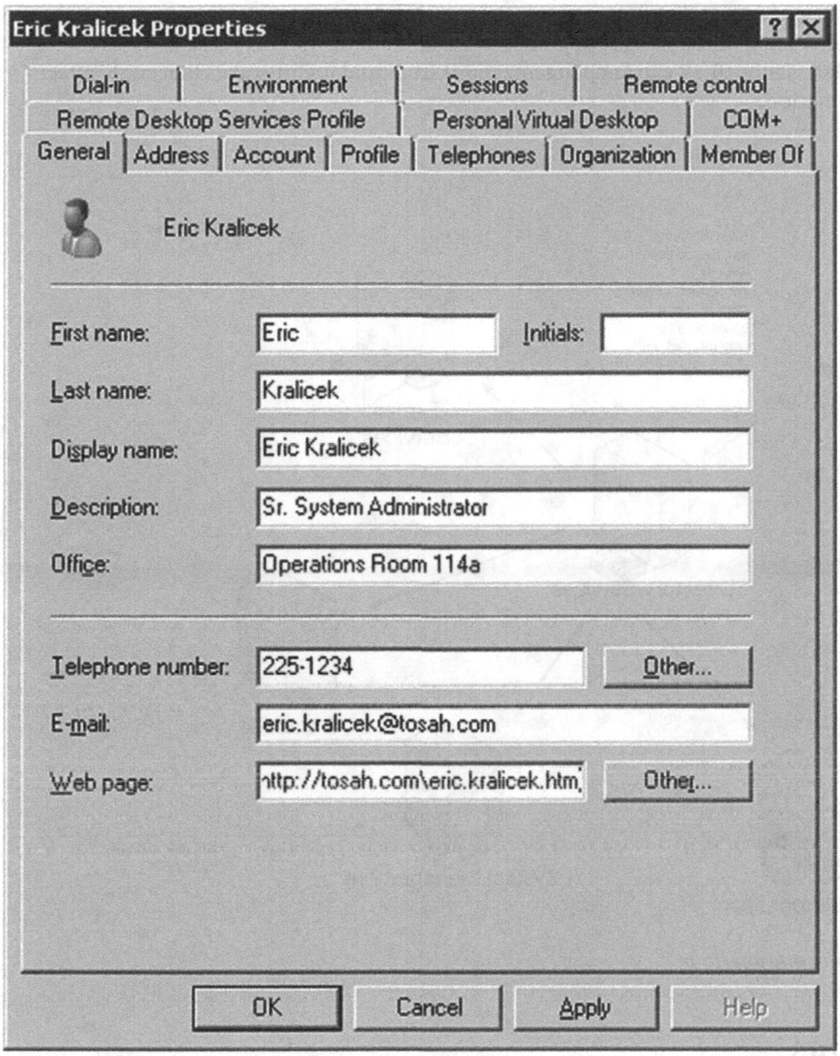

Figure 10-16. *Directory searchable Information*

When you search for people you need only know the first name, last name, title, office, or phone number and you can find the associated user account information. This information also becomes the foundation for other services such as e-mail, portal information (which can be further displayed in organizational charts), binding office IT assets to users (for incident management and inventory), and much more.

Some larger companies use their human resource applications (such as PeopleSoft[9]) to populate this information as new employees are hired. This further closes the loop and ensures that all basic personnel information is managed through a single application and shared through directory services.

---

[9]http://www.oracle.com/us/products/applications/peoplesoft-enterprise/index.htm

Mapping out how important data is distributed across the network helps the organization manage both the current state of data distribution and potential upgrades or modifications that may take place in the future. Something simple like Figure 10-17 can keep organizations from making mistakes that could affect the continuity of user information.

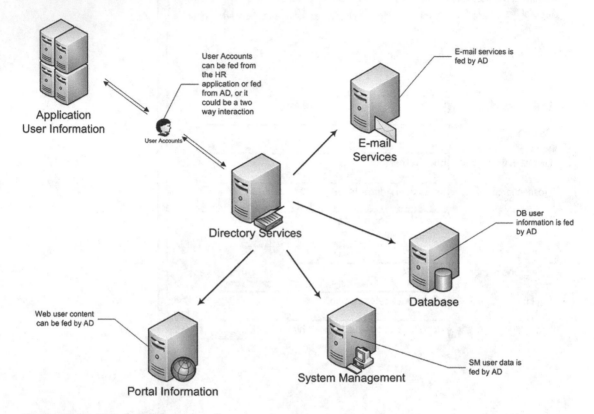

Figure 10-17. *User data information flow*

Computer Accounts

Computer accounts should be planned and implemented. By prepping computer accounts before actually adding computers to the network, you ensure that they end up in the right OU with the right group policies applied to them before users get access to network resources. By default, computer accounts are created in the Computers container. It is a good practice not to let computer accounts get generated there. Containers don't have the ability to apply group policies directly and therefore get only the basic group policy settings.

In Tasah.com, each workstation will use the following naming convention:

- DT—Desktop + wall port (example: DT-101A)

- LT—Laptop + department + increment (LT-SALES001)

For small office spaces such as Tasah.com, this works very well. The naming strategy helps the SysAdmin find the computer and connection point quickly and effectively during troubleshooting.

Using these conventions, the desktop accounts would look like Figure 10-18.

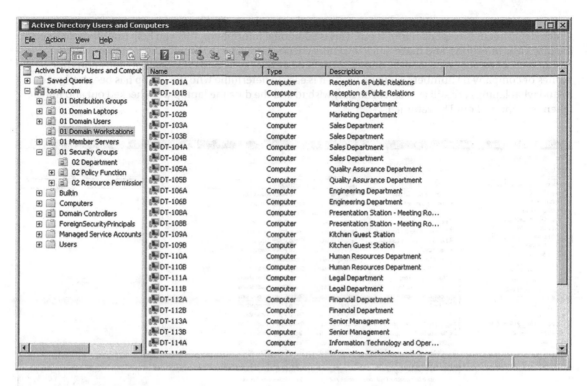

Figure 10-18. *Desktop accounts*

Using these conventions, the laptop accounts would look like Figure 10-19.

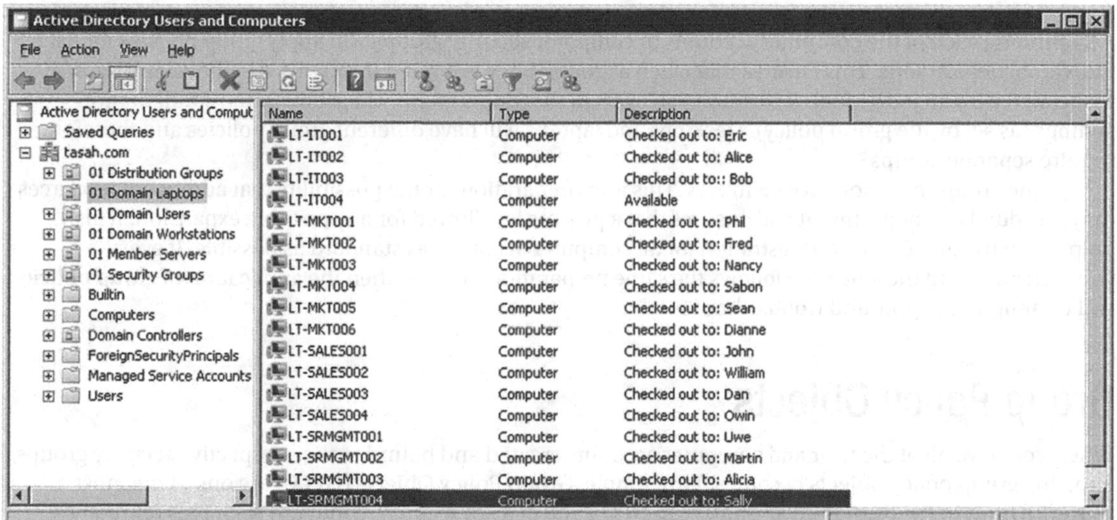

Figure 10-19. *Laptop accounts*

You should note that additional information is added to the computer accounts in order to understand which department is responsible for them. This is additional information that can help troubleshoot issues, localize virus infections, and make quick inventory checks. Using the description field to show who the laptop is checked out to (in small businesses, first names are okay, whereas in larger organizations full names or company ID numbers could be used), it is easy to determine who the laptop has been assigned to and what laptops are still available. You may wish to add the date the laptop was checked out and maybe when the laptop should be returned.

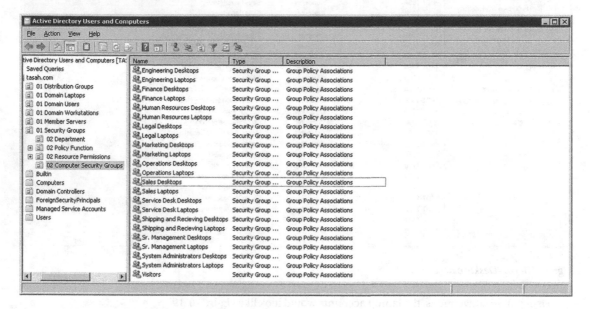

Figure 10-20. *Computer security groups*

Binding each of the computer accounts to computer security groups will apply group policies for each individual department. This ensures that when a group policy is filtered through a specific security group associated with an individual department, all users in that department will get the same configuration settings (as set by the group policy). Desktops and laptops will have different group policies and therefore require separate groups.

Some groups may not have members. This is in preparation for the possibility that additional resources may be added to a department and ensures that a process is followed for any possible expansion. It also helps keep the process of administration for all computer accounts as standard as possible. If every computer account modification follows the same preparation process, then the application of group policies will be simpler to apply and troubleshoot.

Group Policy Objects

When you have all of the user and computer accounts created and bound to their respective security groups, applying group policy objects becomes fairly simple. Group Policy Objects (GPOs) are one of the most powerful tools in the SysAdmin arsenal. With GPOs, you can set security, configure resources remotely, and manage the distribution of applications. You can ensure that standards are applied for everyone while allowing for unique configuration settings to be applied to departments. Almost everything you can do during an installation of an application can be pushed out to network resources automatically.

GPOs are applied by location and security group associations. In other words, GPOs affect accounts within an OU to which the GPO is attached (and all child OUs beneath it). GPOs are filtered by security groups. If an account belongs to an associated security group and that group is added to the Security Filtering list within the group policy object (see Figure 10-21), then the GPO is applied.

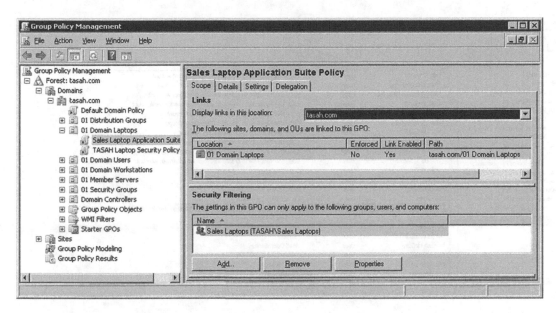

Figure 10-21. *Sales laptop application suite policy*

Even though all of the laptops in the Tasah.com are in the same OU, only those that are members of the Sales Laptop security group will get the Sales Laptop Application Suite Policy.

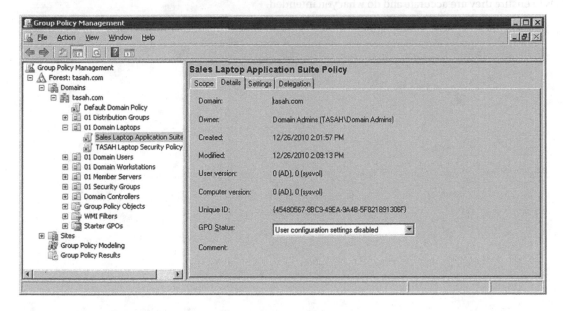

Figure 10-22. *Disabling user configuration settings*

In the Details tab of the GPO, you can fine-tune what inside of the GPO will be processed when the GPO is scanned and applied. The GPO status in the Sales Laptop Application Suite Policy is set to only apply the computer configuration settings. This improves performance and reduces confusion over where to look inside the GPO when configuring or troubleshooting it.

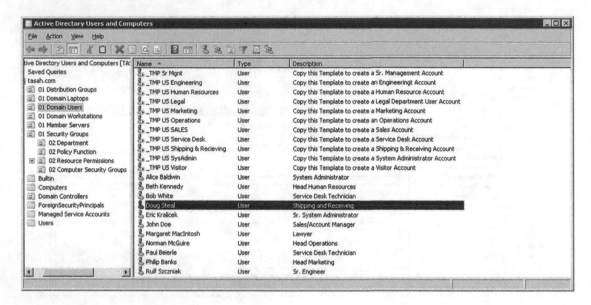

Figure 10-23. *User accounts and account templates*

Because the user account templates were created with security group associations, they can be used to make and test new GPOs without affecting real users. Using the GPO modeling tool, you can build and test GPOs to ensure they are accurate and do what you intended.

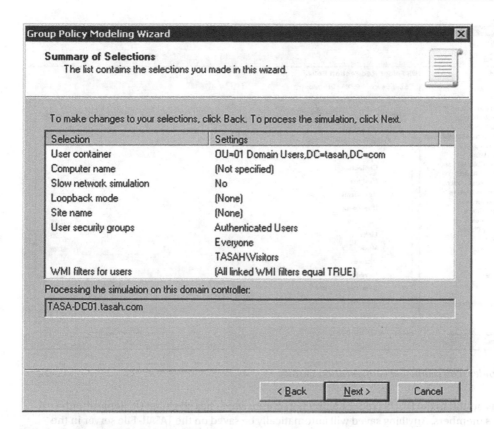

Figure 10-24. *Visitor GPO modeling*

In the US Folder Redirection Policy, all the user data is relocated to the file server redirection share point: \\TASAH-FileServer\Users\%username% (see Figure 10-25).

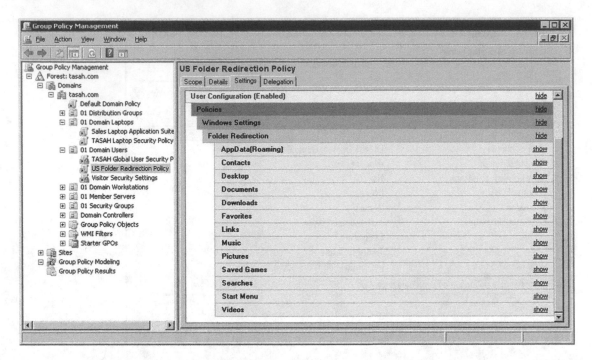

Figure 10-25. *Folder redirection user configuration settings*

This policy is bound to the DL US Folder Redirection group, which has all global US department security groups as members. Anything saved will automatically be saved on the TASAH-File server in the Users share under the user's account name. Laptops will use loopback processing to ignore this policy when the users are working on their laptops and have file synchronization active.

Since Group Policy Objects are powerful, complicated, and have the potential to affect many users with a single mistake, it is wise to keep a log (spreadsheet, table, etc.) of all GPOs created, why they were created, who authorized them, and who tested their configuration settings. Figure 10-25 is a sample page from the log created for TASAH.com.

Much of the detailed information can be easily extracted from the GPO itself as needed, but the general information should be kept in a log so that system administrators can verify and validate GPO settings and the impact of additional GPOs as needed. There should be a clear and specific process in place for creating and deploying GPOs that should follow an authorization and testing process (documented in the log). Any changes, deletions, or additions should follow the same process.

Tasah.com Authorized Group Policy Objects

GPO	Location/OU	Primary Association	Description	LoopBack?	Default Settings?	Enforced	Disabled Configuration Settings	Authorized By	Tested By
Default Domain Policy	Root	Authenticated Users	Root domain security policy for account and password settings	No	Yes	Yes	None	Eric	Alice
Default Domain Controller Policy	Domain Controllers	Authenticated Users	Default domain controller configuration settings	No	Yes	Yes	None	Eric	Bob
US Folder Redirection Policy	Domain Users	DL US Folder Redirection	Redirects all user data to the file server (\\TASAH-FileServer\Users\%username%)	No	No	No	Computer Configuration	Eric	Alice
TASAH Global User Security Policy	Domain Users	Authenticated Users	Custom account configuration settings in support of the current SLA	No	No	Yes	Computer Configuration	Eric	Alice
Visitor Security Policy	Domain Users	G US Visitors	Custom account configuration settings in support visitors using the wireless network	No	No	Yes	Computer Configuration	Eric	Bob
US Intranet Default Settings	Domain Users	Authenticated Users	Default intranet portal settings with security	No	No	No	Computer Configuration	Eric	Bob
US High Resolution Printer Access	Domain Users	DL US High Resolution Printer Access Pool	Authorizes and binds high resolution printers to global user groups that are members of the DL US High Resolution Printer Access Pool group	No	No	No	Computer Configuration	Eric	Bob
TASAH Workstation Security Policy	Domain Workstations	Authenticated Users	Sets the default physical security policy settings for all desktop computers in the TASAH root	No	No	Yes	User Configuration	Alice	Bob
US Default Printer Pool	Domain Workstations,	DL US Default Printer Pool	Binds all US based available "general use" printers to desktops and laptops in the TASAH root	No	No	Yes	User Configuration	Alice	Bob
US WSUS Workstation Configuration Policy	Domain Workstations	Authenticated Users	Configures all US Desktop Computers to access and deploy system updates, patches and hotfixes from the TASAH-WSUS server	No	No	Yes	User Configuration	Bob	Alice
US WSUS Laptop Configuration Policy	Domain Laptops	Authenticated Users	Configures all US laptop Computers to access and deploy system updates, patches and hotfixes from the TASAH-WSUS server	No	No	Yes	User Configuration	Bob	Alice
US WSUS Exchange Server Settings	Member Servers	G US Exchange Servers	Configures all exchange servers to access TASAH-WSUS, bind with the WSUS Exchange container and deploy all authorized patches, hotfixes and	No	No	Yes	User Configuration	Alice	Bob
US WSUS Intranet Server Configuration	Member Servers	G US Intranet Servers	Configures all Intranet servers to access TASAH-WSUS, bind with the WSUS Intranet container and deploy all authorized patches, hotfixes and updates.	No	No	Yes	User Configuration	Alice	Bob
US WSUS W2K8R2 Member Servers	Member Servers	G US W2K8R2 Member Servers	Configures all General Purpose Windows 2008 R2 servers to access TASAH-WSUS, bind with the WSUS W2K8R2 container and deploy all authorized patches, hotfixes and updates.	No	No	Yes	User Configuration	Alice	Bob

Figure 10-26. *Group policy object Log*

For the TASAH.com root domain, all basic applications, antivirus clients, and security settings (including Windows Update Services—WSUS) will be managed by GPOs. If the organization outgrows the ability to deploy applications via GPO, then they can easily move toward Microsoft's SCCM (System Center Configurations Manager) or any of the other large-scale application deployment products (such as Symantec's Altiris[10]).

In any event, it's very important to maintain the GPO log, not only to document GPO deployment, but also to ensure the GPO deployment process is being followed. Finding out that there are unauthorized GPOs out there can be more than just embarrassing.

Delegating Authority

The two main reasons for creating OUs are for the deployment of GPOs and the delegation of authority. The OU structure in TASAH.com also separates security groups which is more for organization purposes, to help find group types more efficiently. Delegating authority allows user groups that are not members of special

---

[10]http://www.symantec.com/business/deployment-solution

groups (such as Domain Administrators, Account Managers, or any of the special groups found in the Users and Builtin containers created when installing Active Directory) to manage select objects in Active Directory.

The old saying "too many cooks in the kitchen" is relevant to administrating Active Directory. Giving everyone in the IT department Domain Admin permissions can quickly lead to chaos. In small to medium sized domains, two domain administrators is plenty. Enterprise Admins, Account Operators, etc. being special groups, need to be doled out sparingly, if at all. This leads to the value of authoritative delegation. Instead of using special groups for everyone in IT support, you should delegate the exact authority required to perform a specific role. This is not the easy way to grant permissions, but it is the most effective to ensure that members are able to do their jobs but won't accidentally do something they are not authorized to do.

Before setting up delegation, you will need to set the view in the Active Directory Users and Computers management console to display Advanced Features (see Figure 10-27).

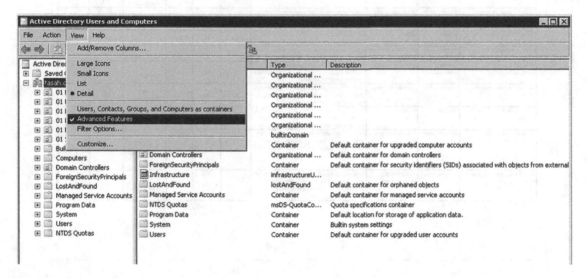

Figure 10-27. *Advanced Features view option*

Most of delegating authority is provisioning access to containers and OUs. Since it is important to ensure that new workstations and servers do not end up in the "computers" container, it becomes necessary to limit access to that container. This is done through the Properties option of the container (see Figure 10-28).

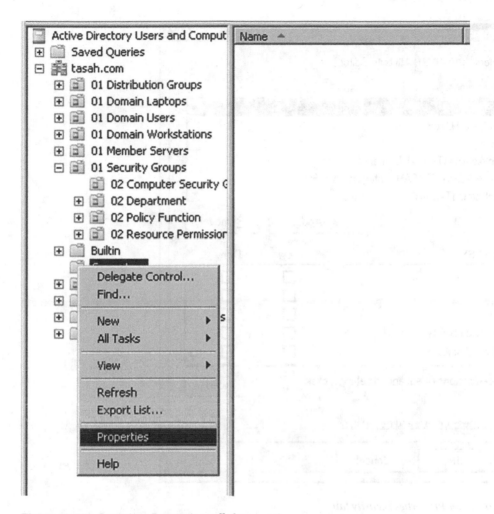

Figure 10-28. Container Properties pull-down option

Within the Security tab of the computer's container's properties dialog box, locate and remove the Authenticated Users group (Figure 10-29).

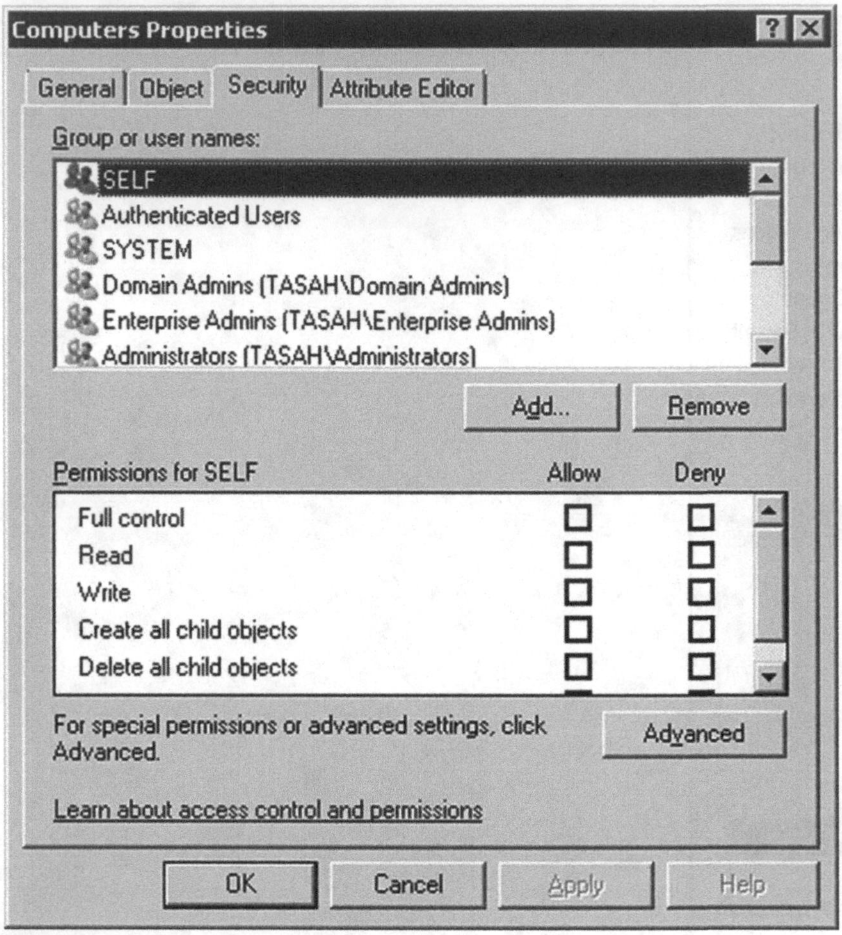

Figure 10-29. *Computer Properties Security tab*

By removing the Authenticated Users group, you limit who can create computer accounts in Active Directory to only those who are members of the special groups (such as Domain Admins, Account Operators, etc.) or those who are given delegated authority to create computer accounts. The default in Active Directory is to allow Authenticated Users to add their workstation to the domain—this removes that default setting.

Within the same pull-down menu, the first option is Delegate Control (see Figure 10-30).

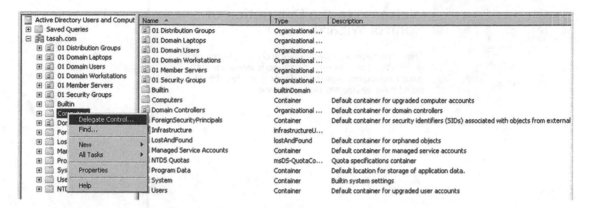

Figure 10-30. *Delegation option*

As an example, the G US Service Desk global group will be granted appropriate permissions to manage user accounts and reset or disable computer accounts. This group may also need Exchange account management permissions as well as access to some GPOs. If you were to give this group Account Operators permissions, you might not provide them with all of the permissions they need (or maybe too much). If you set up proper delegation (and test permissions thoroughly), you can ensure that the Service Desk permissions reflect the Service Desk role. There are three OUs that will require delegation for the Service Desk:

1. Domain Users

2. Domain Workstations

3. Domain Laptops

Delegation is performed using the Delegation Control wizard. You can also use the permissions/security tab options, but that can be complicated. Right-click on the OU you wish to delegate and select Delegate Control.

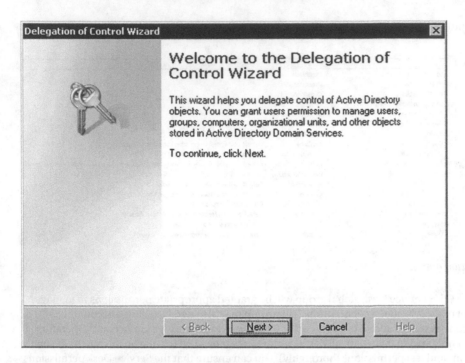

Figure 10-31. *Delegation Control wizard*

Add the G US Service Desk security group to the Delegation Group list.

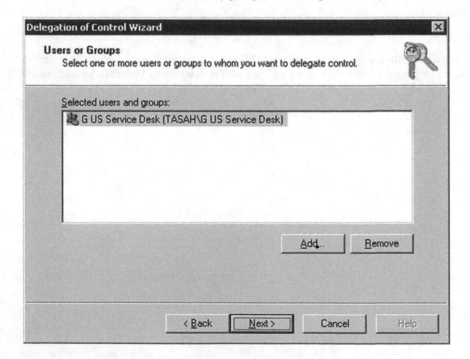

Figure 10-32. *Delegation group list*

Select the permissions you wish to grant to the group (see Figure 10-33). These permissions can be detailed further by selecting the Create a Custom Task to Delegate radio button. However, when selecting the Create a Custom Task to Delegate, you should test your custom task permissions completely—it is easy to either give too much permission or not enough. The best practice is to use the pre-designed "common" task options.

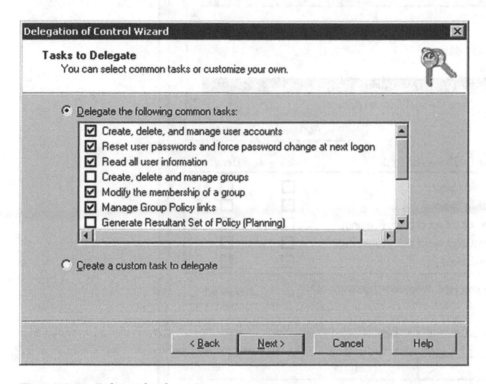

Figure 10-33. Delegated tasks

Once you've completed and exited the Delegation Control wizard, you can verify your work by going to the properties/security tab of the OU.

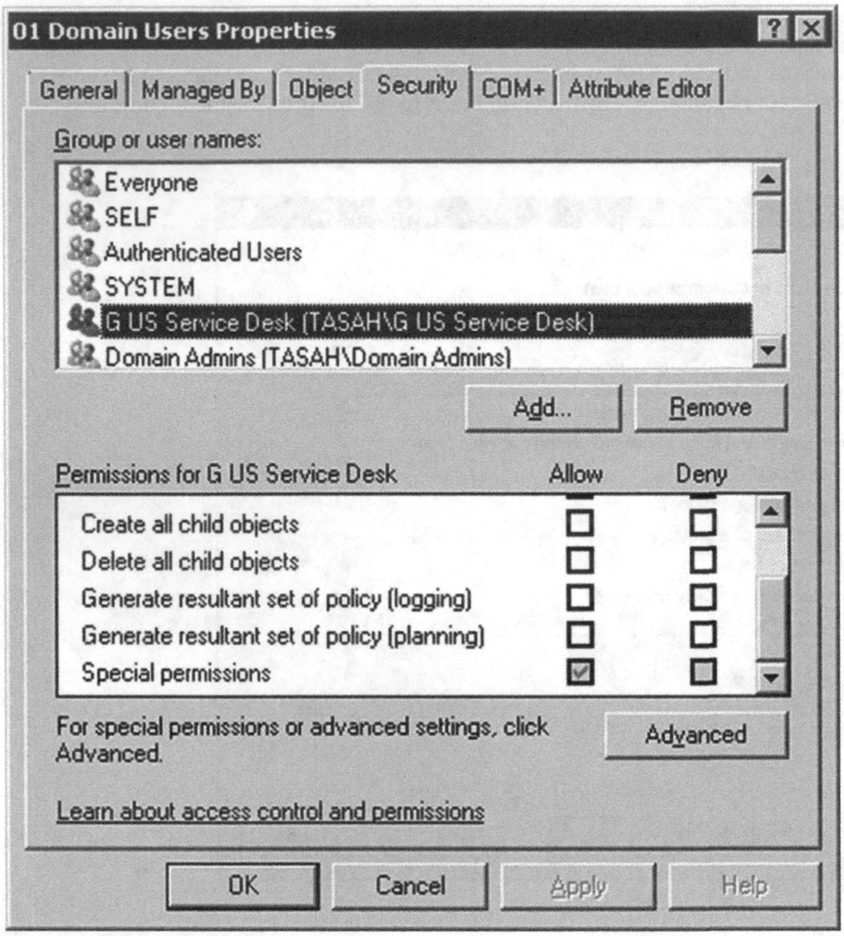

Figure 10-34. *Delegation Control permissions verification*

All delegated permissions are special permissions found in the OU security properties. If you expand the permissions view by clicking on the Advanced button, you will see all of the special permissions granted to the delegate authority group.

You would repeat this process for each OU to be granted delegated authority (Domain Workstations and Domain Laptops). As other security groups require delegated authority, you would first assess the requirements, plan the delegation process, and perform the delegation control wizard setup. It is also important to document all delegation activities to ensure that you have a record of any modifications to permissions granted in the domain.

Summary

A directory service offers the fundamental toolset for managing user and computer account across the forest. It helps manage support permissions through delegation and special security groups. Keeping things simple through binding permissions by group (and not individually) helps make administration uniform and practical. Mapping out roles based on SLA requirements and organizational structure helps make IT practices follow business strategy. Using account templates helps ensure that everyone gets what they need to do their job and leaves little confusion during the troubleshooting process. Keeping the OU tree structure limited to three tiers deep ensures that GPOs will act as they are intended.

Using a standardized naming convention promotes better housekeeping practices and makes it much easier to understand where the computers are and who is using them. Documenting the group associations makes it easier to maintain and expand domain architecture. Numbering the depth of each OU ensures that you understand how deep objects are within the tree structure.

Limiting the permissions granted to specific groups reduces the overall potential for accidental misconfiguration and possible mischief. Promoting standardized processes for making modifications (incorporating an authorization and testing procedure) helps limit blame and/or confusion as to who and why changes were made. Establishing complicated passwords with required password change cycling helps promote security.

The key is to keep things simple. Don't make things more complicated than they already are, and document any and all changes so that there is an audit trail that can be used to resolve issues that come up when something goes wrong. Keep paper copies of all of the documents so that you can refer to them when the system is unavailable. Limit the number of GPOs, OUs, and delegation points. Always plan as if you have a larger network so that as the domain grows you are ready to support it.

CHAPTER 11

■ ■ ■

DNS, DHCP, IPv4, and IPv6

DNS

DNS[1] is one of the three main pillars supporting domain services (DNS, Kerberos,[2] and LDAP[3]). Inside the local network, DNS acts to translate IP addresses into hostnames and vice versa. Fundamental to the Internet, DNS also translates domain names into IP addresses. There is a long history of DNS-related RFCs[4] that document the many changes and adaptions DNS has undergone since its conception. Current DNS supports both IPv4 and IPv6. Basically, DNS is a network of databases established to resolve IP addresses and spans the world supporting all Internet traffic.

To resolve hostnames or domain names into IP addresses, DNS uses *forward* lookup zones. To resolve IP addresses into host or domain names DNS uses *reverse* lookup zones. A "zone" is a contiguous portion of DNS name space. These zones consist of records:

- A records are host records in IPv4.

- AAAA records are host records in IPv6.

- Pointers records (PTR) resolve an IP address into a hostname.

- CName is an alias used to give an IP address multiple names.

- MX record is a mail exchange record to quickly locate mail servers.

- SRV records are service records used by Active Directory to quickly locate directory services through DNS.

Active Directory integrates DNS zones and stores its data in the application partition of the NTDS.dit file. Because Active Directory is a multimode model, all DNS servers are able to read and write DNS entries. DNS zones are usually represented using circles instead of the domain triangles used in Active Directory diagramming (see Figure 11-1). The top-level (or ROOT) DNS zone is represented by a . and consists of many DNS servers supporting a host of DNS databases. It is the interaction between DNS databases that allows for hostnames to be resolved outside their respective zones.

---

[1]http://www.webopedia.com/TERM/D/DNS.html
[2]http://mit.edu/kerberos/
[3]http://www.webopedia.com/TERM/L/LDAP.html
[4]http://cunde.org/doc/rfc/

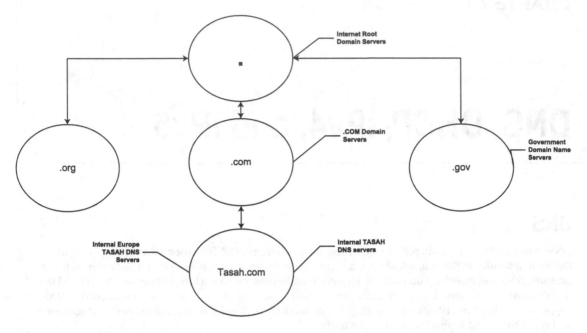

***Figure 11-1.** Simple DNS zone tree*

IXER (incremental zone transfer) is the primary to secondary DNS replication found in Windows 2000 and newer (as well as UNIX). This replaced the AXFR zone transfer in Windows NT, which was a single point of failure. Both are considered standard zones and use a file based DNS.

Figure 11-2 shows where the DNS database file is located on the Windows 2008 R2/ 2012/2016 DNS server.

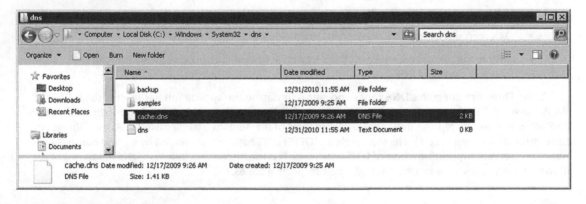

***Figure 11-2.** DNS file location*

The example in Figure 11-3 shows Microsoft's DNS Manager and all of the records represented have static addresses. As noted in earlier chapters, DHCP will be used for guest laptops and the remote deployment of workstation operating systems. The records are using traditional IPv4 but they can easily deploy IPv6 as well. The main benefit to using IPv4 is the relative ease at understanding the IP addresses. Since these are CIDR addresses, they are not routable and must use NAT to translate their IP addresses to access the public Internet.

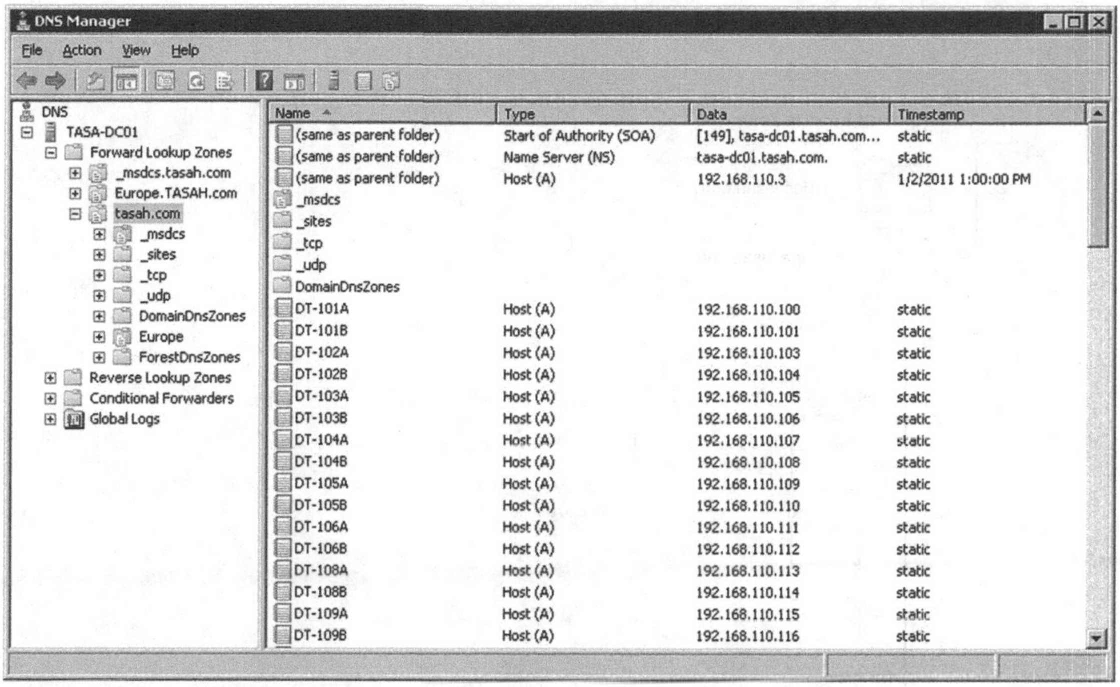

Figure 11-3. *Tasah.com forward lookup zone*

Simply looking at the DNS Manager, you can quickly tell where the hosts are located (DT-101A is in room 101 and connected to the wall socket 101A). This allows the ability to physically trace the network connection all the way back to the network switch port. Since servers are directly connected to the switch (not requiring a wall port), they are labeled by service function (i.e., tasah-DHCP, tasah-DC01, etc.). Printers are named PRN-hallway-port number. In effect, the IP hostnames either reflect their location or service association.

While Microsoft Active Directory comes with its own DNS service, that does not mean you have to use it. There are far more mature versions of DNS (Lucent VitalQIP[5]), which provides large-scale DNS/DHCP integration. Major organizations throughout the world depend on non-Microsoft DNS products to keep their organization's directory services stable. While it is not easy to get it going, it can be a powerful tool for managing large-scale integration. It should be noted that the UNIX DNS BIND version to integrate with Windows 2008 R2 Active Directory should be 8.1.2 or later. If you use UNIX DNS, you may have to create all srv records and their supporting lookup zones (_msdcs, _sites, _tcp, and _udp) manually.

---

[5]http://enterprise.alcatel-lucent.com/?product=VitalQIP&page=features

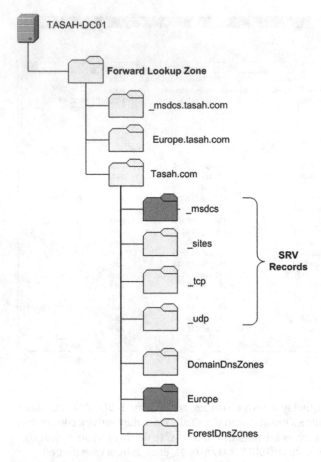

Figure 11-4. *SRV record locations in DNS*

In the srv records, you can set priority for domain controllers and other domain services. You set this through the Priority option in the srv properties dialog box.

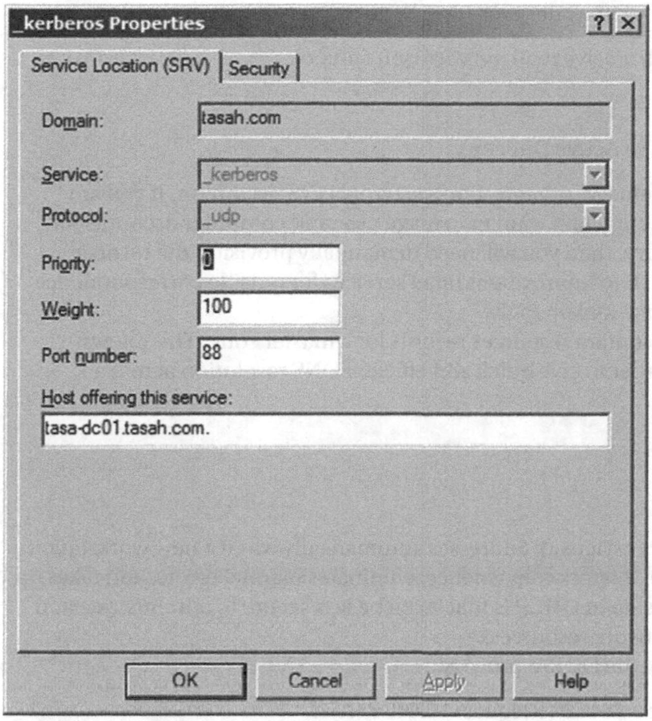

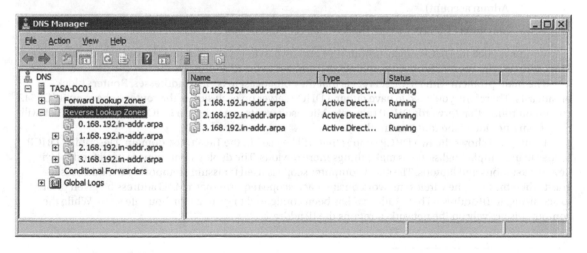

Figure 11-5. *Kerberos SRV Properties dialog box*

In UNIX DNS, you must set the srv priority manually.

Reverse lookup zones are listed by their reverse IP address scope. You create a reverse lookup zone for each of the subnets within your organization.

Figure 11-6. *Reverse lookup zones*

Some of the benefits of creating reverse lookup zones are:

- Increased performance with send/receive mail for Microsoft Outlook

- Binding classless[6] subnets

- Adding Apple's OSX workstations to Active Directory[7]

In most cases, a reverse lookup table benefits an organization's external DNS resolution. If you are adding Apple OSX workstations to Active Directory and want to manage user and computer accounts for non-Microsoft systems through Active Directory, then you will need to manually provision the reverse lookup table with the OSX A records. If you wish to improve sendmail services for outside correspondence, you will need to add an MX record in the reverse lookup table.

There is also the use of "stub" zones that contain resources records for a master zone. This allows organizations to bind multiple DNS sites together to give quick and efficient DNS resolution across a seemingly fractured organization.

DHCP

Dynamic Host Configuration Protocol (DHCP) assigns IP addresses automatically when a new workstation, server, printer, etc. is registered in the domain. It offers convenience, eliminates manual errors, and takes up less time to maintain DNS records. The downside to DHCP is that it can be less secure to administrate and could allow unauthorized clients to access network resources.

In DHCP, a client gets an address through the DORA[8] process:

- DHCP (D)iscover > DHCP (O)ffer > DHCP (R)equest > DHCP (A)ck

The DHCP server must have the following in Windows 2008 R2:

1. A static address.

2. The DHCP server role installed.

3. DHCP must be authorized, if you use Active Directory (using the Enterprise Admin account).

4. You must establish a scope (with exclusion IP addresses and reservations).

Windows 2008 R2 DHCP supports both IPv4 and IPv6. When a client requests an address it presents a MAC address[9] (for reservations you map the MAC address to the IP address).

The main problem with DHCP servers is that they broadcast to issue IP addresses. Routers block broadcasts. Therefore, you need to have either a DHCP server on each side of the router or have an RFC 1542 compliant router that forwards DHCP requests. Microsoft wants you to have a DHCP relay agent (DHCP will relay from one side of the router to another).

Figure 11-7 shows the two DHCP scopes that will be used in the Tasah.com domain. Describing DHCP scopes using simple English helps make things more obvious. The deployment scope is used for deploying new workstations and laptops. The guest computer scope is used for issuing temporary IP addresses to guest while they use the wireless network onsite. Each scope requires that a MAC address be given prior to acquiring an IP address. That IP address has been configured to grant a four-hour life span. While the computer is actively on the network, it retains the IP address.

---

[6]http://www.ralphb.net/IPSubnet/cidr.html

[7]http://forums.appleinsider.com/archive/index.php/t-48772.html

[8]http://www.scribd.com/doc/24445850/DORA-Process-in-DHCP-DHCP-D-Iscover-DHCP-O-Ffer

[9]http://searchnetworking.techtarget.com/definition/MAC-address

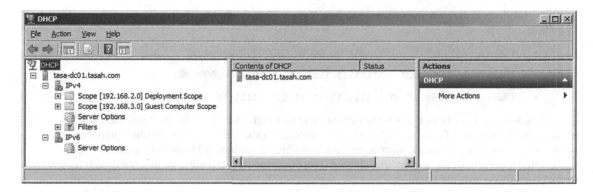

Figure 11-7. *DHCP management console*

The deployment scope is active only when workstations are being prepped through the Windows Deployment Service. The guest scope is manually configured when guests request and receive access authority. If authority is not granted, the DHCP scope does not grant the IP address for access.

The guest scope is also configured to only access the Internet. The deployment scope is only authorized to access the Windows Deployment Server and does not add the workstation to the domain. Both DHCP scopes are viewed as potential risks to the internal network because they are not controlled by the security GPOs that would normally install antivirus, apply password settings, and redirect user data to secured file systems. By configuring DHCP this way, you get the benefits of remote deployment for workstation management and you limit guest access to only external network resources. You may also wish to add a printer to the guest network so that guests can print without being part of the domain.

IPv4 and IPv6

Internet Protocol version four (IPv4) is a system of addresses used to identify devices on a network. It dates back to 1981 and is first described in RFC 791. To date, it is the most widely used Internet layer protocol. IPv4 is a 32-bit addressing space.

Routable IP address schemes are leased through your ISP based on the business package selected. Internal non-routable IP addresses can be generated by the IT department as needed.

There are three types of IPv4 network addresses:

- Class A—Large - 16,000,000+ computers

- Class B—Medium - 65,536 computers

- Class C—Small - 254 computers

The subnet mask is used to limit the search for hosts by the set of numbers assigned to a particular IP class.

Address Class	Dotted Decimal Notation
A (/8 prefixes)	1.nnn.nnn.nnn through 126.nnn.nnn.nnn
B (/16 prefixes)	128.0.nnn.nnn through 191.255.nnn.nnn
C (/24 prefixes)	192.0.0.nnn through 223.255.255.255

An IP address is divided into four octets[10] (nnn.nnn.nnn.nnn), whereas the network number is defined by a class:

- Class A - 255.0.0.0 - 11111111.00000000.00000000.00000000

- Class B - 255.255.0.0 - 11111111.11111111.00000000.00000000

- Class C - 255.255.255.0 - 11111111.11111111.11111111.00000000

Class A networks (where 1- 128 is the network and nnn.nnn.1 would be the host number) will search a larger number of computers (16,000,000+) to locate a specific computer. Further, there can be more computers in that network unaccounted for (possibly not authorized to be part of that network). Class A networks are usually broken into smaller (more manageable) networks so that the search time is decreased—this is covered later.

Class B networks (where 128.nnn - 191.nnn would be the network number and nnn.nn1 would be the host number) will search a smaller number of computers (65,000) to locate a specific computer. This is still a large number of IP addresses but more manageable. This environment would be found in branches of larger networks or medium size businesses.

Class C networks (where 192.nnn.nnn - 223.nnn.nnn would be the network number and nn1 would be the host number) will search an even smaller number of computers (254) to find a specific computer on the network. Currently we are using a Class C license (192.168.1.n).

Supernet

The key is to minimize the search to a reasonable size (allowing for growth of the business) so that computers can communicate with each other in the quickest manner. You can reduce the search path even smaller by dividing the class C network into a supernet.[11]

In a class C license the subnet mask would normally be 255.255.255.0 (leaving the search scope to 254 possible computers in the local network). If you set the subnet mask to 255.255.255.192 you limit the search scope to *64* hosts, which increases network performance and reduces the number of local IP addresses. If you set the DHCP scope (limiting the amount of dynamic IP addresses to 40, which is the number of possible hosts' ports available on the switch), you can use the rest of the IP addresses in the subnet for static addresses.

Subnet range—192.168.1.1 - 192.168.1.64 (IP addresses in the local network)

Static addresses—192.168.1.1 - 192.168.1.22 (IP addresses for servers, printers, and the router)

Dynamic addresses—192.168.1.23 - 192.168.1.64 (IP addresses for workstations on the network)

---

[10]In computers, an octet (from the Latin octo or "eight") is a sequence of eight bits. An octet is thus an eight-bit byte. Since a byte is not eight bits in all computer systems, octet provides a non-ambiguous term.

[11]Supernetting, also called Classless Inter-Domain Routing (CIDR), is a way to aggregate multiple Internet addresses of the same class. The original Internet Protocol (IP) defines IP addresses in four major classes of address structure, Classes A through D. Each class allocates one portion of the 32-bit Internet address format to a network address and the remaining portion to the specific host machines in the network. Using supernetting, the network address 192.168.2.0/24 and an adjacent address 192.168.3.0/24 can be merged into 192.168.2.0/23. The 23 at the end of the address says that the first 23 bits are the network part of the address, leaving the remaining nine bits for specific host addresses. Supernetting is most often used to combine Class C network addresses and is the basis for most routing protocols currently used on the Internet.

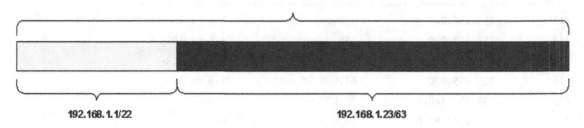

Figure 11-8. *Example of supernetting*

There are four supernets in this class C subnet:

192.168.1.1/64 (used by our network)

192.168.1.65/128 (unused)

192.168.1.128/192 (unused)

192.168.1.193/254 (unused)

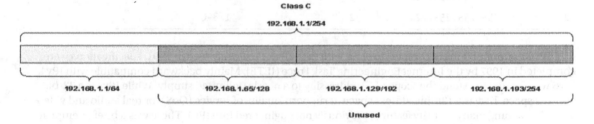

Figure 11-9. *Supernet map*

In the tasah.com network, the supernet used is inclusive to bind three class C subnets together:

- 192.168.0.1 – 192.168.3.254

This provides 1016 internal IPv4 non-routable IP addresses for the local area network. The ability to reduce or expand the network subnet mask is an important tool in fine-tuning network performance.

Supernet Cheat Sheet

CIDR Prefix Length	Dotted Decimal	Number of Individual Addresses	Number of Classful Networks
/13	255.248.0.0	512,000	8-B or 2048-C
/14	255.252.0.0	256,000	4-B or 1024-C
/15	255.254.0.0	128,000	2-B or 512-C
/16	255.255.0.0	64,000	1-B or 256-C
/17	255.255.128.0	32,000	128-C
/18	255.255.192.0	16,000	64-C
/19	255.255.224.0	8,000	32-C
/20	255.255.240.0	4,000	16-C
/21	255.255.248.0	2,000	8-C
/22	255.255.252.0	1,00	4-C
/23	255.255.254.0	512	2-C
/24	255.255.255.0	256	1-C
/25	255.255.255.128	128	½-C
/26	255.255.255.192	64	¼-C
/27	255.255.255.224	32	1/8-C

IPv6 is more a bit more complex to work with than IPv4. First conceived in 1991, specifications were completed in 1997 by the Internet Engineering Task Force (IETF). Mainly backward compatible with IPv4, IPv6 was created to extend the scope of IP addressing to a nearly unlimited supply. While IPv4 is a 32-bit address space, IPv6 is a 128-bit address space. It supports quality of service (QoS) for real audio and video as well as adding many security features previously not engineered into IPv4. There was a brief attempt at creating IPv5 but its limited structure quickly lost interest.

The new IPv6 address space support 2^{128} (about 3.4×10^{38}) addresses, which eliminates the need for NAT (which allowed non-routable IP addresses to use a proxy routable IP address in communicating across the Internet). For many government agencies, IPv6 addresses the potential security issue that allows criminals and hackers to attack data traffic across the Internet.

Some of the new features found in IPv6 are:

- Stateless Address Auto-configuration (SLAAC)[12]

- Network security integrated into the design of the architecture[13]

- IPsec as a fundamental interoperability requirement[14]

---

[12]http://www.openwall.com/presentations/IPv6/img36.html;

[13]Penny Hermann-Seton GIAC GSEC Practical Assignment b1.4 – SANS Institute 2002: http://www.sans.org/reading_room/whitepapers/protocols/security-features-ipv6_380

[14]Steve Friedl's Unixwiz.net tech tip: http://unixwiz.net/techtips/iguide-ipsec.html

The first IPv6 RFC was RFC 1883,[15] which was published in 1995. RFC 3513[16] directly specifies the IPv6 addressing syntax. Since IPv4 and IPv6 will be deployed together for some time, there has been a slow movement by some IT organizations to fully embrace the new standard.

There are three types of IPv6 addresses:

- Unicast—Associates a single interface in the scope of the type of address (RFC 2373).

- Multicast—Identifies zero or more interfaces and delivers packets to all interfaces identified by the address.

- Anycast—Identifies multiple interfaces.

Some common reserve ranges are:

- Fe80:: (APIPA[17] address with the 169.254.nnn.nnn equivalent)

- Fc00::/7 (Private non-routable addresses equal to the 10.0.0.0/172.16.0.0/192.168.0.0 CIDR addresses)

- 2001:db8 (Display address for illustrations)

- ::1 (Loopback address)

Subnetting for IPv6 is a two-step process:

1. Determine the number of bits to be used for subnetting.

2. Enumerate the new subnet address prefix.

Subnetting Bits a

Subnetting IPv6 use techniques to divide the 16-bit subnet ID field for a range of 48-bit global or unique local address prefix. Most system administrators have come to understand and quickly apply IPv4 subnetting and supernetting. Understanding IPv6 subnetting is just as difficult as it was in the beginning when learning IPv4 subnetting. Much like you would subnet IPv4, the number of bits that you allocate

---

[15]The first RFC for IPv6: http://tools.ietf.org/html/rfc1883
[16]Address syntax: http://tools.ietf.org/html/rfc3513
[17]Automatic private internet protocol addressing: http://msdn.microsoft.com/en-us/library/aa505918.aspx

to a subnet prefix (aka, the network address) determines how many hosts exist in that subnet. There is a calculation used to construct subnet regions:

$$f + s + r = Subnet\ Prefix$$

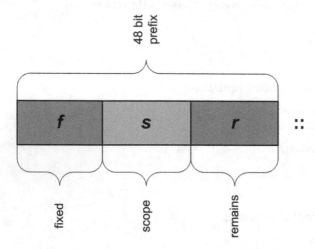

Figure 11-10. *Subnet prefix*

f (number of bits fixed by the previous level of the hierarchy) + s (the number of bits used for subnetting at the current level) + r (the number of bits remaining for the next level down in the hierarchy) = *Subnet Prefix.*

Enumerating Subnetted Prefixes

f (the number of bits fixed in the prefix) = m (the prefix length of a prefix being subnetted) – the 48-bit global address prefix.

$f = m - 48$

n is the number of address prefixes you will obtain

$n = 2^s$

i is the incremental value between each successive subnet

$i = 2^{16-(f+s)}$

p is the prefix length of the new subnet address prefixes

$p = m + s$

As you can see, calculating subnets can be extremely complex. You can use a subnet calculator[18] (created by Rhys Koedijk from the Wellington Institute of Technology) on the Internet to help get the answers more quickly.

All in all, IPv6 is here to stay. It will work side by side with IPv4 for the foreseeable future. It will take time to fully understand but the potential for improving and expanding the IP scope/features is worth the effort. UNIX, Microsoft Windows, and Apple OSX all support IPv6 and integrate both IPv4 and IPv6 side by side by default.

RFC 4291[19] details the implementation of IPv6 and provides valuable information on why it was implemented. It also covers the architecture and expanded scope of IPv6. While most network users will never really need to learn and understand how best to use IPv6, system administrators will become more familiar with its architecture and implementation as they roll out servers and networked devices across cloud computing and large-scale customized networking environments.

Summary

DNS, DHCP, and IPv4/6 all play an essential role in networking systems, directories, and binding hosts throughout the world (both on and off the Internet). They are complex services and protocols that can easily get out of hand if not managed properly. And if they begin to fail, so does directory services and Internetworking operability.

DNS is not something to put in place and then leave alone. You must spend time each month to evaluate the performance and health of your DNS servers and services.

DHCP, while used minimally in this book, is widely used everywhere else (especially with IPv6). It is the cornerstone to Microsoft's Window Deployment Services, and provides extensive functionality for remotely managing configuration of network services to hosts in a local area network. There should always be two DHCP severs for redundancy (as should be for all essential services), but these servers should augment each other and not overlap.

Understanding both IP versions is a must. If you cannot troubleshoot network IP traffic, you cannot ensure connectivity between nodes. Building an understandable IP address scope and binding your hostnames to the network wall ports will help you to troubleshoot physical connection issues more quickly and effectively. If also helps you better understand how your network is built.

---

[18]http://www.subnetonline.com/pages/subnet-calculators/ipv6-subnet-calculator.php
[19]https://tools.ietf.org/html/rfc4291

CHAPTER 12

■ ■ ■

Deploying Workstations and Printers

There are a host of ways to deploy workstations and printers. But there are things you need to do before that. Each box you open should be inventoried, examined for defects, and prepped for deployment. Any books, CDs, DVDs, or other materials should be set aside for later storage. You need to save a few shipping boxes in case you need them to RMA[1] defective equipment.

Each workstation and laptop should be examined internally to see if there are any loose parts prior to powering up. Perform a 24-hour burn in using a diagnostics[2] program that automatically tests basic components. Update BIOS versions to the latest revision to ensure that the hardware you're deploying is up to date.

Each system should also be registered on the vendor web site so that you get automatic notifications regarding BIOS updates, hotfixes, and warrantee information. There should be generic e-mail accounts made for laptops, workstations, printers, servers, etc. These e-mail accounts should be accessible to all of the IT staff responsible for managing the hardware. These e-mail accounts should never be personally associated with any individual. The following would be created for the tasah.com network:

- workstations@tasah.com

- laptops@tasah.com

- Servers@tasah.com

- printers@tasah.com

- switches@tasah.com

- routers@tasah.com

These mailboxes would be shared, thereby allowing each of the IT staff to view, extract, and manage notifications.

Download any updates, make physical copies, and post those copies in the software library.

---

[1]RMA stands for Return Merchandise Authorization (required by a vendor when returning defective products).
[2]http://www.pc-diagnostics.com/

Figure 12-1 is a basic pre-deployment flowchart. While this process does not completely ensure that the hardware you deploy will be 100 percent, it eliminates the obvious system failures and documents hardware readiness. You also ensure that you have the right BIOS versions, most up-to-date patches and hotfixes, and that you are notified by the vendor of any known bugs or issues associated with the hardware you are deploying.

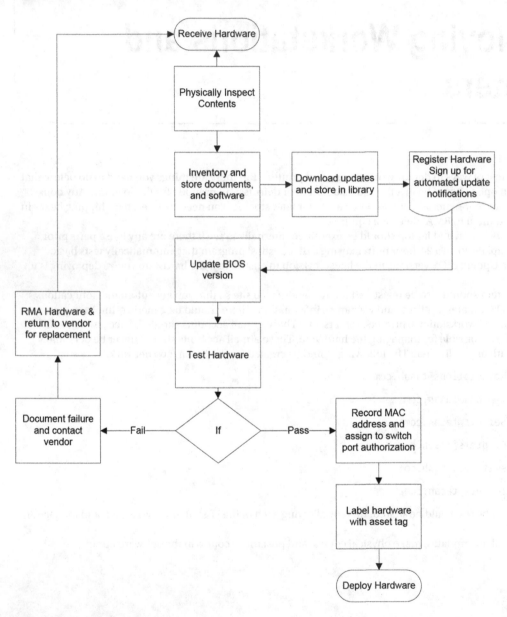

Figure 12-1. *Hardware pre-deployment process*

You also lock down the network switch ports. This ensures that only authorized hardware is plugged into the physical network. Locking down laptop access via MAC addresses ensures that only authorized laptops can use the wireless LAN. In both cases, you ensure that the IP addresses assigned to each system are bound by name (and that workstations are also tied directly into the physical port number).

Deploying Workstations and Laptops

Workstations

It is always easier to deploy workstations in quantity when they are made with physically identical hardware. That is not often the case in organizations that buy workstations on a continual basis. You can get batches of workstations that have the same components but you must be careful. Most consumer quality systems are built with similar components but may not be completely identical. Business quality systems are specifically built to be as identical as possible so that when they are deployed in mass they can be provisioned equally.

As time goes on, one batch of systems (even with the same model number) may have components that come from different manufacturers. While the component model number may be exactly what is advertised, the OEM manufacturer may be change due to cost savings. An example is when a vendor says that they install a NVIDIA 9800 GTX video card in every system of a given model but in reality, they install a MSI[3] OEM product in one batch and a Sparkle[4] OEM product in another batch. These two products require different video drivers and can make provisioning systems more difficult.

For every batch of systems deployed with different sets of components or OEM products inside, there have to be supporting drivers. The ability for system administrators to keep all of the unique provisioning data in order becomes more and more difficult as time goes on. It is therefore essential to keep the differences at a minimum and document specific components as best you can in the service desk inventory library so that when a trouble ticket is raised for any given piece of hardware, the service desk can quickly understand what they are dealing with. Many issues that crop up from hardware malfunctions come from wrong drivers being installed, and this can look very much like a bad or broken component.

To make deployment less complicated, system administrators must work hand in hand with their procurement staff to ensure that only business class systems are purchased, and that those business machines follow a standardized configuration. It is inevitable that batches of systems will have different components from previous purchases. It is best to limit the purchasing of system batches so as to minimize the variety of system versions out there and maintain the smallest possible OEM driver library.

Workstations can be deployed individually or in batches. They can use the software that came with them or have Enterprise-licensed software deployed later on. The difference between the two is important.

---

[3]http://us.msi.com/index.php?func=prodpage1&maincat_no=130
[4]http://www.sparkle.com.tw/

Out of the Box

Deploying computers out of the box is quick, easy, and ultimately unmanageable. Each computer purchased with an operating system comes with something called *bloatware*. These are unwanted applications that market products from the desktop. They take up space, promote software that may not be authorized by your organization, and consume resources that would be better used by authorized software. Getting rid of bloatware takes time and can cause the system to work less efficiently.

Each operating system out of the box has a unique user license that only applies to the workstation it came with. If you're a mom and pop operation, the cost of buying groups of licenses may force you to use these limited licenses. If you're an organization that has a substantial staffing, limited licenses will cost more than group licensing. When the system needs to be rebuilt, it takes longer to ring back online. Additionally, many out of the box operating systems come with low-risk spyware that is designed to benefit the vendor.

If the organization does pursue the out-of-the-box deployment model, it is imperative that the right version of operating system be purchased so that it can work in a business environment. Consumer versions of Windows (such as Windows 7 Home Premium) are not Active Directory compatible. They are not made to join the domain or work in an office environment where centralized account management exists. The organization needs to purchase directory compatible operating systems like Windows 7 Business Edition, Professional Edition, or the Ultimate edition. Depending on the office environment, each domain-compatible edition has its benefits and drawbacks.

As you can see from Figure 12-2, there are parallel processes that should be followed in order to deploy workstations straight from the box. Keeping track of all of the individual copies of software can be complicated and take up additional space. If the workstations are purchased in bundles with identical internal components, you should be able to keep one copy of restore disks for that bundle but it may be wise to talk to your vendor and verify that that is the case.

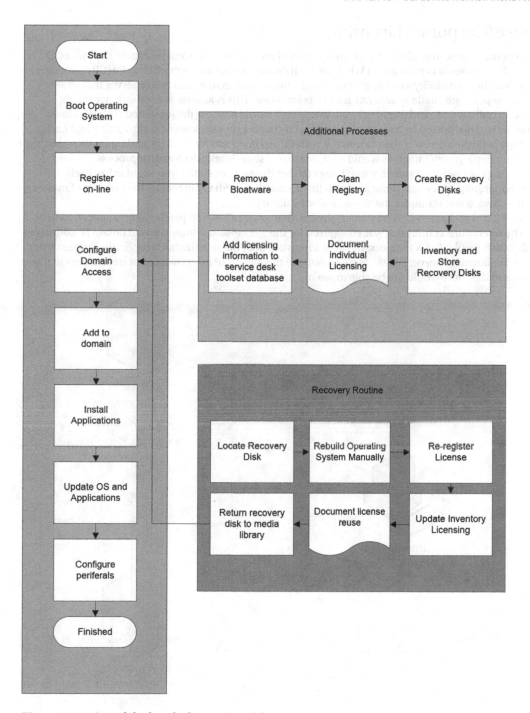

Figure 12-2. *Out-of-the-box deployment model*

In any event, the complication of maintaining individual workstation licenses increases dramatically with the number of workstations deployed. The recovery process becomes just as complicated.

Enterprise/Corporate Licensing

Enterprise (volume[5]) licensing allows you to build copies of the operating system that share the same CD Key. The installation media is posted on a Windows Distribution Server and accessed via DHCP client over the network. Another possibility to remotely deploying workstations is to use an image server that allows you the ability to push pre-made system images to workstations. This is known as a static image. Static images must be built, tested, and then deployed, whereas dynamic images (those pushed via a Windows Distribution Server) are posted on a server and updated through a process known as slipstreaming.[6] Each dynamic image is pushed down to the workstation with the updated service pack (or update) without having to build another deployment image, as would be the case in a static image deployment process.

By deploying the operating system via an image (either dynamic or static), you standardize each workstation's operating system and limit access to the installation media. You reduce the number of master copies of the software and minimize the master software library.

In Figure 12-3, a separate VLAN was established so that any workstation patched into a special switch (located in the operations center) that was configured for the 192.168.2.x subnet would obtain IP addresses from DHCP, which would direct the workstation to a network boot menu to install an operating system from the Windows Deployment Server (WDS). Systems outside this switch IP range would not have access to the WDS service and therefore would not be able to see it.

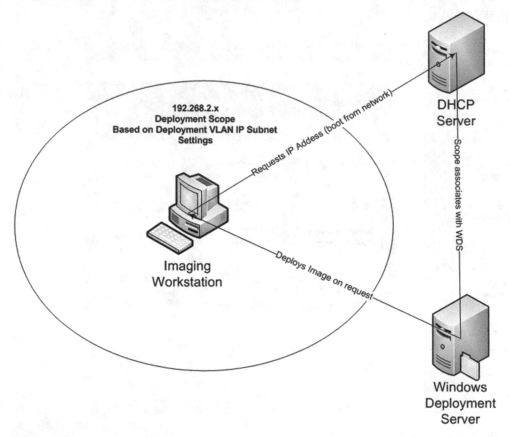

Figure 12-3. *Dynamic imaging strategy*

---

[5]http://www.microsoft.com/licensing/about-licensing/how-volume-licensing-works.aspx
[6]http://www.windowsnetworking.com/articles_tutorials/Slipstreaming-Windows-Service-Packs.html

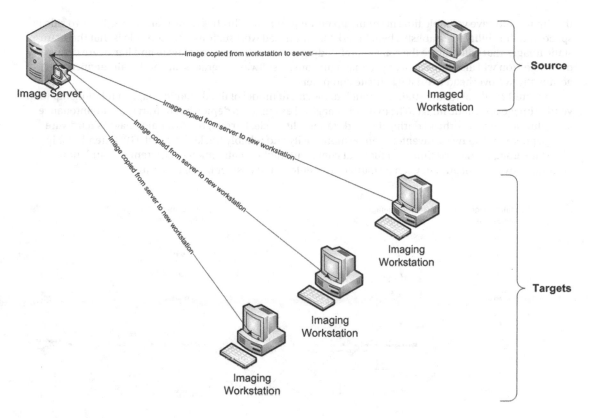

Figure 12-4. *Static image process*

The static imaging process can be done on a standalone network. It simply needs the source workstation, a server with imaging software, and target workstations. The imaging server can house and deploy multiple workstation images. You can even multicast images to groups of target workstations based on a scheduled task. But each image you deploy needs to be made. Every time you make an image you need to use a clean source workstation to build the image from. And every time you finish one image you must wipe the source workstation clean and start over again. All of this takes time, and it requires testing and verification to ensure that each image is error free.

Many organizations build complete static images (operating system, antivirus client, office application, etc.). These images take even longer to build, test, and deploy. Their main benefit is that you end up with an image that is tested and verified. The downside is that it becomes more difficult to upgrade and remove preinstalled software. It is also harder to perform an ad hoc inventory. And any software you push via group policies will have difficulty modifying pre-imaged software.

Trying to maintain operating systems and applications currently supported by the manufacturer is essential to minimizing overall cost. In other words, if your client software is past end of life, the upgrade path will increase in cost, complexity, and impact to business operations. Making sure that OS and application upgrades fall within the window of support decreases cost, increases security, and maintains interoperability with business partners.

Some organizations have chosen to have their vendors build workstation images with all of the predefined applications installed prior to having the workstations shipped. If your organization is large enough and has a working relationship with the vendor to do so, this could be a cost saving opportunity. It will still require your local IT department to build the image, but once built, the vendor would pre-deploy that image and save valuable time in setting up new equipment. This has its pros and cons. The pro side is speed and the ability to establish a benchmark for purchased workstations. The con side is that these are static images that will require the constant rebuilding of newer images as software and hardware changes over time. You will also have difficulty in managing onsite software upgrades and add maintenance and administrative overhead to existing on-site equipment.

Figure 12-5 displays the straight through deployment model of the dynamic image in relationship to the vendor image and static image. The dynamic image takes longer to deploy but requires less maintenance and administrative overhead during the workstation's lifecycle. Further, the dynamic image is hardware independent and software inventory can be more easily and reliably tracked through GPO membership. The static images take less time to deploy but come with higher maintenance requirements and more administrative overhead. They can be harder to inventory and costlier in the long run.

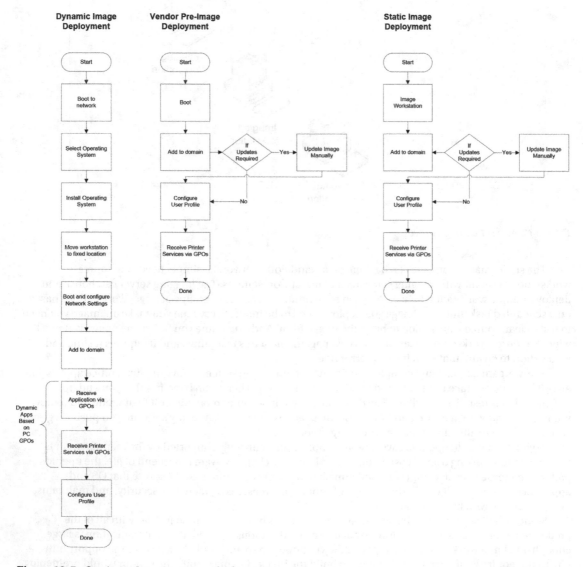

Figure 12-5. *Static vs. dynamic image deployment*

The deployment model chosen for the `tasah.com` network workstations is the dynamic imaging scenario using 64GB USB Flash memory sticks for the operating system. In doing so, each workstation comes without a hard drive. The USB Flash drives can be pre-installed on imaging workstations in the operations center prior to being installed into the production workstations. While the imaging is being performed in the operations center, network technicians can take the production workstation (without the boot device) to its destination and lock down the network port on the switch.

Once the USB Flash drive is ready, it can be inserted into the USB port on the production workstation and the system can be booted, added to the domain using the pre-assigned hostname and IP address, and then receive all of the security GPOs, application GPOs, etc. While this process may take an hour or more, it ensures that the workstation application base is centrally managed, self-repairing, and easily inventoried ad hoc. If the system fails at any time, the replacement process is the same for the USB Flash drive and there is no need to disassemble anything. In the evenings, staff can turn off their workstations, remove the USB drive, and lock it up. In the morning, staff can re-insert the USB drive and boot the system normally.

Laptops

Laptops can be built much the same way as workstations. They can be used straight from the box or imaged dynamically or statically. The administrative overhead is the same as that of workstations. But laptops must be protected differently than workstations. They are used during travel and can be lost or stolen. The data inside the hard drive is more easily susceptible to attack. This requires greater care in provisioning security measure and managing data.

Apple has engineered its laptops to be a bit more difficult to replace its hard drives, mainly to ensure that most of their customers will go to Apple certified support centers for servicing. While this ensures that the Apple laptop is professionally maintained, it makes in-house maintenance less desirable. Unlike Apples laptops, with almost all PC laptops, the hard drive is easy to remove and replace. Using a disk drive docking station,[7] you can image hard drives, reproduce laptop content, and prep new laptops for use. This makes PC laptops a bit more corporate friendly in terms of maintenance and administration.

Unlike workstations, laptops leave the confines of network security. The antivirus and update services should reflect that. Instead of pointing the antivirus client to the in-house antivirus server, it is more reliable to update that service through the vendor's support sites. This does make managing each laptop a bit more difficult, but it ensures that long durations away from in-house update services will not result in a contaminated system. There are alternatives to this. You can post update servers in a DMZ that allows workstations and laptops to connect both inside and outside the LAN, but this requires greater oversight on keeping those servers secure and protected. Of course you can simply have the laptops update only when they are connected to the LAN, but you must depend on your staff to bring their laptop in at least once a week to get their updates.

Each disk must be encrypted. Each BIOS must be password protected. Each laptop must synchronize its user data on a scheduled basis to ensure that data can be secured on a server hard drive. All of this adds to the deployment time (and maintenance time) for each laptop.

There also needs to be extensive testing and verification of laptop images to make sure that they remain secure. It is good practice to have a monthly or quarterly checkup done for laptops. This does not have to be an extensive process, simply one that performs a virus scan, verifies synchronization is up to date, and performs basic maintenance procedures (such as defragmentation of the hard drive, etc.). Since all of this can be done on a workstation at any time since they are always connected to the LAN, this becomes much more important with laptops.

There should be some log kept for each laptop to ensure that they are properly managed and maintained. Each laptop should have an extended warrantee that covers the asset depreciation lifecycle so that they can be maintained by the vendor when parts fail. Since laptops are carried around and can get physically damaged by their movement, it is more cost effective to have the extended warrantee than not.

---

[7]http://www.frozencpu.com/products/10276/hdd-tta-03/Thermaltake_BlacX_Duet_HDD_Docking_Station_-_25_and_35_Hard_Drives_ST0014U.html

Mobile Devices

Mobile devices need to be secured so that users cannot install apps on their own. They need encryption installed as well as antivirus, lo-jacking software, and any other security feature that may be required to maintain business intelligence control. Keeping a list of approved applications and available features to standardize mobile devices will help simplify the deployment model and manage user expectations.

Each device should be documented (serial number, model, applications, features enabled/disabled, and user information). A history of how well particular devices fare in the field would be very useful when it comes time to replace broken equipment.

Workstation Lifecycle

The average lifespan for workstations and laptops is about three to five years (that of the average operating system lifespan or generally applied asset depreciation in accounting for such things). While hardware can survive for longer periods of time, they lose much of their viability as a mainstream workstation and require ever-increasing expense to maintain. Most that do outlive their expected lifespan are either repurposed as test machines or given away to employees. Understanding this lifecycle can help predict purchasing cycles, maintenance cost fluctuations, software and hardware warrantees, etc.

Figure 12-6 assumes the following scenario:

- Initial bundle purchase = 60 workstations, 30 laptops

- Replacement parts = 10 workstations, 5 laptops

- Expansion purchase = 20 workstations, 10 laptops

- Next bundle purchase = 90 workstations, 45 laptops

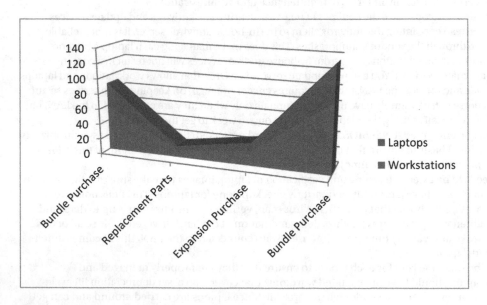

Figure 12-6. *Four-year hardware purchase forecast*

In Figure 12-6, each bundle purchase represents the beginning of a new hardware lifecycle (one where the old computers are replaced with newer systems). Replacement parts as those computers that may have been damaged outside of the warrantee agreement. The expansion purchase is the forecasted growth potential over the given hardware lifecycle. While no two organizations have the exact same lifecycle tied into their asset depreciation table, each organization can build a forecast such as this to determine when money will be needed to maintain a properly running group of workstations and laptops. The same concept can apply for servers, printers, switches, etc. (each group of systems will need to be forecasted based on their given lifecycle). This forecast can also be used to argue the level of IT personnel required to support the equipment. This cycle is repeated over and over until the organization is dissolved, stagnates, reduces in size, or is absorbed by another organization.

To get an idea of when funding will be required, there should be a timeline built with all of the basic components required to support the hardware lifecycle. Since the basic warrantee is one year, Figure 12-7 assumes that replacement equipment outside of the basic warrantee will begin to affect funding one year after the initial purchase is made. The expansion costs can be expected anytime during the lifecycle. Neither expansion nor replacement should occur in the last quarter of the last year of the lifecycle because the next bundled purchase should absorb that quarter's hardware purchase funding. This is a best-case scenario where the organization is fully supportive of asset allocation and IT funding. In most organizations, this is not always the case. Having a timeline like this one helps prepare the fund managers to expect such costs and helps the accountants build a supporting devaluation of assets to better recover any tax credits that can be gained.

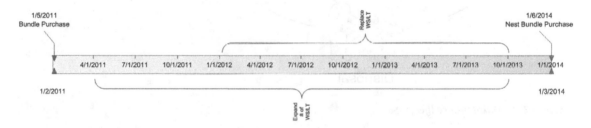

Figure 12-7. *Schedule of purchases*

There needs to be periodic maintenance performed on equipment over the hardware lifecycle. This maintenance should include a physical cleaning (vacuuming workstations internally), disk defragmenting, registry cleaning, and replacement of dysfunctional operating systems.

There should be a yearly physical inspection of each workstation (and quarterly inspection of laptops). This inspection should include the internal cleaning of dust, CD-ROM drives, and keyboards. You should inspect for loose (or missing) parts, damage due to physical abuse, and/or normal ware. Preemptive maintenance will ensure that you know your hardware and how your users maintain that hardware. You should also do a defragmentation of the hard drives on a quarterly basis and perform a registry cleanup at the same time.

Upgrades to software should always be performed using centralized software (WSUS, etc.). If possible these should always be done outside of working hours to limit the downtime users may experience. This also gives the IT department more time to resolve any issues that may transpire during the update process. There is nothing more irritating to users than having to wait for their computers because the IT department is updating their services. The customer should always come first.

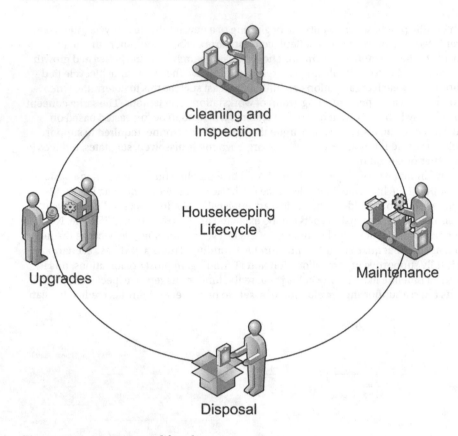

Figure 12-8. *Maintenance lifecycle*

Any formal maintenance that requires replacement of parts or whole systems should be performed in the IT operations center. If possible, you should have a temporary workstation or laptop that you can give the users while their systems are being serviced. This takes the pressure off of the maintenance staff to get the job done quickly and allows the users to continue their work unobstructed.

Keeping users updated on the status of their defective equipment is a must. But you should not make it a burden on the users by constantly updating them without valuable information. If there is no change in the progress of a workstation's repair, don't remind the users of that, but if the duration of the last update has been an unusual timeframe, you may want to send a quick note that you are still working on it. The bottom line is that the users not be hampered by the maintenance cycle, and that they are not overly reminded that their equipment has not been fixed in a timely manner.

Disposal of old equipment should be done in parallel with the distribution of new equipment. The old hardware should be set aside while the new equipment is put in place. Once the new equipment is operational, the old equipment should be removed from the workplace and set aside in the operations center for proper disposal. There should be a grace period for any workstations that have internal hard drives so that the users are completely sure there is nothing on that hard drive they may still require.

Once assured it is no longer required, the hard drive should be wiped clean of any data. This is done using a program like WipeDisk[8] so that no data can be retrieved by anyone once the hard drive leaves your organization. Disk wiping programs can take 24 to 48 hours to clean a disk completely, so time should be allocated for that (usually running the program unattended during the weekends so that the process does not interfere with normal daily operations).

Deploying Printers

Printers have come a long way from the old dot-matrix printers of the 70s and 80s. They not only print in publishing quality with color, but they can store, fax, copy, and collate. They come in all sizes. The one thing you can say about almost every printer made now is that they have redefined the quality of print for everyone. And now even the cheapest printers are networkable and/or wireless.

But printers are an expense that never seems to end. They cost money to purchase. They cost money to operate and supply. They cost money to repair. And they cost money to dispose of. They are often temperamental, requiring IT personnel to manage and maintain. But printers are here to stay. The idea of a paperless office has been around since the late 1980s when Steve Jobs touted the NeXT[9] computers as the beginning of the paperless office generation. Over two decades later, printing has grown exponentially in almost all organizations.

The main problems with printers stem from availability, usability, and convenience. Printers are frontline devices. When they are available, easy to use, and provide a convenience that makes them utilitarian, they are almost invisible to the user. The users expect printers to be there when they select print. Users don't like to have to go far to retrieve their printouts. And users are very unhappy when printers fail to perform. Making printing a utility is often one of the more difficult services for system administrators. The more complicated a printing scenario, the less utilitarian printing becomes.

Print Servers

A common way of sharing printers on a network is through print servers. These are servers dedicated to sharing centralized print queues. There are special print server devices that connect un-networked printers to the network. There are servers that simply maintain the networked print queues and share them with the LAN community. In either case, printers are secondary devices that must rely on a host to provide access. Print servers are a throw off from earlier networking restraints that managed un-networked printers on a LAN so that users could share devices.

As printers became networkable, print sharing continued to use print servers because they were a well-established way in which to centralize printing resources. There was a single place to push printer driver updates and you could control printer access remotely using a common printer spooler format. The downside to print servers was that the server itself had to be up and running at all times in order to provide printer access. If the print server was down, all of the printers connected to that print server were unavailable. This created a single point of failure.

---

[8]http://www.diskwipe.org/
[9]http://simson.net/ref/NeXT/

As you can see from Figure 12-9, the print server is the proxy for all print services. Each workstation and laptop directs their print jobs to the print server. The print server temporarily stores each job on a hard disk in the spooler, and directs those jobs to their respective printing device. This requires the print server to have both sufficient RAM and hard disk space to process multiple print jobs. Users can automatically manage their own jobs on the print server. However, if another user's print job fails, all other print jobs are held in queue until the print job in error is corrected or deleted. This usually requires the intervention of the system administrator to clear the queue if the user whose print job failed is not able to correct their printing problem on their own.

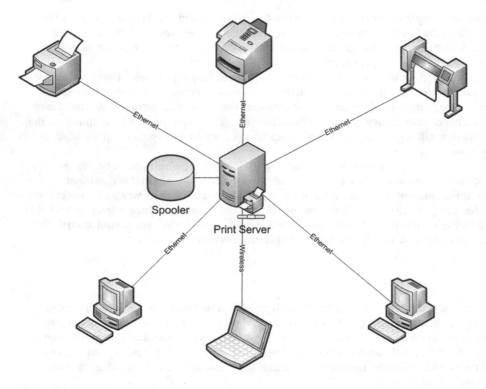

Figure 12-9. *Print server services*

Naming of printers connected to print servers is subordinate to the print server. For instance, if the print server is named TASAH-PS1 and it is the spooler for the printer PRN-101AA, the printer would be named \\TASAH-PS1\PRN-101AA. Each additional printer connected to that print server would also start with the print server's name followed by the backslash and printer name. (\\ represents networked device, TASAH-PS1 is the name of the print server, \ is a separator, and PRN-101AA is the name of the print queue on the print server).

Many organizations have multiple print servers to provide failover (in case one or more print servers are unavailable). This of course is more costly to build and maintain and requires additional administrative overhead to keep updated, but it does provide a strategy for maintaining print services. Multiple print servers could maintain redundant print queues or complementary print queues based on the need for redundancy. Complementary print queues would divide the printer into two or more groups supported by separate print servers. No printer would have queues on more than one print server.

Printers on print servers would be published in directory services. They could also be assigned to workstations and laptops via GPOs or manually dependent on the administration model. It is always a good idea to manage print queue access automatically if possible. The more you leave to the users to configure, the less attractive the resource becomes. It is the job of the system administrator to ensure that the proper resources are made available to users with the least amount of user intervention.

IP Printing

IP printing removes the need for print servers and helps eliminate the single point of failure in the printing process. Instead of having a proxy spooler in between workstations and printers, printers are connected directly to each workstation and laptop via direct network connections. In this scenario, the spooler exists on the local workstation or laptop and print jobs are directed to the printer. If the printer is busy printing another user's print job, your print job remains in the local workstation print queue until the printer becomes available.

Microsoft has added the ability to pool[10] printers locally. The system administrator would set up two "like" printer queues on a workstation (via GPO). If one of the print queues is busy, the printer pool manager will look for another printer queue that's available and direct the job there. The printer pool manager will then notify the user that the print job has been redirected to another printer.

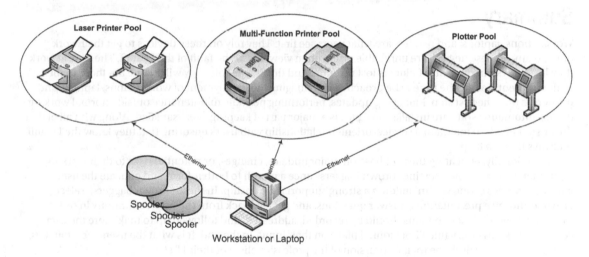

Figure 12-10. *Print pooling*

Setting up print pooling takes a bit of time to get used to but it can save on valuable resources, and improve both performance and reliability of printing services. Managing printer drivers can be a bit more complicated than that of in the print server scenario, but this can be automated as well by creating the proper driver distribution GPOs. Only the GPOs need be updated, tested, and then deployed in order for each of the workstations and laptops to get their proper driver updates. If a print job fails, users can clear their internal queue or go to the printer and release the job from the printer menu.

---

[10]http://technet.microsoft.com/en-us/library/cc958172.aspx

Shared Printers

Sharing a printer from a local workstation is much the same scenario as that of a print server. A locally connected printer is shared by the owner of a workstation so that others can use the device. You should discourage this practice. This is an error-prone scenario that requires the local workstation to be up and running in order for others to print. If the user goes home and turns off their workstations, anyone who relies on that printer to print is unable to. This can result in extra work for the system administrator to not only figure out what's going on, but to get everything back online as quickly as possible. Making sure that users cannot attach local printers and share them is essential to managing printer services locally. If someone must have a local printer connected to their workstation (i.e., financial managers, human resource managers, etc.), then it should be managed as a local printer and the responsibility of the workstation user to support.

For the `tasah.com` network, all printers will be IP printers, set up in printer pools and managed by GPOs. This helps automate printer access, makes managing printer queues easier, and makes printing more reliable. Shared printers are placed in the hallways adjacent to office space so that the printer's noise is minimized but each of the printers is conveniently accessible. Printers are labeled by their location and port association. Printer pools are named by the type of printer that is supported. Since system administrators have local administrator access to workstations and laptops, they can manage problematic print queues.

Summary

Workstations, laptops, and printers are what users see first. They rely on these devices to get their work done. If any of these devices are unreliable, users often view this as the fault of the IT staff. The time at work they lose to system or printer failure is lost revenue. And the first people they will blame are those in the IT department. Taking the time to be proactive in managing the deployment of workstations, laptops, and printers is only the first step. Managing updates, performing periodic maintenance outside normal working hours, automating software installations, etc., is a major part of keeping users satisfied. Along with all of that, the IT staff needs to maintain a service-oriented relationship with users ensuring that they know the IT staff is always there to help.

Additionally, educating the user base on major updates, changes, or potential risks to their working equipment is invaluable. Hosting "brown baggers" once a month to both inform and educate the user community goes a long way in building a strong support relationship. In these "brown baggers," select IT personnel give presentations, answer questions, and get feedback from the user community in order to improve services. Action items should be recorded, addressed, and followed up to make sure the user community knows the value IT personnel place on their input. In the end, it is what the users sees, touches, and relies on that will shape their impression of the professionalism of their IT staff.

CHAPTER 13

■ ■ ■

Antivirus, Spyware, Windows Updates, Spam Protection, Security, and Disaster Recovery

What makes networked computers susceptible to malicious software attack? Why do you need to have antivirus, anti-spamware, and never-ending service pack and updates to keep your system safe? Who are these guys that are trying to get into your system? What can you do to minimize their success? All of these questions have complex answers. But a protective umbrella of security applications is only part of any solution. Everything depends on user education and responsible use practices. You can have the best security in place and fail to protect your systems just because someone in your organization was sloppy and clicked on the wrong thing at the wrong time. Education is one of the most important keys to LAN stability and security.

Even closed networks suffer from virus attacks. As long as users can transfer data from outside sources (as they must to do their jobs), those bits and pieces of data can become contaminated during the process. In fact, secure closed networks have the hardest time maintaining their antivirus software. The process of updating service packs, antivirus clients, etc. is manually performed to bridge the gap between open and closed networks. And as in any manual process, mistakes are made and contaminants get in.

What helps ensure most that closed networks are as secure as they can be is the contractual obligations their organization imposes upon users through legal means as well as monitoring processes. Closed network managers place great emphasis on educating their user base. They spend a great deal of money to test, verify, and refine security measures so that when a breach is discovered, it is dealt with quickly and effectively. Most small to medium sized organizations cannot afford such a regime. What they can afford to do is educate their user base, install the best possible protective software, and be prepared to deal with whatever happens.

As long as there are organizations managing data electronically, there will be people interested in either gaining access to that data or trying to damage it. Most of the worst cases of malicious intent have included people from within the organization's own user base. It is not only important to protect from outside hackers, but also from those people within who have bad or misguided intent.

Antivirus

There are varying stories of when the first virus came about. One such story dates the first viruses were created on the Univac 1108 and IBM 360/370 named "Pervading Animal" and "Christmas Tree,"[1] which would have taken place around the end of the 1960s or early 1970s. However, theories of self-replicating software were first conceived in 1949. Being such as it may the first real virus to hit the public was released in 1981 on Apple II computers.[2] However the first PC-based virus (called "Brain"[3]) was released in 1986. It was designed to protect against software piracy.

In fact, early viruses were based on academic research and software protection schemes. This of course quickly grew into more malicious intent as time went on. The *Washington Post* stated that from 2003 to 2005, home users invested more than $2.6 billion on scanner-based software to protect their computers (Krebs, 2005). Virus protection has become an industry of its own with many large-scale corporations providing solutions to public, corporate, and personal customers.

There are honest discussions going on relating to conspiracy theories that purport dishonesty by antivirus software manufacturers. While it is nice to contemplate these conspiracy theories, it is dangerous to ignore the threat at hand. Viruses, Trojan horses, worms, whatever—these have real consequences for your network if you fail to implement a strategy and provide due diligence.

Home computer owners have many free options to help protect their systems from attack. Microsoft provides free antivirus software that can be downloaded from their site.[4] There are other antivirus programs that can be freely downloaded from the Internet that work just fine. This has impacted the antivirus industry greatly by reducing their potential customer base. This has also resulted in a more educated and resourceful customer base that has forced the antivirus industry to be more forthcoming and responsible with their products. In fact, as more modern operating systems have come about (such as Microsoft's Windows 8 and 10), antivirus solutions have become part of the system itself.

So what makes computers on the network susceptible to getting viruses? Poor protective measures, lack of an antivirus solutions, lack of maintaining operating systems and software updates, and of course user actions.

No user, whether working on a workstation at home or in the office, should be logged in with administrator privileges. If an action requires administrator privileges, the user should either inform the system administrator to assist them (if they are at home) or use the "Run as Administrator" feature to temporarily elevate their account for that limited purpose. No user in an office setting should ever use an administrator-privileged account to do daily work. Viruses, worms, and Trojan horses take advantage of the system based on the current user's privileges. If the current user does not have administrator privileges, it is almost impossible for malicious code to affect the operating system.

That being said, users can be fooled into doing things they thought were okay. There are sites on the Internet that tell you to update your software so that you can use their resources. You agree to do so, thus providing your account's details to allow the software to install and before you know it you have a virus. This is what antivirus software should protect you from. It should also provide protection against e-mail born infections as best it can. With all of this in place, there will always be exceptions that get through every possible protective measure. The best method for protecting a workstation or laptop is to make sure that you have antivirus software in place and your operating system is up to date and then only reveal the current user's privileges when you are 100 percent sure of the source.

---

[1]http://www.virus-scan-software.com/virus-scan-help/answers/the-history-of-computer-viruses.shtml
[2]http://www.infoplease.com/ipa/A0872842.html
[3]http://www.news.com.au/technology/the-birth-of-the-first-personal-computer-virus-brain/story-e6frfro0-1225990906387
[4]http://www.microsoft.com/nz/digitallife/security/microsoft-security-essentials.mspx

In an organization there are layers of antivirus protection in place. Each workstation has an antivirus client. Each server has antivirus software configured for that server's application and configuration. And there is a master antivirus server obtaining client updates and providing operational reports and quarantining suspicious files.

While the download of updates from the vendor is usually automated and the push of updates to the client is as well, they need to be monitored and reviewed on a monthly basis. Quite often antivirus clients fail to install their updates or the client is disabled for maintenance and not restarted afterwards. There are times when the updates from the vendor fail to get delivered on time. There are also unscheduled updates that need to be monitored in order to manage a potential outbreak.

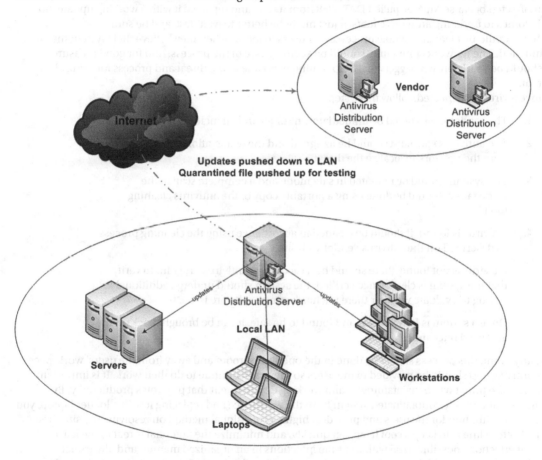

Figure 13-1. Antivirus vendor/client relationship

The local antivirus server provides five basic things:

1. Secure path to vendor/client update distribution

2. Local update distribution

3. Local quarantine

4. Source for downloading virus cleaning toolkits

5. Centralized antivirus management and reporting

The vendor-to-client server distribution is done through an encrypted connection. The system administrator of the local antivirus server controls the distribution of those updates from local antivirus server to workstation/laptop/server farm. Testing the updates before distributing them is strongly encouraged but rarely done.

Most organizations look at the risk factor and believe that the risk of waiting too long to distribute an update outweighs the risk of pushing a bad update. This practice, however, resulted in 2010 in a massive outage of systems worldwide when one update from McAfee, called DAT 5958,[5] deleted the svchost.exe file on client machines, causing uncontrolled rebooting and loss of network functionality. McAfee's support web site was so inundated with requests that it appeared to be shut down. Those who waited to push the updates were unaffected because McAfee pulled DAT 5958 from its site and replaced it with a working update. So when it comes to updating antivirus clients, it just might be better to wait, test, and be sure.

There should be clear and simple processes for users to follow when they believe their system may be contaminated. The network community should be keenly aware of the process. And for good measure there should be yearly brown baggers that help remind everyone of the threat and process for minimizing the threat.

Once a virus is suspected, follow these steps:

1. The service desk should be immediately notified and an incident ticket opened.

2. The antivirus specialist should be assigned and the workstation quickly removed from the network to localize the threat.

3. The system should be rebooted in safe mode and a complete scan of the workstation should be done using a portable copy of the antivirus cleaning toolkit.

4. If a virus is found, it should be cleaned in accordance using the cleaning process as described on the antivirus vendor web site.

5. If a virus is not found, there should be a secondary antivirus program to verify that the system is clean. Once verified, the system should undergo additional testing to evaluate whether there is a hardware or software issue.

6. Once a system is fully verified and found to be safe, it can be brought back online and used once more.

In any event, this process should be done in the operations room and away from the users' workspaces. A temporary laptop should be provided to the users so they can continue to do their work. It is important to minimize the threat while maintaining a calm working environment that promotes productivity. By removing the potentially contaminated system from the workspace and replacing it with a loaner laptop, you deescalate the situation for the users and provide a highly professional method on resolving the situation.

The bottom line is to keep a cool head, act quickly, and minimize the potential threat to the least amount of infections possible. Deal with multiple infections in an organized manner and always act positively with each user. Make sure that when the threat is resolved you give a detailed analysis of what happened and what could have been done to prevent it, and then organize training sessions to ensure everyone is aware of what they need to do to prevent infections in the future. Never blame anyone. Always work with users experiencing infections and let them know that they are not alone in dealing with problems caused by virus attacks. Goodwill can go a long way in preventing future incidents. Document everything.

---

[5]http://www.engadget.com/2010/04/21/mcafee-update--shutting-down-xp-machines/

Spyware

Spyware is software that obtains information about users without their knowledge. This information can be used to market products, monitor computer usage, or record keystrokes for malicious intent. Most spyware is benign and does no real damage to the system. Some spyware can offer criminals password information so that they can break into your system using your login credentials. Other spyware can give unauthorized people control of your operating system or the ability to read data stored on your hard drive. In any case, spyware needs to be minimized and unauthorized spyware needs to be reported to the IT department so that they can evaluate any potential damage.

Usually, anti-spyware comes bundled with antivirus software. Anti-spyware blocks the release of unauthorized information and reports to either the user or antivirus administrator. Since spyware is often loaded through Internet browsing, anti-spyware is usually added to the Internet browsing application. Some spyware comes legitimately bundled with the prepackaged operating system and is much harder to trace. Keeping anti-spyware up to date is as important as keeping your antivirus clients up to date.

The same anti-spyware vendor/client relationship exists as that of the antivirus vendor/client relationship. There is an authorized server on the local network that manages the distribution of updates and reports on anything found through active use and monthly global scans. The anti-spyware server performs the same processes to eradicate infestations and quarantines any potentially harmful files.

Some of the system management agents deployed by the IT department can be considered anti-spyware. These are applications that monitor the health and performance of your workstation or laptop. These applications are usually monitored constantly to help support proactive maintenance and minimize user downtime. Knowing what is being deployed and why will make managing spyware more effective.

Windows Updates

Most people are familiar with the automated Windows Update feature that comes with all newer Microsoft operating systems. Apple and Sun also provide similar services, as most Linux providers do. These have become commonplace annoyances and everyone who uses computers must live with them.

Microsoft, in 2003, first offered their Software Update Server (SUS) free to anyone who wanted to manage their distribution of updates, patches, and service packs to their local area network. The main benefit at the time was to encourage organizations to keep their operating systems and applications up to date. This was not just a PR stunt for Microsoft; it helped to ensure that their customers were better protected from the onslaught of hackers that were finding new ways every day to damage the reputation of the software giant. Almost every day you could find news articles describing weaknesses in the Windows platform. And every week Microsoft pushed patches and hotfixes to close them.

But the first SUS versions were very limited. While they did provide a suitable means to push patches and updates across the network, they lacked reporting features and control over when the patches would be installed. They were (are remain) strongly ties to Active Directory and used GPOs to bind workstations to their SUS distribution source. But it was free, dependable, and fairly easy to use.

As years went on, SUS became WSUS (Windows Service Update Services). It evolved into a fairly complex distribution mechanism that allowed the system administrator to group updates based on system services and applications. It further developed strong reporting features that made monitoring updates across the network easier and more understandable. It went even further and allowed system administrators to schedule updates so that they could be performed at nighttime without system administrator or user intervention.

But administration of WSUS is still a complicated issue. As you can see from the added burden of keeping antivirus and anti-spyware up to date, you need to test everything as best you can before deploying packages. With WSUS this is doubly essential. Pushing the wrong packet to the wrong server can disable a service. If that packet cannot be revoked, you have the difficulty of restoring the server to a pre-updated state.

With every packet that is available for download come warnings regarding its potential problems with specific services (such as Microsoft's SQL services). Some updates to the Windows server operating system can be harmful to Microsoft's SQL Service services. Others can be harmful to Microsoft's Exchange services. Some are only harmful to specific versions of those services. Blindly pushing updates based on bundled download can prove disastrous. Organizations that learn this the hard way understand the value of having a rigorous review of each and every warning for server updates, followed by testing and then deployment. This of course takes time, money, people and extra hardware to ensure that due diligence is performed.

But even when all of this is done, there is still a chance that one packet may go out and cause mischief. This is where having virtual servers come in to save the day. Prior to every update (which by the way comes every week) the very first thing that should be performed is a snapshot of each server. This can be done during the day without causing any downtime. If an update causes a service to fail, the system administrator can restore that server to its pre-updated state in a matter of minutes (during that time the update can be disabled in WSUS for that server) and everything is back to normal without any major downtime.

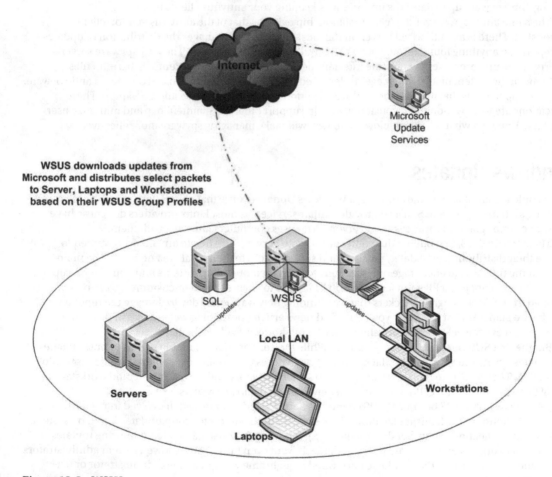

Figure 13-2. WSUS

WSUS works with Active Directory (to point workstations, servers, and laptops to the WSUS service and their selected group profiles) and maintains distribution data in an SQL database that can be reported on. For larger organizations, WSUS servers can be established in a hierarchical structure so that a central office can manage the distribution of tested packets to subordinate site WSUS servers, thus allowing for the delegation of patch management to occur. So a main headquarter can have the master WSUS server receiving packets directly from Microsoft. Test those packets to ensure they will not damage corporate services. And then redistribute those packages to remote WSUS servers so that the administrators of those remote sites can distribute the packet to their workstations, servers, and laptops at their discretion.

Reporting at the top of the hierarchy will reflect the overall distribution of packets across the whole organization. WSUS is now a feature in Windows 2008 R2 and can be implemented without extra cost. The reporting features in WSUS are extremely granular. Many of the installed packets can be revoked from the WSUS console. All of the details regarding installed software, etc. can be obtained from the reporting features.

The key thing to keep in mind is that many large organizations are willing to be anywhere from one week to two weeks behind the distribution cycle in order to review and test all packets prior to pushing them out. While every organization has their own schedule for testing and deployment, the one thing almost everyone agrees on is that blindly pushing packages out to an organization is a very bad thing to do.

Spam Protection

Generally classified as more of a nuisance, Spam does cost organizations time and money. Spam takes up valuable mailbox space on servers, consumes bandwidth, and interrupts users during the workday. It can cause legal issues (some spam received at work could be viewed as a form of sexual harassment). It can also mislead people into making personal financial mistakes (phishing). Defending against Spam costs the organization time and money. Not defending against Spam costs the organization even more time and money.

Unlike antivirus protection scenarios, filtering and removing Spam does not require local workstation or laptop clients. Since Spam originates through e-mail (and more than often from external sources outside of the organization), the Spam guard is considered a boundary protection device. It filters all e-mail going into the internal e-mail server and removes or quarantines all suspicious correspondence. It can be configured to aggressively filter e-mail traffic or not so aggressively depending on what the organization's policy dictates. Figure 13-3 shows a simple antispam installation scenario.

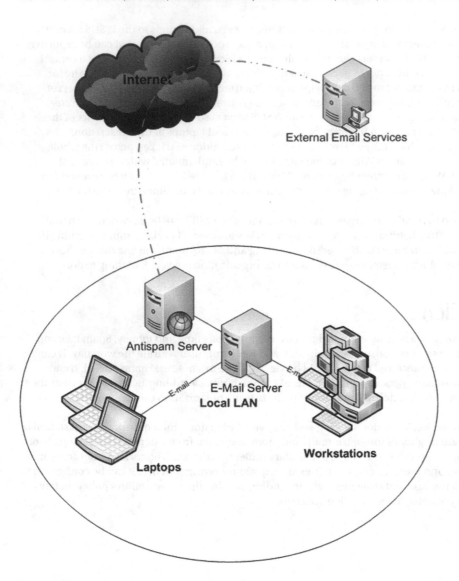

Figure 13-3. *Antispam*

Antispam services can be embedded into the e-mail server or (as displayed in Figure 13-3) as a separate service. They filter and collect e-mail traffic coming into the LAN and quarantine suspect traffic based on an agreed level of filtration. The main reason suspect traffic is quarantined is to provide a temporary storage for e-mails that may seem suspect but are in fact anticipated traffic by users on the network. This quarantine location can be made available for users to check (in case they don't get mail they had been waiting for) to see if the anticipated mail was actually captured by the antispam filter.

E-mail clients have a version of antispam software. Most (if not all) e-mail clients allow users to filter suspicious e-mail traffic into a junk mail folder. This is another temporary storage place for mail that may not be wanted correspondence. The users control their own junk mail folders. Users should be educated on how to manage their junk mail folders to ensure that they get the most of out its capabilities.

The bottom line for antispam software is moderation. It should filter out as much unwanted e-mail as possible but not everything. There is a fine line between one person's spam and another person's acceptance.

Security

Security has been embedded into most of the content of this book. Everything done on an organization's network must be assessed, not only for the benefit of the organization but also to the protection of the network community and integrity of operations. As stated earlier in this book, the protection of intellectual property is the highest priority in system administration. User perception of the importance its IT department places on protecting intellectual property is just as important.

Security is not just imbedded processes in the management and daily operations of IT services, it is the focus of communication, policies, directives, and occasional brown bagger. Every time a user turns on his system, a welcoming banner should be displayed reminding everyone that security comes first. But security is something everyone must embrace. This should never be presented as an "us against them" issue. Every user needs to feel that she is an integral part of the security matrix. When users feel that they are the focus of scrutiny based on security policies or directives, problems will arise.

Of course, there are the technical security mechanisms that need to be in place, including firewalls to keep outsiders from accessing data or systems they shouldn't, proxy servers deployed to filter Internet traffic, antivirus services designed to protect against evil-doers trying to damage or take systems or services, and antispam services embedded in the flow of e-mail traffic to keep things clean and simple. Monitoring agents deployed across the network to evaluate the health of the network and discover acts of malicious intent. All of these and a host of other mechanisms provide the foundation for maintaining a secure network.

There are also the policies and legal mechanisms in place to instruct and dissuade users so that they are able to make the right security decisions. This is the human side of security management. It is the side won through communication, a bit of salesmanship, and top-down support.

For users, the most obvious security measure is their passwords. Many people find maintaining passwords to be a pain. They don't like having to remember password or change passwords. Users just want to get their job done without the whole "IT" thing getting in their way. The fact that passwords are usually eight or more character long, complicated by mixing upper- and lowercase characters with numbers and meta-characters mixed in somehow, which adds to their displeasure. Changing passwords periodically is adding insult to injury for them. But it is one of the most important security precautions put in place to protect the organization's data.

One way system administrators can gain credibility and motivate users to have strong passwords is to give a presentation of how easy it is to crack passwords. As easy as typing "password cracking tools" into Google, you can find extensive password cracking tools.[6] The more complicated the password, the longer it takes to crack it. The longer the password the harder it becomes to figure it out. The best case scenario for setting password policies is to:

1. Make passwords eight or more characters long—Less than that and it becomes too easy to crack. While too many characters makes it more difficult for users to remember their password. Twelve characters are often used in high security environments.

2. Change passwords every 60 days—More often than that just irritates users, while not changing them makes it too easy for hackers to gain access over time.

3. Require that passwords cannot be reused for a period of time—Many people cycle through a small list of passwords they maintain, which makes it fairly simple for hackers to follow the pattern.

---

[6]http://sectools.org/crackers.html

4. Use complicated passwords—Mix characters, numbers, and meta-characters in random order. They should not construct common dictionary words. There are password crackers that use dictionary words to find your password.

5. Run a password-testing tool on your user accounts to look for weaknesses. Microsoft has a great tool called Microsoft Baseline Security Analyzer (MBSA[7]) that will list the weaknesses without compromising any passwords. This process should be done quarterly. Users with weak passwords should be contacted discretely to advise them of the issue.

Systems should not be left open and unattended. Workstation screensavers should engage after ten minutes of non-use and require a password to unlock it. Leaving systems open and unattended can lead to anyone using the logged-on users credentials to send e-mails, access tokened online services, and gain access to possibly restricted materials.

Workstations should have their local firewall active and tuned to allow local server services access. It should be locked down to prevent file sharing protocols such as UTorrent—these are possible ways in which workstations in the organization can be used as data slave sharing systems.

Data should be securely stored on the organizations file system (SharePoint, Intranet, File Server, etc.). Using the deployment model in the `tasah.com` example network, only the operating system and basic applications should be found on the local hard drive. Most (if not all) of the user data should be on the file server (in the folder redirected profile) or in the SharePoint departmental document site. All local data should be disposable. Breaking into a workstation without authenticated user credentials should lead to no intellectual property of significant value.

There should be trained system administrators to manage the technical services and a strong relationship between IT staff and user community. The IT staff should work diligently to ensure that the user community feels as much a part of the security strategy as the IT staff does. Education, communication, and socialization are the human foundation to maintaining a secure networking system.

Disaster Recovery

It is amazing how poorly many organizations' disaster recovery plans are put together (if at all). It's like they don't really believe that things happen, networks go down, and data is lost. That is of course, until it does happen, data is lost, and people are sometimes fired. Even then, there is a short memory span and money gets tight. Trying to keep a plan together and up to date takes time, effort, and an ability to verify the testing process to ensure it will work. It requires the backing of executives and midlevel managers from every department.

Many organizations rely on the "get it back up now" principle. The fact that when systems fail and services go offline, there is always someone capable of bringing everything back online, does not constitute a disaster recovery plan (DRP). It may work out all right, and then again it might not.

But disaster recovery plans don't have to be complicated. The simpler they are, the better they work. When a disaster happens, emotions are high; there is a sense of confusion and people react as best they can. Having simple one sheet checklists for restoring services, a sound archival process to ensure data protection, and the ability to move services quickly offsite to restart operations are the key ingredients to a proper disaster recovery plan.

---

[7]http://technet.microsoft.com/en-us/security/cc184924

For any disaster recovery plan to be successful, it is necessary to back up and archive data. All archive data must be stored offsite. If the building burns down and all of the data is in one building, the business will not have much of a chance for recovery.

■ **Note**   Don't just build your disaster recovery plan. Test it as often as possible and adjust it as needed!

Natural Disasters

Natural disasters can have a devastating effect. Fires, floods, earthquakes, mudslides, etc. can end the life of a business in seconds. If an organization fails, its employees lose their jobs, investors lose money, and the local economy is hurt. If the data is secured properly, then there is a foundation for restoring order in time. Relying on hosted environments can help mitigate these risks. Evaluating the cost of building your own disaster recovery plan or relying on a hosted solution (such as Azure, AWS, iCloud, etc.) is pragmatic and practical.

If people are on-site when a disaster occurs, they need to have an evacuation plan (life before data). The evacuation plan should be posted throughout the organization. There should be a clear understanding that the data is secure in archive and that no one has to endanger their lives to save anything but themselves or their coworkers.

Secondly, there needs to be a means of re-establishing operations offsite as quickly as possible. It could be a mini-version of the organization's infrastructure that can restore data quickly and get communications back online. This will allow managers to reorganize and strategize their recovery. Having used virtualization as the foundation for system services in our tasah.com organization, a less robust virtual environment could be stored in a couple of servers with one or more SANs in a colocation data facility.[8] While somewhat expensive, collocated data facilities offer an extensive array of disaster recovery options and are designed to sustain operations in the worse-case scenarios.

Emergency procedures for service restoration should be kept offsite and readily available for system administrators. There should always be an emergency call roster with protocol for addressing various disaster-based scenarios. The system administrators should practice these scenarios annually to validate and update procedures. While not all possibilities can be fully envisioned you must have a basic plan in place that can reestablish communication for key members for the infrastructure team to coordinate strategy with management. From that, you can improvise as needed.

Ad Hoc Emergencies

Ad hoc emergencies (power failures, etc.) are situations where services are disrupted and the IT team needs to take action to normalize operations as quickly as possible. Since the tasah.com IT department invested in UPSs and backup generators, it has a basic threshold for managing ad hoc emergencies. UPSs need to be maintained and batteries replaced from time to time. Having a maintenance cycle that ensures the reliability of all UPSs on site will minimize a potential UPS failure. Again, having a backup generator is nice, but you need to test the equipment annually to make sure that it performs as advertised. Fuel goes bad when left sitting and components may become unreliable when not used over time. Testing the backup generator over a weekend to clear the fuel lines and verify failover processes work accordingly are mandatory procedures.

---

[8]http://searchdisasterrecovery.techtarget.com/generic/0,295582,sid190_gci1508005,00.html

But unfortunately, even UPSs and backup generators can fail. Having a plan "B" in place is crucial. Plan "B" starts when power fails and the UPS systems turn on. You can think of it as the 15-minute drill. Most UPS systems are designed to give a 15-minute grace period in which system administrators have time to either restore power or gracefully shut down services. A simple checklist should be used when proceeding to plan "B":

1. Contact facilities maintenance immediately and determine scope and longevity of the disruption. If the outage is momentary and within the 15-minute window, use that time to ensure data is protected and that the network community is informed of any possible downtime that may be occurring. Since the `tasah.com` network workstations have personal UPSs and network switching, routers and servers are all on the rack mounted UPS systems, users should be directed to save their files and close their applications just in case. You can inform the user base through network broadcasts.

2. Make a decision based on information from facilities maintenance, if you should begin shutting down services once users have saved their data and closed their applications.

    a. Start with front end services (such as Intranet, e-mail, and shared storage)

    b. Followed by back end service (SQL servers, etc.)

    c. Once all database servers are shut down, shut down Active Directory, DNS, DHCP, etc.

    d. Finally, shut down the virtual servers and virtual server infrastructure

3. Once all server services have been gracefully powered down, you may shut down routers, switches, SANs and SAN interface devices, tap storage devices, firewall services, workstation, laptops, and finally printers.

At this point, everything should be off and reasonably secure.

Recovering from a cold start can be a bit more difficult with a virtualized server base. It is far easier to visualize the booting process for physical servers. However, the process is much the same in both cases. The restore process uses the following steps:

1. Power up the communications infrastructure first (routers, switches, and firewall services).

2. Power up the SAN and SAN interfaces. Wait until the drive sets stabilize and all of the activity lights stop blinking.

3. Power up the non-virtualized servers (the physical domain controller with DNS).

4. Power up the virtual host servers.

5. Access the Virtual Center (in VMware only) and power up the virtualized domain controllers.

6. Power up the virtual SQL servers (if any) and physical SQL servers. Wait until all expected services in the SQL environment are operational.

7. Power up the rest of the back end servers (if any) and verify that all authorized services are operational before continuing.

8. Power up the front end servers. Verify that all front end services are functioning.

9. Test access to the Internet, intranet, service desk, e-mail, etc. for operability.

10. Once all tests are positive, pass the word to the user community to begin powering up their systems. The key is not to bring all of them up at once and flood the electrical system.

11. Send out a broadcast to the network that services have been restored.

Once everyone is back online and working, take the time to generate a detailed account of what transpired and how it was resolved. It is always best to keep the user community informed and partnered with IT operations so that they can become assets to the resolution.

Instead of having a complicated document with hundreds of pages describing each step, you should have individual checklists that can more easily be performed by the IT staff. Each physical server should have a one-page checklist of things to do to restore the system. Each rack should have a priority list of devices to shut down first and bring up first. It is always a good idea to have one system administrator read off the checklist (and checking off each step) while a second system administrator performs each task. This way there is verification of the processes and second opinions when needed.

The more complicated a disaster recovery plan, the more prone to misinterpretation. System configuration is by definition dynamic. Things are constantly changing in an organization and the network service configuration reflects that change. If the disaster recovery plan is a large document, it becomes difficult to update with the changes made to the network. Keeping the plan based on checklists allows the system administrators to more easily update the checklist, submit it for review, and put it into practice.

This by no means covers disaster recovery as it should be done in an organization, but it does provide basic guidance as to what should be discussed and agreed to. The disaster recovery scenario is part of the Service Level Agreement (SLA) and should reflect both sides (IT and user community) so that everyone accepts the processes that will be taken when unplanned outages take place.

Summary

How an IT staff reacts to unforeseen circumstances—how they protect their environment and user community—displays their level of dedication and professionalism. Minimizing the effects that protective software can have on workstation performance while you maximize uptime is a very difficult balancing act. Engaging users to become active participants in protecting their network environment can ensure that the balancing act is not impossible. The key is to communicate at every level and seek comments and suggestions from the user community. You will find people a bit more willing to understand your position as a system administrator and to support you when the going gets tough.

CHAPTER 14

■ ■ ■

Intranet and Internet Support Services

The intranet/Internet medium has changed the way business is done today. Gone are the days of big rooms with file cabinets and complicated manual indexing strategies. Now you store your data electronically. What makes storing and finding data on most networks difficult is that there are usually way too many options. Organizations have a hard time getting their network community to put data in one easy to find place. Technology has had a lot to do with creating this problem. Most workstations have huge local hard drives. Most organizations still support shared drives on file servers. Not enough effort has been made to steer users into using document-handling systems such as Microsoft SharePoint, instead of dropping their files anywhere they want.

Organizations are getting better at "herding the cats" by limiting local hard drive space (or not providing local hard drives at all), limiting shared drive space on file servers, and making the intranet more user friendly. But anything that requires users to perform manual tasks and follow complicated protocol faces a difficult task in getting people to comply.

Branding plays an important part in making users accept intranet storage. Providing a uniform content structure that makes it easy to know where to look for documents and resources is essential. Extending this out to the Internet presence binds the two worlds together (internal and external). If the customer using the Internet can use your services and find things easily, so will your intranet community.

But intranet and Internet services are much more than a repository for documents. They are used to market, sell, support, and schedule organizational activities and products. They are integral to the business model. Molding these services into a functional and operational environment to facilitate business goals is essential in today's organizations and without them organizations could fail.

Intranet

The System Administrator's Perspective

Generally system administrators have little to do with the "branding" of intranet services. A system administration usually focuses on availability, connectivity, security, and data storage. Web content managers provide content design and act as the host application administrators. However, the relationship between content managers and system administrators is give and take. Content managers rely on the system administrator's insight to engineer a robust and dependable application environment that benefits from strong back end architecture. While content managers are responsible for the overall branding of the intranet, it is the system administrators who provide the foundation that extends (or limits) the technology scope that the content manager can work with.

Having a virtual environment makes the `tasah.com` SQL/portal solution affordable for small to medium sized organizations. Since the infrastructure already exists, creating clustered SQL servers and a redundant MOSS[1] farm is based mostly on the cost of licensing and installation.

Figure 14-1 represents the virtual relationship that creates the intranet environment while Figure 14-2 represents a logical depiction of how this relationship works. The back end is a clustered database server set that allows for redundancy, rolling upgrades, and shared storage for maximum uptime. The front end MOSS farm provides redundancy and load balancing by creating a virtual entry point for workstations.

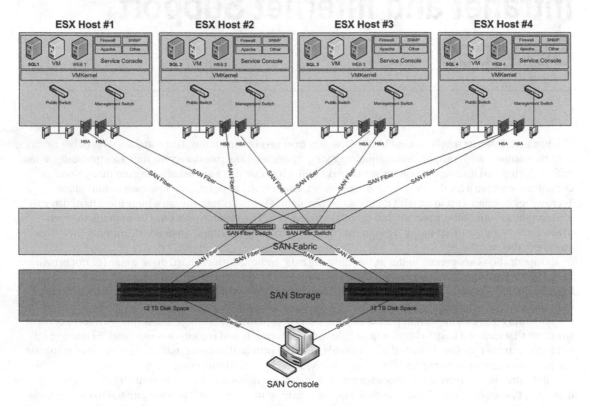

Figure 14-1. *SQL portal virtual servers with redundant SAN solution*

---

[1]http://sharepoint.microsoft.com/en-us/Pages/default.aspx

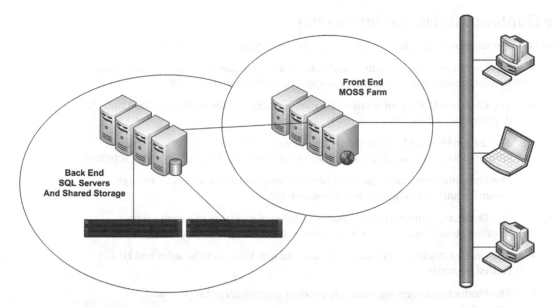

Figure 14-2. Logical front end to back end design

To the network community, they see a single virtual MOSS server that they connect to. In reality, they are redirected (based on a round robin balancing algorithm[2]) to one of the MOSS farm's servers that interact with the SQL cluster to retrieve and store data. Both front end and back end provide multiple servers so that neither service is interrupted by any single system failure.

The four ESX servers add resilience by providing their fault-tolerant environment to ensure uptime and load balancing. The main benefit to this multi-layered redundancy is that no one layer is bottlenecked and no single server (or storage device) on any level can disrupt services. This does add to the overall administrative overhead by requiring system administrators to maintain all of the individual operation systems and applications, but it also allows for each of the individual servers to be upgraded without affecting either access or performance.

The complexity of redundant layers of services and systems also requires thought-out processes for updates, upgrades, service intervention, and training. It is one thing to put a redundant hierarchy in place to support operations; it is another thing to maintain and support it. In many organizations, contractors are hired to build and implement complex services like the one in this example. Once completed, the contractor goes, and with them is the knowledge and experience that is needed to maintain and support the environment. Having an in-house expert who has a fundamental understanding of how each layer is built, as well as how the interaction between levels occurs, is essential to the services lifecycle.

The coordination between system administrator and content manager is not only essential to the catalog of services that the portal will provide, but more so in the continual maintenance and quality assurance that the systems infrastructure can support. Keeping a system alive (even through the maintenance window) is very doable; forecasting change management that aligns both the service layers and the expansion of application scope can be much more difficult. It requires a sound understanding of all of the components that make up the server/storage/application environment as well as what the potential risks will be in altering a stable service to meet the needs of added functionality and "yet to be tested" technologies.

---

[2]http://www.dabcc.com/article.aspx?id=15898

The Content Manager's Perspective

Figure 14-3 represents an example of a higher-level intranet home page logical content.

- The Departments subsection would contain all individual department home pages and the storage space for member documents to be shared internally.

- The Common Library subsection provides business-related documentation that all departments will share.

- The Information Technology subsection provides easy and quick access to user support and remote applications (applications that have a shared licensing scheme).

- The Shipping Receiving subsection provides easy and quick access to manage incoming and outgoing products, resources, etc.

- The Contact Information subsection is an internal directory of names, phone numbers, e-mail addresses, office locations, and emergency contact information.

- The Human Resources subsection is easy and quick access to benefits and HR related inquiries.

- The Products subset is the complete product listing with full service and support details.

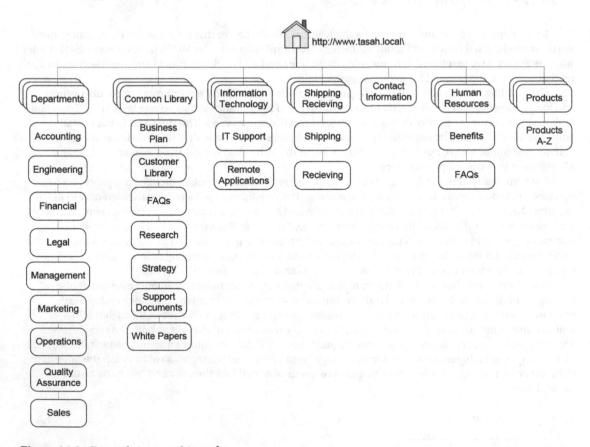

Figure 14-3. *Example intranet hierarchy*

Figure 14-4. *Web-based intranet home page*

The goal of the intranet is to make everything that internal users need three clicks (or fewer) away. This helps get things done quicker and more effectively, and promotes internal usage.

Each department might have its own content manager to reflect the subtle differences within the organization. However, branding should ensure that subgroup maintains one standard skin, font type, look, and feel. Further, each subgroup should place its content type in the same locations so as to limit the need to reorient the readers as they go from subgroup to subgroup. There will be unique requirements for specialized subgroups (such as IT support, Remote Apps, and any other set of pages) that provide custom services that fall outside the general categories of document handling, but these should be limited to a few at most.

Content managers will have a reasonable understanding of administrating portal technology (i.e., Internet Information Services, Apache, SharePoint, and MOSS). The content manager needs to coordinate with the DBA[3] and the system administrators to ensure that only the appropriate updates, patches, and hotfixes are applied each week to keep things going effectively. There are many patches that are applied to the server operating system that may affect either the SQL services or portal technology. There may also be scheduling conflicts that happen from time to time that may require updates to be suspended.

There is also the need for all three (content manager, DBA, and system administrator) to evaluate service processes to ensure that any maintenance being performed does not affect performance in any way. As the portal has become the central point of managing business intelligence in-house, any disruptions in service will have an impact on all levels of operations. No one trusts a document handling system that is constantly unavailable. And regaining trust after repeated failures is extremely difficult to achieve.

Department Sites

Figure 14-3 represented the logical design for the top portal site. Each of the department subsites would share a different logical design based on document sharing, interdepartmental information sharing, and operational requirements.

Figure 14-5 is a sample department subsite home page that links basic online document storage with a quick organizational chart for the Sales department. Most organizations have more complicated pages, but this one offers the foundation for document handling and information sharing.

---

[3]http://ww2.prospects.ac.uk/p/types_of_job/database_administrator_job_description.jsp

Figure 14-5. Web-based sales department subsite

Shared Planning Calendar

For the example in this book, an organization-wide calendar has been added to the menu bar so that no matter where you are on the intranet, you can view what is on the global calendar. Each department can post its individual scheduling so that management can get a macro perspective of what's going on in the organization. This calendar can also feed each member his or her scheduled tasks in association with the calendaring scheme. The main benefit to this calendar is to provide everyone in the organization with an understanding of who is doing what and how that fits into the organization's objectives.

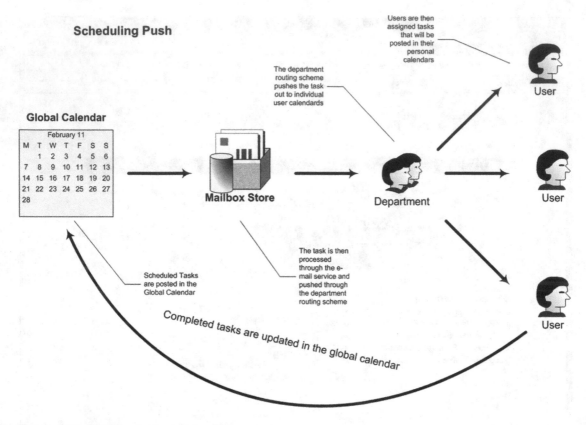

Figure 14-6. *Global calendar tasking process*

One of the benefits of the global calendaring tool is to provide a centrally managed tasking process for all users based on department and upper management goals and objectives.

Remote Applications

The use of remote applications has been touched on several times in this book. It is a way to share limited application licenses across a larger group of users while reducing costs. By allowing users to access and connect to remote applications without a middleman (i.e., IT staff) to install applications individually, there is a direct reduction in administrative overhead. Remote applications allow users to add applications to their desktops at their own convenience. Because the use of these specialized applications is random and these applications (i.e., Microsoft Visio, Microsoft Project, Adobe Illustrator, etc.) are used infrequently, a handful of licenses can be shared easily between many users.

It is necessary for the system administrators to repackage and post application packets on the intranet, but once posted, they become accessible to everyone given proper rights to use them. They can be set up so as to allow users to install a pointer to the application in their Start menu on their desktop. A small initialization application is then downloaded to improve runtime. To the user, the application (once added to the Start menu) looks to be local to the workstation. The only time users know it's remotely accessed is when there are no licenses available for them at the time of request.

Additional license can be bought and added to the remote application site. This allows for the expansion of licensing without having to rebuild application packages or touch desktops. All of the applications are stored on the SAN and backed up accordingly. Upgrading applications can be done centrally without interfering with the user's daily workload. A simple notice to the network community letting them know that a newer version is available and that the older one will be given a terminating date that allows the users to upgrade at their convenience. This offers the network community a highly professional and positive service that promotes the relationship between the IT department and the organization. It gives the network community more control over their IT application choices and does not impose unnecessary scheduling conflicts based on service timetables.

Another advantage is that most, if not all, applications can be converted to remote applications. This allows organizations the ability to buy products from multiple vendors and build one distribution point to support them. Since the applications are accessible only when attached to the local area network, they are protected from use outside the organization. Laptops may require local licenses (due to their need to be mobile), but desktops, once moved outside the LAN, will not have access to either their data or extended application base. This provides better control over those expensive licensing investments and promotes security.

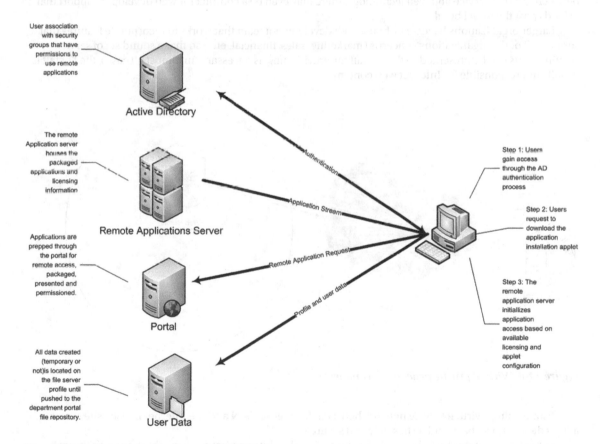

Figure 14-7. *Remote application relationships*

Internet

The Internet is the "shop window" for most organizations today. More often than not it presents customers (and/or clients) with their first impressions of what your organization has to offer and how professional your staff may be. But your Internet presence is more than that. It's your storefront, warehouse ordering mechanism, customer support, etc. When your Internet presence is unavailable to your customers or clients, your organization is unavailable as well.

Once again, the IT department is not directly responsible for how web pages are designed, but they are responsible for the infrastructure that makes it work. Most organizations use web hosting companies to manage the web servers, certificate servers (for SSL), etc. The internal IT staff is responsible for providing the access to Internet services from internal IT services (such as a customer service desk, links between financial data, shipping and receiving, etc.). The reliability of these services is the responsibility of the IT staff.

Many smaller organizations hire web developers to design their Internet presence. This requires some communication between the IT staff and the web developers. Most of that communication is focused on the IT staff providing the appropriate level of data access, coordination of linked services, and basic support to provide a secure connectivity between web site and internal LAN. Depending on the level of complexity between internal service and web technology, there may even be a contract for web developer support that extends past the initial build.

Larger organizations have an in-house web development team that works to incorporate features that support all of the organizations concerns (marketing, sales, financial, etc.) so that a sound set of service requirements can be presented to the IT staff for provisioning as necessary. In almost all cases, the IT staff is usually not responsible for Internet web content.

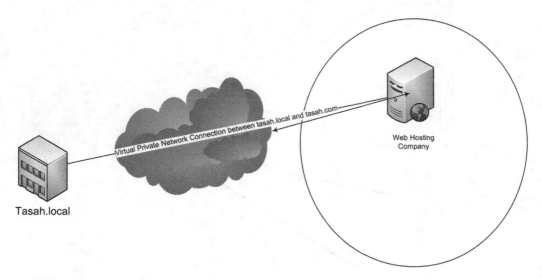

Figure 14-8. *Virtual private network for commerce*

Establishing a virtual private network between the internal LAN and the Internet housed site server allows data to travel back and forth safely and securely.

Some organizations host their web site internally. They hire someone internally to produce the web page as one of their many jobs. While this can work for smaller business, it can reflect on the perception you give as an organization to potential customers or clients. There are a lot of security risks undertaken by these companies. While they are possibly saving money in the short run, they may be losing money overall.

Marketing

Publishing on the Internet does not make the organization obvious to others. There is the need to market the web site to potential customers and clients. This is where companies like Google, Yahoo, Ask, etc. come in. They make money advertising your web site and helping you to market your products and services. Every time a potential customer "Googles" your site, Google receives compensation as part of an agreed to advertising fee. Organizations sign contracts with these firms to work out pricing schemes, etc. It is lucrative for both the search engine provider and the organization wishing to advertise. It's worldwide and reduces the overall traditional marketing costs substantially. Now you have the customers using their own printers and ink to print your brochures, VoIP to handle overseas calls, SSL to ensure security and, of course, a worldwide tool for directing everyone to your site.

External Collaboration

Providing the organization's network community with an outreach service (so that they can access internal documents while their traveling) takes a bit of planning and discussion. By opening up the firewall to allow internal documentation to flow outside the LAN, you are weakening your defenses and taking risks. Providing these services must be done with caution, legal substance, and balancing of the risks and benefits based on the organizations business model.

There are several choices in securing communication between two or more points across the Internet. The least expensive options all incorporate IP tunneling technologies. The most expensive is to buy a leased line. Since it would be impractical at best to buy leased lines for individual file sharing, it is not generally a viable option.

There are hardware solutions available that create a secure connection between two or more points using cryptographic hardware (having one on each end of the connection). This is expensive and used mostly for government and military purposes. However, large corporations may use hardware linked cryptographic solutions based on their need for security and financial disposition.

Most firewalls come with a VPN option (the emphasis on "option" meaning additional cost). This allows you to create an IP tunnel (or encrypted secure link) between two or more points across a network. This works well for protecting communication across the Internet and allows people who are traveling flexibility, security, and (based on their connection) reasonable bandwidth.

Of course, Microsoft provides a free VPN solution with its operating systems and line of server solutions. Using IPsec[4] communication between connection points are securely encrypted and protected from outside snooping. While this is a viable means to secure communications over the Internet, you need to keep in mind that it is not as secure as many of the moderately priced VPN solutions provided by vendors such as Cisco.[5] There are also VPN services, which will provide added support and security based on a monthly charge.[6]

There is also RSA technology,[7] which provides additional security by giving you a password calculator that changes the password every time you log in from outside the firewall. Many banks use this technology to verify customer access to their accounts over the Internet. A digital device is synchronized with the RSA server so that a set of numbers is generated to give access. This set of numbers change frequently and are synchronized with the RSA server to authorize access based on the limited time the number would be valid. It works with addition access codes to ensure that anyone wishing to access the network must have all of the access tokens (both static and dynamically generated) in order to successfully log in. If the number of attempts exceeds the authorized limit, the digital device is temporarily disabled until the user brings the device in to get resynchronized.

---

[4] http://technet.microsoft.com/en-us/network/bb531150
[5] http://www.cisco.com/
[6] http://www.start-vpn.com/category/vpn-offers/?type=0&orderby=meta_value_number&key=hits&order=desc
[7] http://www.start-vpn.com/category/vpn-offers/?type=0&orderby=meta_value_number&key=hits&order=desc

For access to the tasah.com network, the solution that would work best would be to buy Cisco VPN licenses for each client and use an RSA digital calculator to generate synchronized verification numbers. This gives a reasonable, fairly inexpensive secure access to the internal network.

Along with all of the technical security mechanisms in place, it is also necessary to have a legal binding contract for each remote user to ensure that they will properly use the remote access for work-related matters and contact the IT department immediately if anything is stolen or lost.

Summary

This book has detailed the building of a fictitious network from preparing the building to having an operational work environment. While it does not detail everything you should know as a system administrator in support of such an effort, it does provide a reasonable array of the things you should know and offers links to places on the Internet to find out more detailed information.

Best practices are applied throughout the book with some possible controversial options given to help you think outside of the box (i.e., the use of USB sticks for hard drives). The overall goal is to help new system administrators have a basic knowledge of what to expect in an organization's IT department and where to look for answers when topics come up that you can't answer.

No two IT departments are the same. Many of the topics covered in this book will not look exactly like that in your organization. But having a different view of what is used and what's not in your organization helps keep you open to new ideas and suggestions. It may be that you find something in this book you might like to offer as a change to your organization's way of providing IT services.

Any public IP addresses used in this book were randomly chosen and do not reflect real IP addresses associated with any actual known network at the time of this book's writing. Any names used were generated randomly and do not reflect any real or known persons. All topics in this book are factual and useful and are the culmination of over 30 years of experience in the networking industry.

APPENDIX A

■ ■ ■

Checklist Templates

Daily Check

Reporter: _____

Date: _____

Time: _____

Network

Services	Scope	Status U/D[1]	Trouble Ticket Reference #	Notes
Network Access				
Intranet Access				
Internet Access				
VoIP				
DNS				
DHCP				
WINS				
LDAP				
Switch/Router Access				

---

[1]U = Up, D = Down

Servers

Services	Scope	Status U/D[2]	Trouble Ticket Reference #	Notes
Mail Server(s)				
LDAP/Directory Server(s)				
Print Server(s)				
File Server(s)				
Backup Server(s)				
Application Server(s)				
Web Server(s)				
Database Server(s)				
Security Servers(s)				
Monitoring/Management Server(s)				
Antivirus Server(s)				
OS/Application Update Server(s)				

Weekly Check

Reporter: _____

Date: _____

Time: _____

Network

Services	Scope	Status U/D[3]	Trouble Ticket Reference #	Notes
Switch Configuration Backup				
Router Configuration Backup				
Firewall Data Log Review				
VoIP Log Review				
DNS Backup				
DHCP Backup				
WINS Backup				
LDAP Backup				
Switch/Router Access Review				

---

[2]U = Up, D = Down
[3]U = Up, D = Down

Servers

Services	Scope	Status U/D[4]	Trouble Ticket Reference #	Notes
Mail Server(s) Backup				
LDAP/Directory Server(s) Review				
Print Server(s) Backup				
File Server(s) Backup				
Backup Server(s) Test				
Application Server(s) Backup				
Web Server(s) Backup				
Database Server(s) Backup				
Security Servers(s) Review				
Monitoring/Management Server(s) Backup				
Antivirus Server(s) Update				
OS/Application Update Server(s) Deployment				

Monthly Check

Reporter: _____

Date. _____

Time: _____

Network

Services	Scope	Status U/D[5]	Trouble Ticket Reference #	Notes
Internal Network Report				
Router Activity Report				
Firewall Activity Report				
VoIP Usage Report				
DNS Change Report				
DHCP Change Report				
WINS Change Report				
LDAP Change Report				

---

[4]U = Up, D = Down
[5]U = Up, D = Down

Servers

Services	Scope	Status U/D[6]	Trouble Ticket Reference #	Notes
Mail Server(s) Usage Report				
LDAP/Directory Server(s) Activity Report				
Print Server(s) Consumption Report				
File Server(s) Usage Report				
Backup Server(s) Report				
Application Server(s) Usage Report				
Web Server(s) Usage Report				
Database Server(s) Report				
Security Servers(s) Report				
Monitoring/Management Server(s) Report				
Antivirus Server(s) Report				
OS/Application Update Server(s) Deployment Report				

---

[6]U = Up, D = Down

APPENDIX B

■ ■ ■

Network Environment Inspection Templatves

Supporting Documentation Checklist

Table B-1. *Initial Building Inspection Document Checklist*

#	Documents and/or Title	Date Prepared	Available	Not Available	Signature
1	Detailed Floor Plans				
2	Electric Circuit Distribution Diagram				
3	List of False Walls				
4	List of Physical Firewalls				
5	List of Access Points				
6	List of Exit Points				
7	Fire Exits				
8	Air Conditioning BTU Report				
9	List of Available False Ceilings				
10	Preexisting Network Cabling Diagram				

Network Environment Inspection Templates

Supporting Documentation Checklist

APPENDIX C

■ ■ ■

Electrical Circuits and Outlets

Supporting Documentation Checklist

Date: _____

Table C-1. *Initial Building Inspection Document Checklist*

Room #	Port #	Port (A/B)	Type (Data/Common)	Fuse #	Amps

APPENDIX D

■ ■ ■

Uninterrupted Power Supply Maintenance

Supporting Documentation Checklist

Date: _____

Table D-1. *Initial Building Inspection Document Checklist*

Room #	Port #	Port (A/B)	UPS Manufacturer/Model	Date Installed	Date Battery Replaced

Uninterrupted Power Supply Maintenance

Supporting Documentation Checklist

Index

Get the eBook for only $5!

Why limit yourself?

Now you can take the weightless companion with you wherever you go and access your content on your PC, phone, tablet, or reader.

Since you've purchased this print book, we're happy to offer you the eBook in all 3 formats for just $5.

Convenient and fully searchable, the PDF version enables you to easily find and copy code—or perform examples by quickly toggling between instructions and applications. The MOBI format is ideal for your Kindle, while the ePUB can be utilized on a variety of mobile devices.

To learn more, go to www.apress.com/companion or contact support@apress.com.

Printed in the United States
By Bookmasters